Solidarity Under Siege

El Salvador's long civil war had its origins in the state repression against one of the most militant labor movements in Latin American history. *Solidarity Under Siege* vividly documents the port workers and shrimp fishermen who struggled yet prospered under extremely adverse conditions during the 1970s only to suffer discord, deprivation, and, eventually, the demise of their industry and unions over the following decades. Featuring material uncovered in previously inaccessible union and court archives and extensive interviews conducted with former plant workers and fishermen in Puerto El Triunfo and in Los Angeles, Jeffrey L. Gould presents the history of the labor movement before and during the country's civil war, its key activists, and its victims into sharp relief, shedding new and valuable light on the relationships between rank-and-file labor movements and the organized Left in twentieth-century Latin and Central America.

JEFFREY L. GOULD is the Rudy Professor of History at Indiana University. His books include *To Lead as Equals: Rural Protest and Political Consciousness in Chinandega, Nicaragua, 1912–1979*, *To Die in This Way: Nicaraguan Indians and the Myth of Mestizaje, 1880–1965*, and with Aldo Santiago, *To Rise in Darkness: Revolution, Repression, and Memory in El Salvador, 1920–1932*. He has also directed and codirected three documentary films, *La Palabra en el Bosque*, *Scars of Memory: El Salvador, 1932*, and *Port Triumph*, which accompanies this book and is available through Indiana University Press: www .iupress.indiana.edu/9780253046017.

Solidarity Under Siege

The Salvadoran Labor Movement, 1970–1990

JEFFREY L. GOULD
Indiana University Bloomington

CAMBRIDGE
UNIVERSITY PRESS

CAMBRIDGE
UNIVERSITY PRESS

University Printing House, Cambridge CB2 8BS, United Kingdom

One Liberty Plaza, 20th Floor, New York, NY 10006, USA

477 Williamstown Road, Port Melbourne, VIC 3207, Australia

314–321, 3rd Floor, Plot 3, Splendor Forum, Jasola District Centre, New Delhi – 110025, India

79 Anson Road, #06–04/06, Singapore 079906

Cambridge University Press is part of the University of Cambridge.

It furthers the University's mission by disseminating knowledge in the pursuit of education, learning, and research at the highest international levels of excellence.

www.cambridge.org
Information on this title: www.cambridge.org/9781108419192
DOI: 10.1017/9781108297394

© Jeffrey L. Gould 2019

First published 2019

Printed and bound in Great Britain by Clays Ltd, Elcograf S.p.A.

A catalogue record for this publication is available from the British Library.

ISBN 978-1-108-41919-2 Hardback
ISBN 978-1-108-41019-9 Paperback

In memory of two great historians:
Emilia Viotti da Costa
Our mentor
Fritz Stern
My uncle
A mi compañera de siempre
A nuestros hij(a)os
A nuestros niet(a)os
Al pueblo de Puerto El Triunfo en el puerto y en la Diáspora

Contents

Figures

Acknowledgments

Since I began this project in 2011 I have depended on the kindness and assistance of numerous people. Very early in the project I met Ovidio Granadeño in Puerto El Triunfo, who proved to be an invaluable informant. Moreover, he facilitated access to the now decrepit union hall where he showed me stacks of papers that he described as the archive. Luckily, I found a brave and able research assistant, David Segovia, who withstood the rigors of the port and photographed all the disorganized papers and provided a rudimentary organizational scheme for the archive. After meeting Adela Amaya and Ruperto Torres, former Sindicato Agua activists, I gained access to their union's small but invaluable archive, which David also photographed.

In the port, I also benefited from interviews with Migdonio Perez, Migdalia Chavarría, Virginia Reyes, and Maura de Zelaya. Juan Raúl Alberto and Ivette Bará communicated valuable information and perspectives to me through e-mail and in person. I interviewed and consulted with Ricardo Jovel in San Salvador and in the port. However, I developed the longest and deepest relations with three exiles from the 1980s: Gloria García in Los Angeles, Alejandro Molina Lara in Los Angeles and Puerto El Triunfo, and Ana Alvarenga in Montreal and in the port. Angel Escobar (Los Angeles) also offered a fascinating perspective as a former fisherman as did Rolando Franco (Los Angeles) a union leader during the late 1980s. I also interviewed Noé Quinteros in Houston and developed a valuable e-mail correspondence with him. I owe to him a highly detailed description of the production process. Yvette Bará, who worked in management at Pezca S.A. right before the strike of 1987 and returned to do sociological field work, also was extremely helpful.

I owe a deep debt of gratitude to Carlos Henríquez Consalvi (Santiago) with whom I collaborated on two documentaries and on my recent Puerto El Triunfo. Santiago provided the transportation, collaboration on the interviews, and companionship (along with his highly creative son Camilo) on all our trips to the port. The filmmaker Guillermo Escalón also often accompanied us and constantly made witty and intriguing remarks about the interviews (and the interviewer). I also made ample use of the archive and facilities of the Museo de la Palabra y la Imágen (San Salvador), which Santiago directs.

I also benefited from the highly competent work of several other research assistants during the course of the project: Luis Rubén González, Herberth Stanley Morales, Jonathan Warner, and Casey Korducki. Chris Eichstedt provided copies of material he located in Amsterdam.

Verónica Guerrero the librarian at Centro de Información, Documentación, y Apoyo a la Investigación at the Universidad Centroamericana provided invaluable assistance both at the library and long distance. She responded immediately to numerous e-mail requests and then scanned documents and photos. I remain deeply indebted to this indefatigable librarian.

At the Institute for Advanced Study (2012–13), where I was able to enjoy a year of research and reflection, Marcia Tucker, the librarian, went out of her way to be helpful. The rest of the staff at the IAS were also very helpful, especially Marian Zelazny.

At the Charles Warren Center at Harvard University, Monnikue McCall and Arthur Patton-Hock provided much appreciated administrative assistance. Fred Burchsted provided much help in navigating the resources of Widener Library. Kirsten Weld and Brandon Terry did an excellent job running a fascinating seminar in which I was afforded the opportunity of presenting some of this work.

At the Warren Center, I was also fortunate to form part of a small group of Latin Americanists. Carlota McCallister, Forrest Hylton, and Kirsten Weld exchanged chapters. Their comments were extremely helpful, and I thoroughly enjoyed reading and discussing their work.

I also presented earlier versions of this work at the Universidad de Costa Rica and Yale University. Thanks to David Díaz for arranging the presentation in the former and to Gil Joseph for doing so in the latter.

I also presented papers based on preliminary research at the following conferences:

"Global Labour in the 1970s: A Research Agenda," ReWork, 2015, Humboldt University. Thanks to Alex Lichtenstein for organizing such a fine workshop and to Paulo Fontes for his commentary.

"From Proletariat to Precariat: Changing Labor Relations in the Twentieth and Twenty-First Centuries," Indiana University, 2014. Thanks to Eddie Brudney for his organizational skill and to John French for his commentary that forced me to reevaluate some of my early assumptions.

Several colleagues provided invaluable comments on the manuscript. In this day of increased service loads on faculty, I recognize just how much of a commitment it is to read an entire manuscript (or significant portions of one). My deepest gratitude to Purnima Bose, David Díaz Arías, Heidi Tinsman, Peter Guardino, Danny James, Heather Vrana, and Kirsten Weld.

At Indiana University I am grateful for the administrative support of Becky Bryant and Deana Hutchins. Luis González, our Latin American librarian, has proved enormously helpful throughout my career.

I have had the great pleasure to work with my editor at Cambridge University Press, Deborah Gershenowitz. I have never had such an intense and profitable working relationship with an editor. She meticulously read every chapter making astute observations on every page. The book is infinitely better than it would have been without her assistance.

Once again, I am profoundly indebted to Ellie for putting up with travels, fears, and frustrations during yet another Central American project. Gabriela, Mónica, and Carlos have also been supportive from afar. When I insisted to Sofía, our five-year-old granddaughter, that I had to go to my office to finish the book, she responded, "You go to work looking like that?"

My dress code was hard to explain to her, but she inspired me nonetheless.

People, Terms, and Acronyms

Matthies Regalado, Roberto	– co-owner of Pezca, accused of participation in fraud
Mena Lagos, Alfredo	– rightist politician; 1982–85 president of Pezca
Molina Lara, Alejandro	– SIP and FENASTRAS leader (1972–81); exiled 1981
Romero, Oscar Arnulfo	– Archbishop of El Salvador; assassinated March 24, 1980
Saravia, Alvaro	– part of plot to assassinate Archbishop Romero; worked as head of security for Atarraya
Torres, Ruperto	– Sindicato Agua activist
Wright, Juan	– principal owner of Pezca; owner of expropriated La Carrera – largest cotton plantation in country (very close to Puerto El Triunfo)

FACTORIES

APEX	– textile
APLAR	– electronics
Atarraya	– second-largest processing plant and fishing operation
Diana	– cookie and cracker
La Constancia-Tropical	– bottling
IMES	– textile
Mariscos de El Salvador	– third-largest shrimp processing plant, owned by Rafael Guirola; closed in 1984
Pezca S.A.	– largest processing plant – 10 fishing companies under its control
PRONACSA	– vegetable oil, located near Puerto El Triunfo; owned by Wright

UNIONS, POPULAR ORGANIZATIONS, AND PARTIES

BPR	– Bloque Popular Revolucionario – Popular Revolutionary Bloc – 80,000 – affiliated with Fuerzas Populares de Liberacion (FPL) – guerrilla group
CLAT	– Central Latinoamericana de Trabajadores – Christian Democratic/democratic socialist/anti-communist

FAPU — Frente de Acción Popular Unificada – Unified Popular Action Front – 1974 – 10,000–40,000 members in 1979 – affiliated with guerrilla group Fuerzas Armadas de Resistencia Nacional (FARN)

FENASTRAS — Federación Nacional Sindical de Trabajadores Salvadoreños, Left-leaning labor federation (founded 1972) – linked to FAPU (1979–89)

JRG — Junta Revolucionaria de Gobierno – October 15, 1979–January 2, 1980, replaced by another junta led by José Napoleón Duarte

LP-28 — Ligas Populares 28 de febrero – Popular Leagues, February 28, 1974 – 5,000 members (many were campesinos from Morazán) affiliated with Ejercito Revolucionario del Pueblo (ERP) – Revolutionary Army of the People

MNS — Movimiento Nacionalista Salvadoreño – also FAN – Frente Amplio Nacional – precursors to ARENA

OP — Organizaciones Populares – refers to BPR, FAPU, and LIGAS POPULARES

ORDEN — Organización Democrática Nacional – state-founded peasant organization involved in rightist paramilitary activity in 1970s; more than 100,000 members; abolished by JRG in November 1979 but continued under another name

PDC — Christian Democratic Party – Duarte

Sindicato Agua – SGTIPAC — Sindicato General de la Industria Pesquera y Anexos – Fishermen's Union – member of CGT (allied with Christian Democrats)

SINDICATO TIERRA — Founded in 1961, more than 1,000 members in Puerto El Triunfo organized in three locals at each of three plants (in order of size: Pezca, Atarraya, and Mariscos de El Salvador). There was another local in la Unión with several hundred members. Fishermen at Pezca belonged to another union, commonly called Sindicato Agua.

SIP Sindicato de la Industria Pesquera	(union of the fishery industry)
STECEL	– electrical power worker's union; key union in FENASTRAS; outlawed 1980
UNOC	– Union Nacional de Obreros y Campesinos – founded March 1986 by pro-Duarte forces to counter Left and opposition – includes many peasants
UNTS	– Unión Nacional de Trabajadores Salvadoreños – Left labor and popular coalition – includes FENASTRAS
UPD	– Popular Democratic Unity – coalition of labor and peasant groups that backed Duarte in 1984 elections. Most members from agricultural cooperatives benefited with 1980 Agrarian Reform

OTHER ACRONYMS AND TERMS

AIFLD	– American Institute for Free Labor Development – international arm of AFL-CIO – funded by AID, accused of being part of CIA operations
ANDA	– Water and Sewage National Administration (SETA corresponding union) ARENA – right-wing party, founded by D'Aubuisson with Mena Lagos; won Congress in 1988 and the presidency 1989
BAC	– Banco Agrícola Comercial
Eventuales	– seasonal, temporary workers (or fishermen)
"La Movida"	– practice whereby fishermen would illegally sell shrimp on the high seas; originally a form of resistance to the shrimp companies
Marinero	– fisherman
Patrón de Barco	– captain (employee of company)

Introduction

An Arc of Triumph and Despair

Let us hope that, in the next century, historians will be able to pick up
the pieces in this field littered with fragments and create a richer and less
chaotic vision that may help them (and others) to free themselves from the
straitjacket of narcissism, to reinvent new forms of solidarity, and to find
new roads to a more open and truly democratic world, where all people of
different genders, classes, ethnicities, religions, and nationalities will come
together to participate equally in the wealth of the world.

    Emilia Viotti da Costa, "New Publics, New Politics, New Histories"

We approached the corner store along a dusty side street of Puerto
El Triunfo, El Salvador, 70 miles southeast of San Salvador. Guillermo
leaned out the car window and asked a young man who was sweeping in
front of the store for directions to 14th street. We were going to film an
interview with a former packinghouse worker. The young man replied
with equanimity, "here everything is 18th street," referring to the Calle
18 gang. As we turned around and headed out of the neighborhood,
I pondered how the high level of loyalty, legitimacy, and solidarity
that several decades ago had been associated with the Sindicato de la
Industria Pesquera (SIP: the fishing industry union) now belonged to the
Calle 18 gang, which, in addition, commanded widespread fear.

    Today, on the way to the dock the few remaining fishermen walk
past the corroded shells of the packinghouses, perched on the edge of
the heavily polluted Bay of Jiquilisco. The oldest of them remember the
din of machines, unforgiving odor of shrimp, and wild nights after their
return to port. They recall how, during the 1970s, the shrimp industry
was booming (third among El Salvador's exports) and its 2,000 organized

workers were among the more privileged in the country. After battling the companies, backed by the military dictatorship for nearly a decade, by 1980, their hopes for a dignified life for their children seemed on the verge of realization. But by the early 1990s, the collapse of the industry had extinguished those aspirations.

In an echo of US rustbelt anguish, many of the 16,000 inhabitants of this gang-ridden port blame the unions – in particular Sindicato Agua, the fishermen's union – for the destruction of their community and their livelihoods. That blame derives from two strikes that Sindicato Agua spearheaded; the latter one, from 1987 to 1991, the longest in Latin American history, coincided with the closing of Pezca S.A., the main shrimp processing plant. Yet, as we will learn in this book, the primary cause of the demise of the industry was a more than US$20 million fraud perpetrated by the rightist owners of the company and the director of a state-controlled bank. Like so many of the financial machinations during the onset of neoliberalism, the details of the fraud were largely illegible and invisible.[1] It was more plausible to blame those whose intransigent militancy was impossible to justify in a memory shaped by the triumph of neoliberalism that also swept away many private-sector unions in El Salvador and throughout the hemisphere.[2]

Solidarity Under Siege presents a case study of workers who struggled and prospered under extremely adverse conditions during the 1970s only to suffer discord, deprivation, and eventually the demise of their industry and their unions over the following decades. Their stories are instructive by revealing a road not taken. Initially crushed by state terror in 1980 and 1981, the workers were unable to maintain the dignified life and relative power for temporary and permanent laborers that they had achieved. Several years later, the workers reorganized. Gender differences, union politics, and political discord, however, obstructed their path forward

---

[1] Carlota McAllister and Diane M. Nelson, "Aftermath: Harvests of Violence and Histories of the Future," in *War by Other Means: Aftermath in Post-Genocide Guatemala*, eds. Carlota McAllister and Diane M. Nelson (Durham, NC: Duke University Press, 2013), 33–40.

[2] In addition to numerous interviews with residents who often used the refrain "mataron a la gallina que puso huevos de oro" (killed the hen who laid golden eggs), José Isidrio Arias Segundo (*Puerto El Triunfo: 487 años de Antología Histórica* [Puerto El Triunfo, El Salvador: Centro de Tecnología, 2009], a popular history of Puerto El Triunfo) encompasses such common sense when he writes: "We had to watch with sadness as one by one the companies closed due to lengthy labor-management conflicts." The book makes no mention of the fraud.

and ultimately blocked the possibility of a cooperatively run shrimp industry in Puerto El Triunfo.

A LOCAL TRANSITION TO NEOLIBERALISM

The massive fraud provides a Central American window on to what David Harvey, a pioneering scholar of neoliberalism, calls *accumulation by dispossession*. For Harvey, financialization forms a key component of the process: "Deregulation allowed the financial system to become one of the main centres of redistributive activity through speculation, predation, fraud, and thievery."[3] Harvey views neoliberalism as fundamentally a political project whereby the North Atlantic corporate elite dealt a crippling blow to its labor movements and managed to push national governments toward the promotion of deregulation of financial markets and the privatization of public assets – services and industries. For Harvey, the achievement of a radicalized form of capitalism hinged on the defeat and demoralization of the labor movement in the United States and in Western Europe and on the shift of industries to the developing world where they also had to confront an emboldened labor movement.

Solidarity Under Siege charts a unique, if particularly stormy, path toward neoliberalism that includes an epoch of violent repression marked by accumulation by dispossession, primarily benefiting some of the company owners. Fishermen and plant workers battled against flexible labor strategies associated with neoliberalism. Their two unions, however, waged their battles at different times. Moreover, during the strikes, there was precious little solidarity between land and sea workers.[4] Political differences, various forms of resistance to capital, and gender tensions impeded long-term solidarity between these unions.

Greg Grandin's analysis of the violent transition to neoliberalism in Latin America is apposite with respect to Puerto El Triunfo and El Salvador. State terror broke up alliances and pacified militants.[5] Repression was

---

[3] David Harvey, *A Brief History of Neoliberalism* (New York: Oxford University Press, 2007), 161.

[4] As we will see, though informally referred to as "sector tierra" and "sector agua," or "Sindicato Tierra" and "Sindicato Agua," in fact Sindicato Tierra had many fishermen among its membership, primarily from Mariscos de El Salvador and Atarraya S.A. but also from Pezca S.A. Sindicato Agua, however, particularly in the 1980s, recruited workers from the processing plant.

[5] Greg Grandin, *The Last Colonial Massacre: Latin America in the Cold War* (Chicago: University of Chicago Press, 2004), 196–97. For an excellent case study that substantiates the Grandin thesis, see Lesley Gill, *A Century of Violence in a Red City: Popular Struggle,*

not the only weapon against labor solidarity. During the 1980s, leftist SIP union leaders gradually became practitioners of policies congruent with neoliberalism that were inconsistent with their previous forms of solidarity: they opposed cooperative management of the enterprise, accepted a company subcontracting plan for fishermen, and opposed Sindicato Agua strikes. In short, SIP activists began to act within what some scholars call "neoliberal rationality."[6]

ON SOLIDARITY AND SUBALTERN CONSCIOUSNESS

The Salvadoran labor movement formed part of a Latin American upsurge during the 1970s. As in El Salvador, many strike movements had to contend with military regimes. In the Southern Cone, military coups crushed the massive, dynamic labor movements in Argentina and Chile. In Brazil, by contrast, despite military rule, automobile workers and metalworkers launched a massive and prolonged strike movement that had a decisive impact on the democratization process. Timing played a critical role in labor-regime relations. The Brazilian military government, in power since 1964, began a process of liberalization in 1978 and, more formally, in 1979 prompted in no small part by the strike wave, whereas during the same period, the Southern

---

Counterinsurgency, and Human Rights in Colombia (Durham, NC: Duke University Press, 2016). For an important reflection on related issues see Gilbert M. Joseph, "Latin America's Long Cold War: A Century of Revolutionary Process and U.S. Power," in *A Century of Revolution: Insurgent and Counterinsurgent Violence during Latin America's Long Cold War*, eds. Greg Grandin and Gilbert M. Joseph (Durham, NC: Duke University Press, 2010), 397–414.

[6] Harvey, and to some extent Grandin, represents one pole in a debate on neoliberalism. The other pole has its theoretical origins in Foucault, but other theorists have pushed forward his studies on "governmentality" and neoliberal rationality. Rather than a political project, these theorists view neoliberalism as the invasion of the political by economic liberalism: a "technique of government that has become the dominant rationality and has competition as its first principle ... The drive towards individual responsibilisation and the self as enterprise is a major principle of the neoliberal art of governing. It leads subjects to perform actions that reinforce their own subjection," Mathieu Hilgers, "The Three Anthropological Approaches to Neoliberalism," *International Social Science Journal* 61, no. 202 (Oct. 2011): 358. Two important theoreticians of this this position are Pierre Dardot and Christian Laval, *The New Way of the World: On Neoliberal Society* (New York: Verso, 2014). For a critique of their work, see Bruce Robbins, "The Monster of Governmentality," *Los Angeles Review of Books*, June 10, 2014.

Cone regimes had recently begun their brutal crackdowns on labor.[7] In El Salvador, the labor movement had developed over two decades under military regimes. Labor's militant rise in the late 1970s pushed the regime in a highly repressive direction that, in turn, propelled an expansion of the movement. If we use the number of strikes and strikers as a measure, by 1979, the Salvadoran workers' movement followed Brazil as the proportionately the most combative in the Americas. Moreover, the Salvadoran labor movement followed Argentina, Chile, and Uruguay in the early 1970s as the most militant in Latin American history, if one takes the *toma* (plant occupation) as a sign of militancy.

In many respects, the Salvadoran movement resembled the Guatemalan, so brilliantly depicted and analyzed by Deborah Levinson-Estrada in *Trade Unionists against Terror.*[8] The organized Guatemalan workers also faced an increasingly homicidal regime: presumably, the two governments exchanged notes on their respective situations. The main difference between the two movements was that the Salvadoran radical Left (the Organizaciones Populares, OP) led the majority of strikes in 1979 and 1980, as opposed to Guatemala, where trade unionists not identified with the Far Left headed most of the labor actions; the Salvadorans also employed the tactic of the *toma* more frequently. Regardless of the differences, the union activists of both countries rank among the most heroic and brutalized in twentieth-century labor history.

Solidarity Under Siege explains the success of the Puerto El Triunfo labor movement in achieving major quotas of autonomy and substantial improvements in the workers' wages and working conditions; it had begun the 1970s under the leadership of a regime-controlled labor federation tied very closely to the military regime. That achievement hinged significantly on a major change in the consciousness of a primarily female workforce.

---

[7] For an excellent analysis of the Brazilian labor movement during the late 1970s, see John D. French, *Lula's Politics of Cunning: From Trade Unionism to the Presidency,* Part 2 (Chapel Hill: University of North Carolina Press, forthcoming).

[8] Deborah Levenson-Estrada, *Trade Unionists against Terror* (Chapel Hill: University of North Carolina Press, 1994). The Honduran labor movement had a larger percentage of the economically active population organized in unions and achieved significant gains during the 1970s facing far less repressive regimes. The Nicaraguan labor movement was weaker than its neighbors, though it took off in at least a numerical sense following the 1979 triumph of the revolution.

Like their counterparts in Guatemala, Salvadoran workers struggled for a life in which their children could be adequately cared for, schooled, clothed, and fed in a healthy community free from arbitrary repression. To achieve that basic goal, they entered into alliances that ultimately made them objects of state and paramilitary violence. Faced with a common, homicidal antagonist, the alliances nevertheless endured well into the 1980s.

This book explores the multifaceted transformation of workers' consciousness. In my first book, *To Lead as Equals*, I analyzed the ways in which peasants and peasant laborers (campesinos) in northwestern Nicaragua experienced an endogenous transformation of consciousness.[9] Campesinos used and expanded the meanings of elite concepts – such as private property – to understand and transform their social world. Moreover, they deployed those concepts in ways that first engaged and ultimately disengaged with their elite allies. Rather than a realm of complete autonomy, a dialectic of autonomy and dependency was consistently in play in their contradictory forms of consciousness. *Solidarity Under Siege* follows *To Lead as Equals* in that it emphasizes the endogenous transformation of consciousness yet embarks in a new direction in that it explores the uneven qualities of the changes related to the workers' multiple, coexisting affiliations and identities. Those, in turn, conditioned misunderstandings and discord within the labor movement, rooted to some degree in gendered structural divisions and labor segmentation. To cite a key example, the approximately 500 fishermen based in Puerto El Triunfo engaged in a unique form of resistance, known as "la movida" (the move) involving illegal sales of shrimp that became a realm of dispute among all port workers. Due to its illegality, no one could publicly speak about *la movida*.

The silence conditioned what I call a *desencuentro*, a Spanish word with greater reach and resonance than the individual English synonyms: a misunderstanding, disagreement, disjuncture, run-in, or failed encounter. People in two different groups can have different understandings of the

---

[9] Jeffrey L. Gould, *To Lead as Equals: Rural Protest and Political Consciousness in Chinandega, Nicaragua, 1912–1979* (Chapel Hill: University of North Carolina Press, 1990). My analysis resembled the early work of the Subaltern School, on the one hand, and James Scott's corpus, on the other. Unaware of that important work at the time of my research and writing, it differs in my emphasis on the subaltern use of elite concepts.

[10] For other uses of *desencuentros* see Bruno Bosteels, *Marx and Freud in Latin America, Politics, Psychoanalysis, and Religion in Times of Terror* (London: Verso Press, 2012); Julio Ramos, *Divergent Modernities: Culture and Politics in Nineteenth Century Latin*

same word or concept that, in turn, may condition different practices in a given historical moment.[10] In the words of the Russian linguist, V. N. Volosinov: "Each word, as we know, is a little arena for the clash and crisscrossing of differently oriented social accents. A word in the mouth of a particular individual person is a product of the living interaction of social forces."[11]

I propose to use *desencuentro* as a methodological tool to aid in our understanding of the divisions among oppositional and subaltern forces. In previous work, I noted that, in the 1980s, the Sandinistas and grass-roots peasant activists understood "people's property" differently, with significant political consequences. The peasant notion, rooted in an earlier conceptualization of "private property," emphasized individual access with local, collective control of land whereas the emerging revolutionary notion limited the meaning to state ownership and control. At times, I will use the term in a stronger sense, emphasizing the linguistic impact on political disagreement (*desencuentro* I). At other times, the term will refer to the failure of two groups with shared goals to ally, without specifying a linguistic dimension (*desencuentro* II).

The book also explores a vein of analysis opened up originally by Daniel James that emphasizes the dialectical relationship between formal ideological discourse and practical consciousness.[12] *Solidarity Under Siege* underscores how the labor and peasant movements grew quantitatively and qualitatively when that relationship was able to flourish, and what happened when this dynamic was restrained.

In El Salvador and elsewhere, the disjunction between formal ideology and practical consciousness was related to the contradiction between the revolutionary major utopias and subaltern minor utopias. Those spaces of unfettered horizontal communication at times were not visible to the different actors.[13] In Latin America, these minor utopias, "visions of

America (Durham, NC: Duke University Press, 2001). For another interesting use of the term related to the notion of a failed encounter, see Álvaro Garcia Linera, "Indianismo y marxismo: El desencuentro de dos razones revolucionarias," *Revista Donataria* no. 2 (Mar.–Apr. 2005).

[11] V. N. Volosinov, *Marxism and the Philosophy of Language*, trans. Ladislav Matejka and I. R. Titunik (Cambridge, MA: Harvard University Press, 1973), 41.

[12] Daniel James, *Resistance and Integration: Peronism and the Argentine Working Class, 1946–1976* (Cambridge: Cambridge University Press, 1988).

[13] Jay Winter, *Dreams of Peace and Freedom: Utopian Moments of the Twentieth Century* (New Haven, CT: Yale University Press, 2006), 5. Winter calls "minor utopias": "imaginings of liberation usually on a smaller scale, without the grandiose pretensions or the almost unimaginable hubris and cruelties of the 'major' utopian projects."

partial transformation, of pathways out of the ravages of war, or away from the indignities of the abuse of human rights" were often embedded within a "major" revolutionary utopian discourse.[14] As a result, the organized Left often ignored or misunderstood these utopian, egalitarian experiences, due to their challenge to all forms of hierarchy. There was also a murky space often filled with rhetorical flourishes between the revolutionary nationalist imaginary and the objective possibilities for social and political change most vividly illustrated by the chasm between the leftist Sandinista government's goals and its achievements, however noteworthy.

Regardless of the *desencuentros*, discord, and disillusionment associated with the Central American Left, the enshrinement of fundamental notions of solidarity was a significant collective achievement. Today, the term *solidarity* encompasses elastic meanings ranging from the purchase of fair-trade coffee to support for flood victims. However, during the 1970s the term had powerful salience throughout the world, despite its multivocality. One of the key contributions of Liberation Theology that spread across Latin America during the 1960s and 1970s was to take a strand of Christianity, the early ideas about brotherhood, and create new meanings of solidarity embodied in the thought and practice of tens of thousands of Christian Base Communities (CBC). Solidarity meant a full commitment to aid and support fellow members of the CBCs specifically and the oppressed in general, both locally and nationally, in their struggles for material and spiritual liberation. The Iglesia Popular (Popular Church) also pushed the institutional churches to offer support (solidarity) to the CBCs and to join their attack on the profoundly inegalitarian societal structures that imprisoned the majority of Salvadorans in poverty. These notions of Christian solidarity resembled those of anarcho-syndicalists during the earlier decades of the twentieth century, especially in Spain and in the Southern Cone, and illustrate the philosopher Kurt Bayertz's contention that

The solidarity practiced within social movements thus acquires a dimension which is both archaeological and anticipative. It is archaeological insofar as it uncovers a disposition, buried under established social conditions, towards cooperation, mutual aid, common feeling – in short: solidarity. It is *anticipative* insofar as it also draws a picture of the future human being, who will ultimately be free to develop its cooperative and common strengths unhindered ... It refers directly to a *means* of the battle: solidarity as a weapon. Yet, at the same time, it refers to the

[14] Ibid., 5.

end of the battle: solidarity as an anticipation of future society, as part of Utopia already lived.[15]

These notions of Christian solidarity had a major impact on the development of the campesino movement in El Salvador: the vast majority of the rural wing of the radical Bloque Popular Revolucionario (BPR) had an intimate connection with the CBCs. Campesinos translated the practice of social solidarity within the CBCs, including highly evolved notions of sharing and collective labor, into the radical struggles for land, decent wages, and working conditions. In the BPR and other OPs, the Iglesia Popular's notions of solidarity merged with those connected historically to the labor movement and then to those related to the nascent revolutionary movement that exploded onto the world stage in 1981. As the Jesuit intellectual, Ignacio Ellacuría warned, however, the integration of these distinct strands of solidarity was not seamless. Criticizing the OPs for minimizing the influence of the CBCs, he wrote that former needed the latter "to transform our being itself and the consciousness of the laboring class; this is the deepest and most valuable principle of liberation."[16]

In the port, the transition from the most elementary forms of unionism, a sense of solidarity with fellow workers on the shop floor to a willingness to sacrifice for all union members, was fraught and far from unidirectional. The move from labor solidarity to support for political-military organizations committed to social-political revolution was similarly partial and contradictory.

By 1979 and 1980, as state repression intensified, popular resistance grew. Death squads tied to security forces executed between 8,000 and 11,000 civilians in 1980. Amidst that orgy of violence, opposition to the regime often was equated with support for the revolutionary Left. By the end of the year, when death squads eliminated the entire civilian opposition leadership, that identification between dissent and revolution became a truism.

On January 22, 1980, in the largest demonstration in the country's history, some 150,000–200,000 workers, peasants, and students marched in San Salvador, in what many leftists understood as the high point of revolutionary Left mobilization. The view from the port on January 22, however, allows for a more nuanced interpretation. For labor militants in

---

[15] Kurt Bayertz, "Four Uses of Solidarity," in *Solidarity*, ed. Kurt Bayertz (Dordrecht, The Netherlands: Kluwer Academic Publishers, 1999), 20.

[16] Tomás Campos, "La iglesia y las organizaciones populares en El Salvador," *Estudios Centroamericanos* 33, no. 359 (Sept. 1978): 699.

the port, and perhaps for a substantial minority of union members nationally, the march represented the power of the labor movement. At the same time, the SIP and its parent labor federation employed minor forms of coercion to encourage its membership to join the march. This study suggests that the revolutionary Left enjoyed less support than it purported to have, and that support was at times ambivalent. At the same time, its middle-level leadership was far more *popular*, based in the rural and urban working classes, than some analysts and scholars have posited.

HISTORIOGRAPHY

Recently, there have been several fine studies of the origins and development of the Salvadoran civil war. Joaquín Chávez's *Poets and Prophets of the Resistance: Intellectuals and the Origins of El Salvador's Civil War* examines the evolving alliance between urban intellectuals and peasants during that critical and understudied period.[17] It describes how peasants became educated and then became educators through nontraditional means fostered in general by the Catholic Church. Chávez also provides a first-rate analysis of the mobilization and radicalization process by focusing on the emergence of different types of intellectuals, including peasants.

In *Modernizing Minds*, Erick Ching and Héctor Lindo-Fuentes offer a convincing account of the primordial role of ANDES 21 de Junio, the teachers' union within the anti-regime opposition.[18] Moreover, they unpack with great precision a major division in the governing Partido de Conciliación Nacional, that is the military, highlighting a rift between those committed to social-economic reform and those who fought to maintain the status quo. Ching has also recently published *Stories of Civil War in El Salvador: A Battle over Memory*. This finely crafted, sophisticated study examines the process of memory formation in the aftermath of the civil war. He analyzes four discrete narratives: civilian elites, military officers, Frente Farabundo Martí Para La Liberación Nacoinal (FMLN) combatants, and FMLN commanders. Through a literary analysis of written testimony Ching argues that each narrative, drawing on

---

[17] Joaquín Chávez, *Poets and Prophets of the Resistance: Intellectuals and the Origins of El Salvador's Civil War* (New York: Oxford University Press, 2017).

[18] Héctor Lindo-Fuentes and Erik Ching, *Modernizing Minds: Education Reform and the Cold War, 1960–1980* (Albuquerque: University of New Mexico Press, 2012).

different readings of El Salvador history, are surprisingly coherent within groups despite their individual construction.[19]

Kristin Pirker's recent book *La Redefinción de lo Posible* makes an extraordinary contribution to our understanding of the Salvadoran Left over a 40-year period, especially on the work of the OP during the late 1970s.[20] She notes their democratizing impact on the existing unions. Paul Almeida's work, *Waves of Protest*,[21] an account of the causal relationship between state repression and popular radicalization, is also very useful for understanding the period under study. Finally, Jocelyn Viterna's *Women in War*[22] offers one of the first serious accounts of gender and militancy. Through sophisticated, multidisciplinary analyses, she offers an explanatory framework for understanding the motivations and experiences of the roughly one-third of the FMLN fighters who were women.

Solidarity Under Siege draws intellectual sustenance from all these books yet departs from them in several respects. First, it focuses primarily on industrial unions composed mainly of women. After a flurry of highly engaging studies on the working class and popular movements written in the 1970s and 1980s, there have been very few scholarly studies of Salvadoran labor during that period.[23] This book also focuses on a town that experienced relative peace during a war. In addition, the book deals

[19] Erik Ching, *Stories of Civil War in El Salvador: A Battle over Memory* (Chapel Hill: University of North Carolina Press, 2016).

[20] Kristina Pirker, *La redefinción de lo posible: Militancia política y mobilización social en El Salvador, 1970–2012* (Mexico City: Instituto Mora, 2017).

[21] Paul Almeida, *Waves of Protest: Popular Struggle in El Salvador, 1925–2005* (Minneapolis: University of Minnesota Press, 2008).

[22] Jocelyn Viterna, *Women in War: The Micro-Processes of Mobilization in El Salvador* (New York: Oxford University Press, 2013). Also see an earlier, important work by Gilles Bataillon, *Génesis de la guerras intestinas en América Central (1960–1983)* (Mexico City: Fondo de Cultura Económica, 2008). His sophisticated analysis of the Junta Revolucionaria de Gobierno (JRG) arrives at similar conclusions to our own using a different methodology.

[23] Mario Lungo, *La lucha de las masas en El Salvador* (San Salvador: UCA Editores, 1987); ibid., *El Salvador in the Eighties: Counterinsurgency and Revolution* (Philadelphia: Temple University Press, 1996); Rafael Guido Béjar, in "El movimiento sindical después de la Segunda Guerra Mundial," *Estudios Centroamericanos* 45, no. 502 (Aug. 1990), 871–92; Rafael Menjívar Larín, *Formación y lucha del proletariado industrial salvadoreño* (San Salvador: UCA Editores, 1982); Salvador Samayoa and Guillermo Galván, 'El movimiento obrero en El Salvador: Resurgimiento o agitación'; *Estudios Centroamericanos* 369–70 (July–Aug. 1979), 591–600; and ibid., "El cierre patronal de los empresarios: Prueba de fuego para el sindicalismo revolucionario," *Estudios Centroamericanos* 34, no. 371 (Sept. 1979), 793–800.

with an unusual social-geographical space, a nationally controlled enclave. Puerto El Triunfo resembled a foreign-owned enclave in that the port was geographically isolated from the rest of the country and its residents depended on one industry whose products were mostly sold on the foreign market. The conditions were so enclave-like and the owners were so socially distant from the workers that periodically the unions denounced the "foreign"-owned companies.

THE PORT AND ITS PEOPLE

At the turn of the nineteenth century, John Wright was a prosperous fishing boat captain based out of San Francisco. He married into the Melendez family, leading members of the Salvadoran coffee oligarchy. His son, also called John, eventually made his way to El Salvador where he became integrated into his maternal family and eventually came to own "La Carrera," the largest and most successful cotton plantation in the country, located near the Bay of Jiquilisco in Usulután, some 60 miles east of San Salvador. Following his passing in 1952, his son Juan Wright Alcaine took over his properties and businesses. During the mid-1950s, Wright noticed how a group of Portuguese fishermen, based in Puerto El Triunfo, founded a company and were beginning to catch large quantities of shrimp in the ocean waters just beyond the Bay of Jiquilisco. In 1957, along with others, he decided to invest heavily in the Portuguese-owned company that they baptized Pezca S.A. (to distinguish it from a Guatemalan company, Pesca S.A.). The processing plant and associated fishing companies became part of his growing industrial empire: by 1960, Wright owned 61 enterprises with more than US$20 million in social capital (net worth of company's assets that will not be returned to the stockholder).[24] Most of Wright's companies were related to the cotton industry (insecticides, textiles, vegetable oil, etc.). As shrimp had never been caught in the ocean waters near the Bay of Jiquilisco, the industry had phenomenal success, reaching a production of more than six million pounds in 1961. Production of the more expensive white shrimp, however, declined dramatically over the next decade from 2,030 tons in 1960 to 1,054 tons in 1970. Ironically, that decline was due in large part to the pesticide runoff from the nearby cotton plantations, including Wright's *La Carrera*.[25]

---

[24] The net worth of company's assets that will not be returned to the stockholder.
[25] Peter Phillips and Charles Cole, "Fisheries Resources of Jiquilisco Bay, El Salvador," Proceedings of the Gulf and Caribbean Fisheries Institute, 30th Annual Session

The industry remained highly profitable thanks not only to high prices in the United States but also because the pesticide runoff did not affect brown shrimp and camaroncillos (known locally as *chacalín*). Wright invested much of his profits into the further mechanization of the plant. By the early 1970s, employing some 750 plant workers, it was one of the country's largest manufacturing plants; the company had a balance of US$3 million, and a social capital of US$1 million.

Wright was the leading share owner of five fishing boat companies, with 39 boats that directly supplied Pezca S.A.[26] They were disconnected formally from the main company, in part due to governmental restrictions on the ownership of fishing boats and presumably also due to tax (and possibly labor) questions. Until the late 1970s, Wright tended to stay out of politics. In 1944, however, his family had supported the anti-dictatorial battle against the Martínez Hernández dictatorship. Indeed, Juan Wright's brother was killed accidentally during the uprising.[27]

The other businessmen connected to the shrimp industry also came from oligarchic families. The Alfaro, Salaverría, Daglio, and Dueñas families figured among the leading landholders in the country; they were all major shareholders in Atarraya S.A.[28] For tax purposes, the company was divided into three separate, contiguous plants in turned owned by three companies, most of whose shareholders were the same people. Ward Foods of New York also had a US$250,000 investment. The three Atarraya plants had a total workforce of less than 500. The same owners also controlled several fishing boat companies. Finally, Rafael Guirola, whose family was the second leading landowner in the country and one of the most important coffee producers, owned *Mariscos de El Salvador*, the smallest shrimp business in the port, employing roughly 200 workers and fishermen.[29] He owned another shrimp operation in the department of La Unión.

The heart of El Salvador's shrimp industry was Puerto El Triunfo, founded in 1829, in honor of a military victory of the Liberal forces allied with their leader, Francisco Morazán in the civil war against

(Nov. 1977), 83–84. Pesticides applied from August to January coincide with early life of white and pink shrimp. Brown shrimp do not migrate into the bay until after the rainy season and camaroncillos (called *chacalín* locally) were also not affected.

[26] Eduardo Colindres, *Fundamentos económicos de la burguesía salvadoreña* (San Salvador: UCA Editores, 1977), 251. The book lists 1.7 million colones of *utilidades*.

[27] Fabio Castillo, Servicio de Informativo Ecuménico y Popular, interview with the author, June 27, 2005.

[28] Colindres, *Fundamentos economicos*, 54–55, 158.   [29] Ibid., 158.

Map of Puerto El Triunfo
(by Anne Continelli)

Conservatives. It gained a limited degree of importance during the coffee boom in the late nineteenth and early twentieth centuries as a site of export for coffee produced in the department of Usulután. Then, in the 1960s, the shrimp industry changed everything.

As the shrimp industry boomed in the 1960s, migrants, mainly peasants, flooded the one-street town as production increased from virtually zero in 1958 to more than 10 million pounds in 1966. The port population leaped from 673 to 4,470, with the vast majority of residents in the 1960s and 1970s living in houses made of *mangle* (mangrove). Neither the companies nor the underfunded municipal governments bothered to address the festering problem of sanitation or the lack of electricity outside of the plants. Many people used a drainage ditch for their necessities or public latrines on the edge of the mangrove swamp. Workers referred to the port as "Puerto el Tufo" (Port Stink). What happened when a relatively sleepy port became a boomtown is the subject of the pages that follow in this book.

The Book

The stories of several key union activists in the Sindicato de la Industria Pesquera (founded in 1961) form the core of the first chapter, which also details the production process, paying particular attention to the gendered division of labor. In addition, the chapter narrates and analyzes the role of women and gender ideologies in the mobilization of the 1970s that converted the union into a key member of the leftist labor federation, the Federación Nacional Sindical de Trabajadores Salvadoreños (FENAS-TRAS). The first chapter also introduces the *marineros*, the fishermen, and their unique form of resistance.

The second chapter examines the causes and nature of the growth and radicalization of the national labor movement that erupted with such force during the first months of 1979. The narrative also returns its gaze to Puerto El Triunfo: by the end of August 1979, SIP compelled all three companies to grant temporary workers permanent status with all the attendant benefits. This reversal of the global flexibilization of labor strategy came in part through an alliance with FENASTRAS. In fact, Alejandro Molina Lara, the secretary-general of SIP, became a high-ranking figure within the labor federation. These ties pushed the rank and filers, sometimes against their will, toward more active participation in solidarity strikes and marches.

A critical moment in Salvadoran history is analyzed in Chapter 3: from the coup in October 15, 1979 until the start of the civil war and mass repression during the latter part of 1980. The coup installed a military-civilian junta that included moderate leftists who promised a reformist solution to the economic, social, and political crisis that would prevent a looming civil war. This chapter offers a new interpretation of the first JRG (October 15, 1979–January 2, 1980) and, in particular the six-week truce that represented both a shutdown of the repressive apparatus and the flowering of the rural labor movement. In part, the disjunction between revolutionary rhetoric and the grassroots struggles and necessities impeded a potential alliance between the JRG and the OP. The failed encounter between the two forces conditioned a subsequent explosion of rightist violence. By the end of 1980, death squads arrived in the port, executing some SIP leaders and driving many others into exile.

The early war years are the subject of Chapter 4. During this period, the port was largely unaffected by the war, as the guerrillas used it for recuperative purposes (and perhaps finances) and the military directly profited from the shrimp industry. SIP gradually recovered from the wave of repression in 1980–81, reconstituting itself in the port in 1984, still nominally allied with the Left through FENASTRAS. Sindicato Agua, the fishermen's union, allied itself with the Christian Democratic government and received significant support from the American Institute for Free Labor Development (AIFLD). Sindicato Agua also developed an anti-communist, but nonetheless radical, populist ideology. During the mid-1980s, the union waged a two-front battle to expel SIP from Pezca S.A. (the largest company) and to combat efforts by the company to engage in a form of subcontracting that would effectively take away the bargaining rights of the fishermen. Its union leadership agitated to push the government to expropriate the industry and turn it over to the fishermen and the workers to run as a cooperative. SIP leaders, despite a shared affinity for public ownership of industry, rejected the cooperative.

Rightist politics connected to the shrimp company owners and a related massive fraud form the subject matter of Chapter 5. Although death squad activity in the port cannot be traced to the owners, several of them relocated to Miami where they reportedly financed paramilitary rightist activity in El Salvador. The chapter uses court records to unravel the massive fraud that some of the owners engaged in with the director of the nationalized Banco Agrícola Comercial.

The labor movement was able to reorganize in the mid-1980s in part due to an alliance between the Christian Democratic president Jose Napoleon Duarte and centrist trade unionists. Chapter 6 charts the contradictory relations between the Duarte administration and centrist and leftist union activists in the San Salvador metropolitan area. *Solidarity Under Siege* reveals a contradiction at the heart of Reagan administration policy, namely between its neoliberal goals and its counterinsurgent strategy that involved its opposite – heavy state welfare expenditures, support for labor, nationalized banking, and cooperative ownership. In the port, AIFLD financially supported Sindicato Agua through more than four years of strikes that directly undermined US governmental efforts to stabilize the economy.[30]

The final chapter tacks back to the port where it narrates and analyzes the highly controversial strike that broke out in 1987. Sindicato Agua union pushed back against Pezca's subcontracting plan. Once again, SIP and Sindicato Agua could not overcome their differences, rooted in ideological and gender conflicts, to push for the cooperative ownership of Pezca; instead, the company collapsed along with the unions.

---

[30] Norman Schipull, communication with the author, 2014. He was a former head of AIFLD. He states that the organization could only support the union through funding for educational programs, typically totaling approximately US$20,000 a year. That account was substantiated by Ruperto Torres, former leader of Sindicato Agua (officially known as the Sindicato General de la Industria Pesquera y Anexos, SGTIPAC).

A Note on Sources and the Film Puerto Triunfo

As with my previous books, *Solidarity Under Siege* relies on a considerable amount of oral history. Nevertheless, there are significant differences between this project and the others. The interviews in the port, conducted over a dozen visits, generally coincided with the filming of a companion documentary. Although the interviews were invaluable for the film production (see www.puertotriunfofilm.com), the setting may have affected the quality of the interviews, in that the camera may have intimidated the interviewee. However, the repetition of the interviews on subsequent visits probably mitigated the effects of the camera. Certainly, the informants appeared more relaxed during the follow-up filmed interviews. I also made several trips to Los Angeles where a good portion of the interviewing of labor activist exiles took place away from the camera.

I was fortunate to stumble upon the archives of the Sindicato de la Industria Pesquera and of Sindicato Agua consisting of abandoned documents from its inception in 1961 until 1995.

FIGURE I.I The union hall archive
(photo by Guillermo Escalón)

Those documents principally include extensive minutes from meetings of six locals and transcripts of meetings with company representatives at the Ministry of Labor and in labor-management commissions at the company. Moreover, I was fortunate to find a fine research assistant, David Segovia, who was able to bear the extremely difficult conditions in the stifling hot, boarded-up former union buildings in Puerto El Triunfo to organize and photograph the utterly unorganized archives. To my knowledge, these are the only extensive union archives in the country from this period. I also gained access to a judicial archive in San Salvador, where another research assistant, Rubén Gonzalez, was able to photograph some 3,000 pages of records related to the fraud case. Other than that, I had some success with a Freedom of Information Act (FOIA) request for State Department archives related to the labor movement and the problems in the port. Finally, I availed myself of some Salvadoran periodicals from the period, including those found in the invaluable North American Congress on Latin America (NACLA) archive. Unfortunately, I met the fate of other researchers who failed to obtain access to the military archives despite years of a supposed left-wing government. Although I did obtain some valuable photos from the current owner of Atarraya (now a small fishing operation), I was unable to consult any company archives or to interview former management employees (with one exception). So once again my monograph will lack a certain balance between the views from *los de arriba* and those from *los de abajo*.

Tired of the Abuse

Gender and the Rise of the Sindicato de la Industria Pesquera, 1970–1990

I don't know if we felt liberated but we would even joke during work hours, we were happy. Was it the union support or were we just tired of being in that position? Things changed. We would not get scolded or threatened to have our daily wage taken away from us for talking. We felt free!

Gloria García, 2015

He helped me to build my union hall, he learned me how to talk.

Woody Guthrie, "Dear Mrs. Roosevelt"

Gloria García was born and raised in a tiny seashore village on El Salvador's eastern coast.[1] When she was 10, her father brought her and two sisters to Puerto El Triunfo. She immediately started work on a nearby cotton hacienda. She planted, pruned, and picked cotton for 25 cents a day. She recalls the unrelenting sun, the exhaustion, the prohibition against play, and her infected hands. Gloria's father found work at the shrimp processing plant Pezca S.A. Her older sister also got a job there peeling *chacalín* (sea bob). Even though they paid little rent for their mangrove bark dwelling, they were barely making ends meet. Her dad eventually got Gloria a job in the plant, but they had to change her birth certificate so she appeared to be 14 instead of 12. The foreman complained that she was so skinny that she looked like she was nine. And the work was hard at first. After a day's labor, her hands were cut, raw, and

---

[1] Personal references to Gloria García derive from interviews with the author, Lake Elsinore, 2015; ibid., Los Angeles, 2016; ibid., 2017.

infected but it was better paid and less onerous work than on the cotton hacienda. She got to play on the Pezca baseball team against the other plants, Atarraya and Mariscos de El Salvador. She also went to night school the rest of the year and finished the sixth grade. Despite doing well at school, her work schedule was too intense and unpredictable to continue her education.

Over the next several years, Gloria became increasingly adept at peeling and eventually she gained a permanent position so that she wasn't laid off at the end of the *chacalín* season like 40 percent of the labor force. She also got shifted around to various assignments, alleviating the boredom and allowing her to meet new people among the plant's labor force of more than 500 workers. By the time Gloria was 18 in 1971, she had become accustomed to life and work in the plant and no longer suffered as much from pain and exhaustion. She was able to enjoy a minimum of leisure – occasionally taking the bus 10 miles with her friends to Usulután to the cinema. Sometimes on Fridays she could buy some clothes and makeup from the open market outside of the plant. Almost all her earnings, 18 colones (US$1.00 = 2.5 colones) a week, however, she turned over to her father.

As we shall see, Gloria's frustration with managerial authoritarianism, low wages, and poor working conditions eventually led her to union activism. Her union participation marked her life dramatically. Her husband opposed her leadership role and left her to raise her two children as a single mother. In 1981, death squad threats and violence drove her into exile.

With the exception of her brush with death squads, Gloria's experiences typified those of her fellow rural migrants to Puerto El Triunfo. Gloria and many of her female coworkers, over the course of but a few years, became active in a burgeoning union movement in the port allied with a left-wing labor federation. Their gendered experiences of mobilization, the main subject of this chapter, reflect the process of labor activism and radicalization of the Salvadoran worker and peasant movements whose militancy and courage in the face of violent repression received global attention. There are salient differences, however, to the local story. Most scholars argue that labor and peasant radicalization was a direct response to state repression.[2] Although in November 1977, the National Guard arrested four union leaders and held them for a couple of days,

---

[2] See Charles Brockett, *Political Movements and Violence in Central America* (New York: Cambridge University Press, 2005); Paul Almeida, *Waves of Protest: Popular Struggle in El Salvador, 1925–2005* (Minneapolis: University of Minnesota Press, 2008).

until 1980, there was virtually no other consequential anti-labor repression in the port. The transformation of the Sindicato de la Industria Pesquera (SIP) from a company union, tied to the pro-regime labor federation, into an integral part of a radicalized national labor movement was a largely endogenous process and not a response to state repression. Women's struggles for full rights for seasonal workers (almost all female), for their own specific needs, and for dignity in the work place decisively shaped that process.

Yet the transformation of labor that challenged the shrimp companies and their oligarchic owners was a fraught, contentious, and incomplete process. The insurgent union leadership had to confront three major obstacles. First, the union had to challenge and at least neutralize the political conservatism of the majority of the workforce. Second, SIP activists had to overcome the ideological consequences of a highly gendered division of labor that marked the private and public lives of female workers and their accompanying apathy.

Female workers, the majority of the labor force, were vital to the union's success. Their activism commenced along with a conscious effort to publicly voice their concerns and to overcome internal divisions. The male leadership also had to overcome their biases as women pushed hard to make their concerns those of the union. Third, the union leadership had to deal with the machista lifestyle and ethic of most of the fishermen and their opposition to the militancy of the insurgent SIP leadership. That opposition during the 1970s derived primarily from the pro-company orientation of Sindicato Agua. Moreover, their unique form of resistance to the companies by the 1980s would have an acutely negative impact on the plant workers.

In October 1971, Gloria witnessed the arrival in port of the 39 fishing boats administered by companies tied to Pezca S.A. There was a ceremony in which the captains and fishermen renounced their membership in the SIP and the union leader accepted their resignation. They then founded their own union that locally would be called SGTIPAC.[3] Many fishermen and plant workers believed that the general manager of Pezca, Francisco Varela, had engineered the whole operation on the basis of his friendship with a group of captains. He cajoled the captains into believing that they would receive special treatment from the company unavailable to them as members of SIP. That founding moment of labor/management complicity would condition their harmonious relations with the company until 1979.

[3] The union SGTIPAC was also called "Sector Agua" in contradistinction to "Sector Tierra." We will employ SIP or Sindicato Tierra and Sindicato Agua (or SGTIPAC).

FIGURE 1.1 Pezca S.A. workers in 1970s
(courtesy Migdalia Chavarría)

During that period, they never supported SIP job actions. At the founding of Sindicato Agua, there were no salient ideological differences between the unions, but that would change over the course of the decade as the SIP leadership began to work with the Federación Nacional Sindical de Trabajadores Salvadoreños (FENASTRAS), an independent, Left-oriented labor federation.

Throughout the remainder of 1971, the company took the offensive against SIP. Pezca refused to make any concessions during the contract negotiations. In December 1971, the union launched the first strike in the history of the company. At the same time, workers at Atarraya S.A., the second-largest processing plant, launched another strike; most of the port was paralyzed. The Pezca-affiliated fishermen in Sindicato Agua continued to work, significantly weakening the position of the plant workers. Their strike funds dwindled as SIP General (the district union) had to support the Atarraya workers as well. Both groups suffered through a Christmas with no money to buy toys for their children. The SIP general secretary, Manuel Muñoz, supported by others in the leadership, then pushed the rank and file to accept the deal that Pezca was offering. The company offered raises of only 5 centavos (US$0.02) a day for permanent workers and 3 centavos a day for *eventuales* (seasonal workers). The deal seemed laughable, but Muñoz, a respected leader and highly skilled carpenter, staked his reputation on it and most of the unionized workers saw no alternative. Almost immediately though, rumors swirled around the plant, suggesting that Muñoz had been paid off. To this day, Gloria believes that the raise was really 1 colon 3 centavos and that he pocketed the rest.

Regardless of the truth of the matter, Gloria and her friends were furious at the union leaders, the company, and the strikebreakers. She resolved to get more involved in the union. Up until then, she had belonged to the union but did not attend meetings and did not follow events closely; nor did most of the other young female workers. Gloria approached Noé Quinteros, 23, who had served on the strike committee and had seen close up what he also read as corruption. He was an *eventual* (seasonal worker) who also worked in the cold storage section in Planta II where they processed *chacalín*. Originally from the countryside in the remote, northeastern department of Morazán, Noé had arrived in the port in 1966 at the age of 18, when his father found work as a foreman on a nearby cotton plantation. He got work as an *eventual* in cold storage during the *chacalín* season. When the season was over, he worked as an extra on fishing boats, where his main job was to cut off the heads of thousands of shrimp a day. That experience soured him on life at sea. His brother also worked at Pezca and yet the family income was barely enough to sustain the family of nine. Enraged with the union leadership, Noé looked around for other allies. He saw that the Atarraya strike had worked out much more favorably for the approximately 200 workers. He approached one of their leaders, Evelio Ortiz Palma.

Ortiz Palma was a key union leader in Atarraya. He was a carpenter in the *varadero* (boat maintenance and repair area) section of the plant, made up primarily of skilled workers. That group formed most of the leadership of the Atarraya Local. Previously, he had owned a small carpentry shop in the nearby town of Jiquilisco. When the shrimp industry opened up, he hired on as a fisherman, attracted by the possibility of high wages. As a young man, he enjoyed the work and kept at it for two years, but when the captain recognized his carpentry skill, he was given a job at a boat repair facility.

For the next six years, Evelio worked as a carpenter in the maintenance facility five miles from Puerto El Triunfo on the other side of the Bay of Jiquilisco. There, he enjoyed a fair degree of work autonomy and got along well with the Dutch owner and management. When Atarraya absorbed the small shipyard, he moved to Puerto El Triunfo. He married a plant worker and moved out of the plant barracks and into a small house made of *mangle* (mangrove). They managed to get by. Shortly after the war with Honduras (the so-called Soccer War of 1969), Atarraya brought in José Noltenius as the new plant manager. Noltenius was from an elite background and introduced a new level of authoritarianism into management-labor relations in the plant. His different accent, intonation, and mannerisms caused Evelio and his workmates to believe that Noltenius was a Honduran. The new manager wanted to bring in his own workers, perhaps Salvadoran refugees from Honduras. In the war hysteria of the moment, it was easy to conflate the war with Noltenius and the anger and anxiety he caused in the plant.

Although a union existed in the plant, Evelio only began to become involved with the arrival of Noltenius. In 1970, Evelio helped spearhead a work stoppage that reinstated the workers who had been displaced by the arrival of the new manager and his crew. That year the membership elected him to the Junta Directiva of the Atarraya Local, and he "took the work real seriously."[4] During the fall of 1971, Evelio, along with the Local leadership, initiated contract negotiations with the company. Around this time, they began to hear growing complaints from female workers.

The women had many grievances against the *jefe de personal*, Rafael Villatoro. He was taking young women out of the plant and having them work as domestic servants at his home over the weekends. Even worse, he was abusing them sexually. Atarraya workers' anger heightened even more as the company fired six union activists and used stalling tactics in contract negotiations. In December, the Atarraya Local launched a strike for increased wages and for an end to sexual harassment. The company used strikebreakers including fishermen but also employed other workers from the outside. One worker recalls Christmas that year:

We spent Christmas lulling our kids to sleep with no toys. The babies screamed but we had nothing to give them not even cold tortillas, just sugar water. All this while the radio blares FELIZ NAVIDAD. ... the bosses' servants walked by with their enormous gifts that they had gotten for their servility ... and we got to savor our kids with distended stomachs and the sadness of life.[5]

---

[4] Evelio Ortiz Palma, interview with the author, Los Angeles, 2015.

[5] "Obreras de la industria pesquera," *Pueblo,* Feb. 1979. "Nosotras pasamos la navidad arrullando nuestros pequeñitos, sin juguetes ... los cipotes chillaban a moco tendido y no teníamos que darles, ni tortillas frías, a pura agua y azúcar, no había pa' donde, mientras la radio vociferaba canciones de FELIZ NAVIDAD ... los sirvientes patronales se paseaban en frente de nosotras con sus enormes regalos que el patrón les había dado por su servilismo y nosotras saboreando con nuestros chiquitines barrigudos, y la tristeza de la vida."

FIGURE 1.2 Women working in Atarraya S.A. in late 1960s or early 1970s (courtesy Mario Sáenz)

Despite the extreme and painful adversity, the unionized workers held on for 31 days until Atarraya ceded ground.[6]

On January 21, 1972, SIP reached an agreement with management. The company resisted on the key issue of pay during the strike but promised to give jobs back to the six workers who had been fired for union activities and not to take reprisals against the "agitators." Moreover, they agreed to remove the strikebreakers from the labor force. They offered raises that amounted to 68 centavos a day, or roughly a 20 percent increase. The company also granted the key demand to retire Villatoro because of the charges of sexual harassment.[7] Following the strike, female

[6] For tax purposes, Atarraya S.A. was officially composed of three separate companies: Atarraya, Ballena, and Alimentos Atarraya. There were SIP locals in each section, and theoretically they had to negotiate separate contracts though they were usually identical as the owners of the three companies were the same people.

They were all owned by the same stockholders but different plant managers. The union negotiated contracts for all three divisions.

[7] The salary increase is unclear. The company allotted 50,000 colones (US$20,000) for the approximately 200 workers for the year, to be distributed in accord with a union/

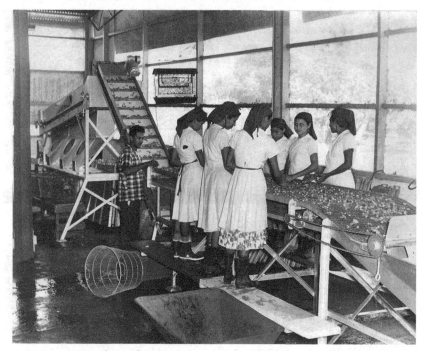

FIGURE I.3 Female workers in Atarraya S.A. in late 1960s or early 1970s
(courtesy Mario Sáenz)

membership in the union soared, representing nearly 80 percent of total
affiliates, far greater than their proportion in the workforce.[8]

Evelio had sat at the negotiating table with a younger union activist,
Alejandro Molina Lara, age 28, who, at the time was second secretary of
conflicts of SIP General. Molina Lara was a rising star, due to his rhetorical
and negotiating skills and his courage. Originally from Usulután, the departmental capital, Alejandro Molina Lara was 22 in 1966 when he arrived in
Puerto El Triunfo on a contract assignment to do some welding on a refrigeration tank. A foreman at Mariscos de El Salvador was impressed with his
work and immediately offered him a job. Accustomed to the insecurity that

---

management commission. The account did not mention the specific charges of harassment.
La Prensa Gráfica, Dec. 22, 1971; *Diario de Hoy,* Jan. 22, 1972. On Pezca, Alejandro
Molina Lara, interview with the author, Los Angeles, Sept. 2012; Noé Quinteros, phone
interview with the author, Houston, Mar. 2013.

[8] Women had 136 members and men had 38 members. The total employees are harder to
calculate, due to the temporal nature of work in various sections, but females had roughly
one-half of the jobs in the company. "Nómina de trabajadores afiliados a SIP por empresa,
la Ballena," 1973 (SIP General Archives, Puerto El Triunfo, Usulután, El Salvador).

plagued artisanal labor, the prospect of a reasonably well-paying steady job appealed to Alejandro. The port, though, was not a major attraction. Recall its nickname, Puerto El Tufo (Port Stink), as virtually no public sanitation existed outside of the packing plants. Most residents depended on public outhouses and many used the bordering mangrove swamps as toilets. Like many port laborers, Molina Lara commuted to work.

He thoroughly enjoyed his work as a welder on the docks; he was good at the job and management and the other workers treated him well. During his lunch break down by the loading dock, he would hang out with a *panguero* (who captained small boats between the dock and the shrimp boats). The *panguero* was a SIP activist. Although they maintained friendly conversations, Alejandro did not see the relevance of the union to his particular situation. Nevertheless, he did recognize the egregious situation of the majority of female packinghouse workers who lacked permanent status and any associated benefits; the company also denied them overtime payment. Despite his lack of interest in the union, company foremen observed those conversations with apprehension. Soon they began to threaten him with the loss of his job. Molina Lara knew that four years earlier, Mariscos de El Salvador had crushed the union. Although the union had legal standing, it had virtually no bargaining power. The harassment drove home to Alejandro the unequal power relations and reinforced in him elementary notions of social justice. In addition, he recognized that a position in the SIP leadership would offer him job security.[9] In 1968, he both joined the union and became a candidate for office. Presumably based on his rhetorical skills and charisma, he won election to the leadership of the Mariscos de El Salvador Local. No one could have realized at the time that he possessed rare leadership gifts that he immediately put to work successfully winning a contract negotiation.[10]

Over the next few years, Alejandro helped spur an organizing drive, among the young female workers, the *peladoras* and *empacadoras*.[11]

---

[9] The labor code stipulated that a member of the junta directiva (the governing board) could not be fired.

[10] In 1969, Molina Lara won election to the position as Second Secretary of Conflicts in the departmental union. In that position, he served on three special commissions, including an organizing mission to aid a union local in the port of La Unión. Although Alejandro and Evelio activated the departmental branch of the union, before and after their terms it was largely ceremonial; the Usulatán branch would meet merely to satisfy Ministry of Labor regulations.

[11] In Salvadoran labor law, closed shops were illegal, hence the importance of plant organizing.

FIGURE 1.4 Alejandro Molina Lara
(courtesy Molina Lara)

Women formed the majority of plant employees and thus necessary to any
serious union mobilization. In 1970, 38 female workers in Mariscos
joined the union.[12] This influx of young female workers doubled the size
of the Mariscos Local. By 1972, virtually the entire workforce belonged
to the union. Like Gloria, most of the young female workers hailed from
large, deeply impoverished families in the countryside. For those who had
started work in the 1960s and early 1970s, their experience, at first, was
quite gratifying. They received their first pay, however small, and were
able to purchase basic consumer goods about which they had previously
only dreamed. The transition to industrial time was not easy and the labor
along the conveyor belt was physically demanding – they were on their
feet all day – and highly regimented. As they matured into adulthood, the

[12] "Nómina de afiliados al sindicato de la industria pesquera subseccional por empresa
Mariscos de El Salvador," 1980 (SIP General Archives).

young women came to resent numerous problems ranging from the degrading hiring practices to the working conditions that ruined their clothes and caused their feet to swell (they often had to work in water). They resented their hunger pains toward the end of the eight-hour shift, the lack of breaks, and the yawning pay differential with male workers.

Molina Lara met constantly with the new female workers, demonstrating a concern for their everyday problems, vowing to fight on their behalf. At the same time, he began to work with Noé Quinteros and Leonel Chávez, another Pezca worker, equally disaffected from the union leadership since the end of the disastrous 33-day strike in Pezca. They all agreed that the leadership either had sold out the strike or simply lacked the will and fortitude to keep the fight going. Within a year, the three activists won election to the key posts of SIP General.[13] Their prestige was not based on their job hierarchy as only Molina Lara was a skilled worker. Rather people admired their negotiating skill and their combative, optimistic spirit. As a direct result, increasing numbers of women joined the union and began to participate in meetings. Between 1968 and 1973, the attendance at SIP General meetings rose from an average of less than 200 to more than 500.

INSURGENT LEADERSHIP

The new union leadership operated on somewhat favorable ground. Labor unions occupied an important space in authoritarian El Salvador. Labor protections, including the right to strike, were enshrined in the nation's constitution. Nevertheless, unionized workers represented only some 5 percent of the economically active population during the 1970s, in part a reflection of the prohibition against labor organizing among rural workers and the size of the informal labor sector.[14] Unions did, however, legitimize the military regime specifically through the operation of a pro-government labor federation. Toward the end of the decade, union legality could also be used as an argument to answer Carter administration demands for democratization. Yet the military regime depended

---

[13] The SIP General, in effect a district union, was made up of all SIP members in the port from the three local unions. Although there was also a departmental SIP, throughout the ensuing decades the SIP general was far more important.

[14] Robert Alexander, *A History of Organized Labor in Panama and Central America* (Westport, CT: Praeger Publishers, 2008); William Bollinger, "El Salvador," in *Latin American Labor Organizations,* ed. Gerald Greenfield and Sheldon L. Maram (New York: Greenwood Press, 1987).

upon an alliance with various sectors of the oligarchy, which included industrial capital. The tension between the regime's discursive support for union activity and its strategic alliance with business interests provided labor militants with a potent rhetorical weapon within their unions and in the broader society. Although management throughout the country often successfully resisted unions, militants could avail themselves of legal standing, however limited.

Despite the advantages of belonging to the pro-regime labor federation, in particular an open door at the Labor Ministry, Leonel Chávez, Alejandro, and Noé engineered the disaffiliation of SIP from the regime-dominated Confederación General de Sindicatos (CGS). At the 1972 congress, SIP militants joined 17 other unions in staging a walkout. The SIP militants promoted this action because they associated the CGS who advised Muñoz with the sellout of the Pezca strike.

The act of disaffiliation did not immediately represent the beginning of a political radicalization process. At that very moment, Alejandro was a councilman in Puerto El Triunfo as a member of the Partido de Conciliación Nacional (PCN), the party of the military regime. Believing he could improve the living conditions in the port, he had agreed to join the PCN ticket in the national and local elections of 1972, widely condemned as fraudulent. Although he was able to push through a major increase in the municipal tax paid by the shrimp companies, Alejandro quickly became disillusioned with the mayor and the PCN, whom he came to view as corrupt. Within a year, he resigned his position and recognized that the corruption of the PCN was tied to that of the regime-controlled CGS.[15]

In the February 1973 union elections, Leonel Chávez won the post of Secretary General; Noé Quinteros became Secretary of Organization; and Molina Lara became the first Secretary of Conflicts. That same year Molina Lara pushed for a new contract at Mariscos de El Salvador so that its salary structure would match that of the other companies. He pursued a strategy that he would follow throughout much of the decade: Following the company rejection of the union demands, he attended Local meetings where he painstakingly presented statistics about productivity, world prices, and inflation to educate the workers about the necessity and potential limits to wage increases. Notwithstanding his efforts, Mariscos de El Salvador responded by laying off nearly its entire workforce.

[15] Molina Lara, interview with the author, Los Angeles, 2015.

Probably due to a loss of prestige caused by SIP's failure to halt the layoffs in February 1974, Molina Lara lost the elections for secretary general to Evelio Ortiz by a vote of 260–190 with another 90 votes going to the former secretary general, Mercedes Muñoz.[16] Evelio Ortiz always maintained a degree of neutrality between the two main factions of the union, those aligned with Alejandro, Leonel, and Noé and those with Muñoz. He sympathized more with the insurgent faction but maintained a strong friendship with Muñoz. Although the image of Muñoz had been tarnished by the accusations of selling out the Pezca strike, he still maintained a base of support due to his affable personality, his reputation as a highly skilled worker (reputedly the best carpenter in the port) and to some degree to his rhetoric of worker-management harmony. Molina Lara only won election to Second Secretary of Conflicts.[17]

THE FIRST LEGAL STRIKE IN HISTORY

Operating from his relatively lowly position in the union hierarchy, Molina Lara led two initiatives. First, he pushed hard to block the introduction of deveining machinery in Atarraya, used for small shrimp and *chacalines* (sea bob). According to the SIP leader, the machinery had cost more than 200 jobs in Pezca S.A. He unsuccessfully argued that the machines were grossly inefficient.[18]

Alejandro was far more successful in a new round with Mariscos de El Salvador, where he faced Rafael Guirola, a powerful oligarch. Among the four wealthiest in the country, Guirola's family owned 52 coffee plantations and businesses worth approximately US$50 million.[19] Guirola rarely negotiated directly with the union but when he did so he remained diplomatic. He shared some other traditional oligarchical values, in particular the right to oblige subalterns to participate in the "don's" rituals. His workers had to revere his patron saint, San Rafael on May 23; he paid workers double time if they worked on that sacred day.

---

[16] *Libro de actas 1974*, Feb. 3, 1979 (SIP General Archives).

[17] Quinteros held on to his key position as Secretary of Organization but the Secretary General Chavez was demoted to Third Secretary of Conflicts. "Acta 1," *Libro de actas 1974*, Feb. 3, 1979 (SIP General Archives).

[18] "Acta 18," *Libro de actas 1974*, Oct. 22, 1974 (SIP General Archives); *Libro de actas*, Apr. 11, 1973 (SIP Departamental Archives, Puerto El Triunfo, Usulután, El Salvador).

[19] María Dolores Albiac, "Los ricos más ricos de El Salvador," in *El Salvador: La transición y sus problemas*, ed. Rodolfo Cardenal and Luis Armando González (San Salvador: UCA Editores, 2002), 159.

Similarly, Guirola named a sister shrimp processing plant, *Pesquera San Rafael*. Located in the port of La Unión, the plant processed shrimp during strikes in Puerto El Triunfo.

In March 1974, Mariscos de El Salvador responded to union demands for a contract renegotiation with the firing of 91 female production workers. Molina Lara mobilized his union base to stage protests and work stoppages and also denounced the move at the Ministry of Labor. Guirola did not respond to the ministry's call for a meeting. From March until June, Molina Lara and Guirola parried continually. The company refused to take back all the workers and, in response, the union staged walkouts. Meanwhile, the SIP General offered significant monetary support to the fired workers. Indeed, in a telling sign of solidarity, workers in the other plants donated a day's pay to help out the Mariscos workers.[20] On May 9, Molina Lara stated to the assembly of SIP workers: "The problem with this company is getting worse each day and now we have broken direct relations and have moved on to the conciliation stage."[21]

Molina Lara navigated the line between direct action and a scrupulous accordance with the Labor Code. Despite the selective work stoppages to protest the mass layoffs, Molina Lara followed each of the strike procedures outlined in the Labor Code: consecutive stages of negotiation, conciliation, and arbitration. Only after following all these stages could a strike be legally declared. A majority of the employees had to belong to the union and a majority had to vote for the strike. Guirola followed the practice of other employers by firing union activists so that fewer than 50 percent of the employees would vote for the strike, thus making it illegal.

At 4:00 PM on June 11, the Mariscos de El Salvador workers walked off the job, declaring a strike against contract violations and most specifically against the firings that they deemed part of an anti-union strategy. Within two weeks, the Juzgado Segundo de Primera Instancia de Usulután (a departmental court that dealt with labor issues) declared the Mariscos strike to be legal, the first such ruling in the history of the Salvadoran labor movement. This remarkable achievement was due in no small part to Molina Lara's tactical brilliance, leading work stoppages, mobilizing broader support, while rigorously following every step specified in the Labor Code. Guirola's arrogance surely was a major factor in the court

[20] "Acta 7," *Libro de actas 1974*, Apr. 3, 1974 (SIP General Archives). The act stated that 3,990 colones had been thus far donated to the Mariscos workers.
[21] "Acta 8," *Libro de actas 1974*, May 9, 1974 (SIP General Archives).

decision. He simply refused to respond to the Labor Ministry at several key moments over the previous three months. Perhaps there was a political dimension as well. The military regime's legitimacy was at a low point following the well-publicized electoral fraud of 1972. In addition, bowing to the concerns of the agrarian elite, the regime had expelled AIFLD in 1973, due to its promotion of a mild land reform program through its support for the centrist Unión Comunal Salvadoreña.[22] That expulsion drew protests from the US government and sectors of the international labor movement.

Regardless of the precise motives, the declaration of the strike's legality proved an enormous boon to SIP. The right to strike was enshrined as an article of the Salvadoran constitution, and the Labor Code essentially placed the weight of the government on the side of the (legally) striking union, forbidding the use of strikebreakers and compelling the company to pay wages during the strike. Following the dictates of the code, the Labor Ministry ordered the National Guard to ensure that there would be no strikebreaking and ordered Guirola to pay wages during the strike and prohibited him from sending shrimp to his facility at La Unión.[23] The National Guard did not, however, carry out the orders, and Guirola managed to ship shrimp to his plant in La Unión before the labor inspectors arrived. Notwithstanding, Mariscos could only find a handful of strikebreakers (including among fishermen) and thus could not effectively operate during the strike. Rather than negotiate, let alone pay wages, Guirola unsuccessfully appealed the decision to the Supreme Court. His refusal to negotiate galvanized more gestures of solidarity from other unions in the port and elsewhere. After three months, Guirola bowed to the key demand to reinstate and provide back pay (before and during the strike) to all the fired workers. The back and strike pay also covered the losses of fishermen who could not deliver the product. Other concessions included vacation and scholarships for children and the promise not to send shrimp caught by fishermen who worked for Mariscos de El Salvador to the San Rafael facility.[24]

[22] Ironically, the withdrawal of AIFLD further weakened the pro-regime CGS. Robert Alexander, *A History of Organized Labor in Panama and Central America* (Westport, CT: Praeger Publishers, 2008), 194. AIFLD, accused of working with the CIA, was the foreign branch of the AFL-CIO.

[23] Asamblea Legislativa, Comisión de Trabajo y Prevención Social, Comité de Huelga to Rubén Alfonso Rodriguez, president of the Legislative Assembly, Aug. 28, 1974 (Archivo de la Asamblea Legislativa [AAL], San Salvador).

[24] Dirección de Trabajo, Sept. 9, 1974. It is important to note that the Mariscos fishermen belonged to SIP.

This was a dramatic victory, one in which all SIP members could take pride: They had contributed generously to the strike fund.[25] The union leadership was so pleased that they contributed more than US$400 to throw a victory celebration.

Molina Lara's prestige grew significantly as a result of the strike victory. In February 1975, he won the SIP general elections for secretary general, 243–97 besting Evelio Ortiz. This was Alejandro's third try for the top office in the union. Well before the victory, Alejandro had a revelation:

I realized that I wasn't at all intimidated by being around management or the company lawyers. I enjoyed being at their level. I was even superior to them because I represented the workers.[26]

Moreover, he had an unflinching goal: to allow the workers of Puerto El Triunfo the possibility to enjoy a dignified life and dignified work. His emotional satisfaction was powerful. He had known psychologically that he was management's equal for some time, but his experience at the helm of the Mariscos S.A. strike and his humbling of don Rafael Guirola had confirmed his intuition.

During the mid- to late 1970s, the three shrimp companies were highly profitable as the international prices soared higher than US$4.00 a pound and the fishing grounds were plentiful.[27] Before each contract renewal negotiation, Molina Lara carefully tracked the companies' profitability and communicated the information to the union membership.[28] In each union meeting, he laid out the inconsistencies in the company's argument against wage increases, while highlighting the deeply felt problem of double-digit annual inflation rate during the mid- to late 1970s. When a given company would not yield in one year, they built up their forces for the following year. Thus, in September 1975, Molina Lara reported on the failure of negotiations with the three main companies. Speaking before more than 300 members of the Pezca Local, he commented, "[W]e did the humanly possible but the company exhibited no understanding nor was

---

[25] The Mariscos Local repaid the strike fund more than 10,000 colones from the settlement with the company.

[26] Alejandro Molina Lara, interview with the author, Los Angeles, 2015.

[27] There were danger signs about overfishing and the effects of contamination caused by pesticide use on nearby cotton plantations. Neither the companies nor the union paid attention to the studies that underscored those dangers.

[28] In front of 112 members in the Atarraya local, he showed charts demonstrating how in the preceding months "la producción ha aumentado en grave escala." *Libro de actas,* Sept. 13, 1975 (SIP General Archives).

there enough solidarity from the assembly to support our demands."[29] He referred to a lack of unity among the rank and file over exercising a strike threat. Without such a threat, all three companies held their negotiating ground. Mariscos de El Salvador, granted a 6 percent raise to plant workers and 8 percent to fishermen despite an inflation rate of more than 19 percent in 1975.[30]

Despite the setback, SIP continued to pressure the companies. In February 1976, after a 10-hour marathon negotiation session, Pezca conceded a 15 percent raise. Although Molina Lara was not satisfied, the rank and file accepted the raise that, combined with the 1975 raise and the decline in the rate of inflation (7 percent in 1976), in effect maintained their real salaries intact, at a time when the rest of the working class faced declining real wages.[31]

Molina Lara (who won three consecutive elections for secretary-general) and the other union leaders engaged in painstakingly slow organizational work. Gradually, the male leaders were able to incorporate increasing numbers of female workers into the local and district leaderships and they became a more active presence in union meetings. By the end of the decade, more women than men spoke during union meetings. In 1977, SIP again fought for improved contracts in the three companies. Noé Quinteros and Leonel Chávez won office in the Pezca Local, opting to mobilize the rank and file and leave Molina Lara in full command of the SIP General Union. In a highly significant change, women won half of the Pezca Local positions. The combination of experienced leadership and female activists fomented greater militancy in the Local.

In 1977, the Pezca Local launched a drive around demands for improvements in salary and working conditions. In July, the company offered a 1.15 colones a day raise with a fixed two-year contract (typically parts of contracts could be renegotiated every year). Molina Lara spoke to the Local assembly of 173 workers and issued a "llamado a la conciencia" (call to conscience) as Noé called for "unity." Molina Lara continued to negotiate as the Pezca Local inched toward a strike. On July 21, the entire Pezca workforce walked off the job for the first time since the failed

---

[29] Union Minutes, Sept. 1975, no. 11, 27, set 75 (Subseccional Pezca Archives, Puerto El Triunfo). We are translating *"Subseccional"* as Local.

[30] "Acta 20," *Libro de actas 1974*, Oct. 17, 1975 (SIP General Archives).

[31] In Atarraya, the SIP local pushed back against a similar wage offer. After a protracted negotiation, the company granted a 16 percent raise along with other concessions that the rank and file then accepted. *Libro de actas*, Mar. 19, 1976 (Subseccional Atarraya Archives, Puerto El Triunfo).

strike of January 1972. This time they won a resounding victory with an immediate wage hike of 1.60 colones per day and a series of other major concessions by the company.[32] As a result of the strike, SIP workers joined the ranks of the country's best-paid industrial workers, the majority of whom had seen their real wages decline dramatically over the previous few years.

Due to the perishable nature of the commodity the SIP unions possessed what Beverly Silver calls "workplace bargaining power ... that accrues to workers who are enmeshed in tightly integrated production processes, where a localized work stoppage in a key node can cause disruptions on a much wider scale than the stoppage itself."[33] Following Charles Bergquist, this power increases substantially when the industry is a key source of foreign exchange (shrimp ranked as the third-highest source in the 1970s).[34] Molina Lara had acute practical knowledge of the commodity chain and the production process. He was able to depend on the union's overwhelmingly female rank and file to carry out work stoppages (or slowdowns) to respond rapidly to even the most minor problems that developed on the shop floor. Combined with a growing union membership and commitment, that is its "associational power," SIP had the potential to transform the lives of its members and to carve out a relatively autonomous space of freedom in an authoritarian society.

POLITICS AND DISCORD

Yet as can be discerned from the *llamada de conciencia* and the lamentations about the lack of solidarity, the achievement of worker unity was a fraught and incomplete process. The first impediment to unity was political. Throughout 1975, Molina Lara, formerly apolitical, had increasing contact with the independent Left-oriented federation FENASTRAS. In the federation, he began to relate to more experienced union militants, including those who belonged to the Salvadoran Communist Party (PCS) and to the Frente de Acción Popular Unificado (FAPU), a group to the left of the PCS. From both leftist organizations, Molina Lara gained access to people and some limited reading material (pamphlets) that allowed him

---

[32] "Acta 20," *Libro de actas*, 10:20 PM, July 22, 1977 (SIP General Archives).

[33] Beverly Silver, *Forces of Labor: Workers' Movements and Globalization since 1870* (Cambridge: Cambridge University Press, 2003), 13. She borrowed the term from Erik Olin Wright.

[34] Throughout the 1970s and 1980s shrimp ranked from second to fourth as a generator of foreign exchange.

and his friends to understand the situation of the laboring classes in the country and more specifically the alignment of political and economic forces that SIP needed to confront.[35] Leonel Chávez joined the PCS, and he frequently engaged with Alejandro in more or less private conversations about politics and labor. Chávez disagreed, at least in practice with Alejandro, Noé, Evelio, and Gloria García for whom it was imperative to keep politics directly out of the union. García recalls how she scolded Leonel Chávez for showing a Soviet film about housing in November 1977: "Aqui se pelea la cuestión laboral" (Here we are fighting about labor issues). He responded that he was showing it "para que se abren los ojos" (to open up eyes). The anti-political position of Gloria and Noé and many others hinged on an understanding that the union represented a rare democratic space but one that the government could easily shut down. Moreover, activists like Gloria and Noé came to believe in a form of militant syndicalism as the best way to achieve more power and improved lives for workers.

At the same time, there was an even more pragmatic side to the anti-political stance because the SIP leadership faced a difficult political reality. Although the opposition Christian Democratic Party (PDC) had strong support in the port, the majority of male workers and many female workers belonged to one of two right-wing parties: the official party the PCN or Partido Popular Salvadoreño.[36] Moreover, many workers belonged to the rightist, paramilitary group ORDEN (Organización Democrática Nacional). Given the strong pro-regime support from the union membership, SIP's affiliation with the increasingly Left-leaning FENASTRAS was a source of potential conflict and concern.[37]

This political concern became more palpable as national-level repression became pronounced. National Guard killings of protesting campesinos at Tres Calles in the department of Usulatán (Puerto El Triunfo's department) and La Cayetana (San Vicente) had galvanized national attention. Similarly, on July 30, 1975 the National Police opened fire and killed at least a dozen protesting university students in San Salvador. On September 26, unknown assailants gunned down a Communist union activist, Rafael Aguiñada Carranza, the head of FUSS (a union federation

---

[35] Most of the reading material consisted of semi-clandestine weeklies or pamphlets.

[36] A likely indicator of the strength of ORDEN was the victory of the PPS in the 1970 municipal elections. The party was controlled by "Chele" Medrano, founder and head of ORDEN.

[37] A strong minority supported the opposition PDC. In the 1980s, most fishermen supported the PDC and a female plant worker won election as mayor.

in which the PCS was strong). Molina Lara joined others in pushing for a national strike of protest. In front of more than 300 SIP members, Leonel Chávez condemned "the constant blows against the labor and peasant movement by the fascists who want to dominate the people."[38] Although the national strike initiative did not get off the ground, the SIP leadership did introduce national politics and a left language of denunciation into the union discussions as they attempted to organize the rank and file to participate in the protest.[39]

Eventually, Molina Lara and his group were able to convince the rank and file to support the independent leftist federation on the grounds of its capacity to deliver solidarity when SIP needed it. Similarly, they developed a language of class solidarity phrased as a logical extension of union activity that had been sanctioned by the constitution. In other words, the constitutional acceptance of the right to organize and strike provided a discursive opening toward expanding notions of solidarity.[40]

Molina Lara was careful to cover his right flank. In fact, during most electoral cycles he recruited an ORDEN member to serve on the SIP's leaderships ticket. He thus co-opted a local branch of an organization that would become the nucleus of right-wing death squads. Molina Lara was able to turn the ORDEN member and many other rightists into good trade unionists in part by guaranteeing that politics would stay out of the unions.

GENDERED DIVISION OF LABOR

The high level of gendered labor segmentation within the three plants was another source of division. Those divisions often translated into sharp differences in perspectives and attitudes toward union organization. Only a minority of workers, both male and female, could count on salary and benefits for the entire year. A substantial sector of female workers, who classified and packed the shrimp were frequently laid off when the supply dwindled. Finally, there was an even larger group of workers who were employed as *eventuales* (seasonal or occasional workers) who had even

---

[38] "Acta 20," *Libro de actas 1974*, Oct. 17, 1975 (SIP General Archives).
[39] The union voted to donate money to his widow. Ibid.
[40] Although unusual, the SIP leaders went so far as to invite a representative of the Liga por la Liberación, tied to a nascent guerrilla group, the Partido Revolucionario de Trabajadores Centroamericanos (PRTC), to address a union meeting of some 500 members. "Acta 23," *Libro de actas 1974*, Dec. 21, 1976 (SIP General Archives).

less job security.[41] In the *La Ballena* processing plant of the Atarraya group, more than 70 percent of the workers were temporary.[42] In Pezca S.A. most *eventuales*, some 40 percent of the workforce, labored in Planta II. The permanent workers in Planta I often exhibited a marked degree of superiority toward those of Planta II. One female worker in Planta I recalls that the workers of Planta II were poorer, less educated, more country ("*más rústica*"), less reliable, and more rebellious.[43] Planta II women recall being treated with disdain by Planta I female workers. One Planta II who eventually became a SIP leader had to endure the nickname, "letrina" (latrine), a word uttered to her face more often than her name. She was called that because she had lived in a *rancho* by the public latrines, when private toilets were virtually nonexistent. Her father supplemented the family income by cleaning the latrines, hence her nickname. That level of intra-class derision was hard to overcome, but necessary to forge a united labor force.

In Pezca S.A., the largest and most modernized of the three packing-houses, employing more than 500 workers, Plant II was exclusively devoted to the smallest species of shrimp, *chacalín*, or sea bob. Previously discarded, the domestic market for *chacalín* emerged in the late 1960s thanks to the introduction of supermarkets in San Salvador; by the mid-1970s an export market opened as well.[44] In 1976, a typical voyage would net 2,333 pounds of *chacalín* and 1,800 pounds of the larger varieties of shrimp. The company paid fishermen 557 colones per ton for white shrimp (it fetched up to US$4.50 per pound in New York) and 191 colones per ton of *chacalín*.[45] During the season, from July to November, several hundred female workers peeled each *chacalín* by hand and then placed it on a conveyor belt that passed over a machine. When the *chacalín* reached a certain point, a rotating cylinder penetrated it, as a high-pressure stream of water removed the vein and rinsed the product that then dropped onto another conveyor belt. For the smallest of the

---

[41] The official nomenclature was different than the popular version. The official contractual terms listed *eventuales* as those who only worked occasionally; they were called *supernumerarios* by workers. The seasonal workers were usually called *eventuales* by workers, but "trabajadores temporales" by the company.

[42] Sixty-seven were listed as temporales, of whom 53 were female. "Lista de los salarios de los trabajadores de La Ballena S.A.," Oct. 24, 1973 (SIP General Archives).

[43] Migdalia Chavarría, interview with the author, Puerto El Triunfo, 2013.

[44] Apparently Red Lobster purchased Salvadoran *chacalín* according to various informants.

[45] In 1975, the three plants processed 2,669 tons of *chacalín* and 903 tons of white shrimp. Ana Eloisa Herrera Schlesinger, "Los trabajadores de la industria pesquera" (law thesis, Universidad de El Salvador, May 1980).

chacalines, a special "peeling machine" peeled and deveined the product.[46] Female workers selected the undamaged *chacalín* and packed them to be frozen and then transported to the airport or to the supermarkets. Men operated all machinery in the plants. The machine operators and maintenance machinists earned as much as 50 percent more than the female workers and occupied the key positions in the union, during the 1970s.

Permanent workers processed the larger shrimp in a less labor-intensive fashion. The shrimp came through a classification machine (rated by the number it would take to make a pound) and then the workers would pick out the nondamaged shrimp to pack into five-pound boxes that would be frozen and stored.

From the companies' vantage point, *eventuales* were disposable, interchangeable, and highly exploitable. At the start of the season, a whistle announced the arrival of the fishing boats and hundreds of women would jostle with one another at the plant gates, trying to get hired. The majority who lived in the countryside were at an extreme disadvantage because they had no information on the arrival of the first *chacalín* boat.[47] Although they performed more difficult work – as they had to shell each *chacalín* – the seasonal workers – mostly women – received roughly one-third less pay than did permanent workers who classified and packed the larger shrimp; the *eventuales* also did not receive overtime pay and did not have health insurance.[48]

From the beginning of their tenure, Alejandro, Noé, Leonel, and others strove to transform the status of the female temporary workers both as an act of fundamental social justice and as a linchpin of a strategy to augment the power of the union. Their earliest focus was on ending the piece rate system and substituting it with hourly pay rates. Female workers overwhelmingly backed this measure. The union won this change in pay structure in each plant during the mid-1970s, thus modifying the work pace for the entire labor force. The SIP leadership also pushed hard against any management employees who behaved hostilely toward union

---

[46] George B. Gross, "Shrimp Industry of Central America, Caribbean Sea, and Northern South America," *Marine Fisheries Review,* 35, nos. 3–4 (1972): 38; Noé Quinteros, interview with the author, Houston, 2014.

[47] Company employees and foremen would inform their novias and mistresses ahead of time, according to various informants.

[48] According to informants, the introduction of social security system to El Puerto in 1968 was a key factor in the companies' decision to promote this two-class system.

militants. In virtually every job action, one of the demands was for the removal of a supervisor or foreman.

Molina Lara, as noted before, worked to organize the previously unorganized *eventuales* and to increase female participation in each of the union locals in the port. By 1979, five of the seven officers of the Pezca Local were women. The top posts in SIP General, however, still went to men. The typical explanation by male and female union activists at the time and in memory was that women were more militant and committed than male workers, but that they shied away from occupying leadership positions due to their domestic labor obligations.

In February 1979, a female Atarraya worker commented on the gendered dimension of the labor struggle in Puerto El Triunfo. She argued that the company fired the primarily female temporary workers whom the company treated like "machos de carga," substituting new ones.

Among us, since we women are the majority in the plants and the authorities beat the men first, and the authorities are always around, in the sessions we women protest first. The men hardly speak out, but when we decide to struggle we form a unified front.[49]

This is a novel enunciation of a position, at once proto-feminist and syndicalist. Echoing a common belief and practice in revolutionary movements, the female activist argues that women are more militant and courageous than men in part because the authorities are more likely to beat males.[50] Through speaking up, the women attempt to shield the men from physical harm. The statement also suggests the remarkable transformation in consciousness experienced by female workers over the previous decade. From apathetic workers, they are now visibly and

---

[49] "Entonces nosotras como la mayoría en esas plantas la tenemos las mujeres, porque los hombres son los primeros a quienes flagelan, y en las sesiones, como siempre anda la autoridá por ahí, las primeras que protestamos somos las mujeres, los hombres casi no opinan nada, pero ya cuando se deciden a luchar formamos un solo frente." It is hard to ascertain to what beating she was referring, Other than the beatings of November 1977, informants recall but few instances of Guardia beating pickets during the strike of February–March 1979. *Pueblo,* Mar. 1979.

[50] By no means was this a novel position for women wither in the United States or in Latin America. I first came across a very similar situation in Nicaragua where women took over the burgeoning campesino movement in the early 1960s as men had to go underground for a period. See Jeffrey L. Gould, *To Lead as Equals: Rural Protest and Political Consciousness in Chinandega, Nicaragua, 1912–1979* (Chapel Hill: University of North Carolina Press, 1990), 225–44; Lorraine Bayard de Volo, *Women and the Cuban Insurrection: How Gender Shaped Castro's Victory* (New York: Cambridge University Press, 2018), 114–43.

vocally in the forefront of the class struggle in the port exemplifying the ideology and practice of solidarity. Female participation in large meetings did increase dramatically over the course of the decade. Whereas mostly male voices were recorded in the minutes earlier in the decade, by 1978, half of the speakers – often in front of more than 500 people – were female. Almost all their declarations encouraged militancy in defense of union demands and worker solidarity within the port and beyond.

The statement by the anonymous female militant also refers to the National Guard mentioned earlier. On November 18, 1977, shortly before the regime declared a state of siege to quell labor, student, and peasant unrest, Leonel Chávez organized the showing of a Soviet documentary. Before the film began, "The authorities arrived in trucks. We had to calm the children who began to cry from fear. We gathered up our courage. Then they entered with bayonets and went straight for the leaders. Everyone hit the floor because we could hear shots ... they beat Alejandro so that blood poured from his ears and mouth. We thought they had killed him."[51] According to various witnesses, the attackers destroyed as much of the union hall as they could and then carried off Alejandro, Leonel, Delia Cristina Hernández, and two other union leaders.[52]

Immediately afterward, dozens of union members followed the National Guard to the departmental capital. Despite a government claim that the National Guard had uncovered "subversive propaganda," union protests helped to free the union activists. Upon their return to the port, workers and their families broke out in a spontaneous fiesta. The beating and the repression only enhanced Alejandro's reputation. As one female union militant commented,

Alejandro is our secretary general of everyone: he is our idol. Because if Alejandro says "I'll be there" when we get off work at 10 pm he'll be there ... He orients us in our struggles: GO TO PEZCA'S GATE, THOSE WOMEN NEED OUR HELP.

Another female worker even penned a poem:

We of Puerto El Triunfo never have lost a strike; we always struggle together; We don't let the deceitful bosses offend us, though they try to every day; Alejandro

---

[51] "llegó la autoridá en camionadas. Los niños comenzaron a llorar del miedo, nostras tuvimos que arrullarlos y nos comenzamos a armar de valentía ... con bayonetas en mano se metieron en el recinto y primeramente ... se dirigieron hacia los directivos en esos momentos todos nos tiramos a suelo, porque sonaron las balas y los culatazos ... a Alejandro le dieron un fuerte golpizo, manaba sangre por oidos y boca; nosotros creimos que ya lo llevaban muerto." "Obreras de la industria pesquera," *Pueblo,* Feb. 1979.

[52] *Diario de Hoy,* Nov. 21, 1977.

Molina Lara is our leader and he is a precious pearl that we found in the sea; all the workers of the fishing industry will die before they do him harm; we won't allow his noble principles to fail.[53]

Yet the dynamic between Alejandro and the predominantly female workforce was far more complex than the paean would suggest. Molina Lara and his male *compañeros* had to undergo a transformation, particularly with regards to their notions of women and femininity. They had to recognize female militant workers as women and not see them as stereotypes framed in derogatory language.[54] Moreover, they had to begin to treat women as intellectual and moral equals. Gloria García recalls, "Alejandro did improve quite a bit. But you know, in the end he always thought that he knew better."[55] García's statement is an implicit recognition that changes in social attitudes among even the most progressive males involved an incremental process.

Similarly, the insurgent leadership learned from the women very early in the game that they could not countenance any forms of harassment on the part of management; indeed, the Atarraya strike of 1971–72 pointed to the issue as capable of provoking mass mobilization. It is remarkable that women recall less than a handful of incidents of sexual harassment during the entire decade. Although consensual affairs took place among the workforce (and between rank and filers and union leadership), there were few, if any, cases of harassment (e.g., sexual aggression or unwanted advances). Women workers recognize the role of the union in militating against any form of sexual harassment in the plant. This

---

[53] "Obreras de la industria pesquera," *Pueblo*, Feb. 1979:

> Nosotros de Puerto el Triunfo, nunca hemos perdido una huelga
> Siempre luchamos unidos como hermanos de clase
> Y no dejamos que nos ultrajan los farsantes patronales
> Que a diario nos quieren dar;
> Nuestro líder es Alejandro Molina Lara
> Es una perla preciosa que encontramos en el mar,
> Todos los trabajadores de la industria pesquera,
> Para que a el le hagan daño primos nos matarán
> Pues no dejaremos fracasar la nobleza de sus principios.

[54] "Marimacha" was a typical derogatory expression used against female workers and militants. See, e.g., Deborah Levenson-Estrada, *Trade Unionists against Terror: Guatemala City, 1954–1985* (Chapel Hill: University of North Carolina Press, 1994) and Barbara Weinstein, *For Social Peace in Brazil: Industrialists and the Remaking of the Working Class in São Paulo, 1920–1964* (Chapel Hill: University of North Carolina Press, 1996).

[55] Gloria García, interview with the author, Lake Elsinore, Feb. 2015.

contrasts sharply with the experience of female workers in other parts of Latin America.[56]

During the mid- to late 1970s, as more and more women became active in the union, they began increasingly to attempt to exert informal control over the production process.[57] In effect, female and male workers neither required nor accepted interference from either the *jefes de producción* or management. That said, there were numerous minor skirmishes over that control. Mauro Granados, for example, often stood on the other side of a plate glass window to observe the workers. When he saw the women pop a candy in their mouths or engage in conversation among themselves, he would come down to scold them. Such managerial actions annoyed the female workers who, by the late 1970s would retaliate by talking back to their superiors and by calling them out in general assemblies. SIP's record of ridding the plant of anti-union managers made those employees wary.

The female workers also developed concrete demands that the SIP leadership adopted. They fought for and, by the end of the decade, obtained the construction of a cafeteria. There had been many cases of women fainting on the job because they had to stand six hours without any food and at times eight hours given that the trip home for lunch was almost impossible to pull off within the allotted half an hour break. As Eloisa Segovia put it, "[T]he union gave us a chance to eat."[58]

That demand accompanied a series of others that if not specifically female in nature, fundamentally benefited that segment of the workforce. For example, they won the right to a first aid center on the premises that treated women who suffered large numbers of cuts from handling the *chacalín*. Similarly, by the end of the 1970s they had gained the right to four uniforms and three pairs of boots per year. In addition, they achieved the right to two coffee breaks. The union also procured 30 high school scholarships for their children. As part of the contract, they received a

[56] John D. French and Daniel James, *Gendered World of Latin American Women Workers: From Household and Factory to the Union Hall and Ballot Box* (Durham, NC: Duke University Press, 1997), 11; Daniel James, *Doña Maria's Story: Life, History, Memory and Political Identity* (Durham, NC: Duke University Press, 2000), 56–70, on the discursive association of factory labor and prostitution; Anne Farnsworth-Alvear, *Dulcinea in the Factory: Myths, Morals, Men, and Women in Colombia's Industrial Experiment, 1905–1960* (Durham, NC: Duke University Press, 2000).

[57] Gloria García, interview with the author, Lake Elsinore, Feb. 2015.

[58] Eloísa Segovia, interview with author and Carlos Henriquez Consalvi, Puerto El Triunfo, Feb. 2013.

FIGURE 1.5 Gloria García with Pezca coworker
(courtesy Gloria García)

right to 5 pounds of shrimp and 10 pounds of fish a month. In the words of Carmen Minero, "Before we worked like burros and could only touch the shrimp, now we could eat it."[59] Although these victories seem minor enough, cumulatively they amounted to a significant improvement in their working and home lives. Without the active participation of the female workforce, those demands might not have been even formulated much less achieved. Those victories also empowered and unified female and male workers as they recognized their collective agency in the everyday betterment of their lives and working conditions. The workers came to view the processing plant, if not as a place of joy, at the very least as their own space in which, within generally prescribed limits, they could work at their own pace, in their own way, with a reasonable degree of amusement. On the night shift, they often played games, even spraying each other with hoses.

Gloria recalls,

I don't know if we felt liberated but we would even joke during work hours, we were happy. Was it the union support or were we just tired of being in that

---

[59] Carmen Minero, interview with the author, Puerto El Triunfo, 2014.

position? Things changed. We would not get scolded or threatened to have our daily wage taken away from us for talking. We felt free![60]

The sense of liberation was generally confined to the plant floor. Yet, female union participation also contributed to personal transformation. Union education seminars had a major influence on Gloria and her *compañeras*. She recounts: "I wasn't always a talker. I was timid. It was when I went to the union educational seminars that I learned to talk. After that, no one could shut me up."[61]

Many female workers were single mothers, most of whom depended on extended family networks to care for their youngest children. According to former plant workers, single mothers saw less incentive to get married. Upon returning from work, however, the "second shift" of cooking, cleaning, and caring for children kicked in. The double shift was intensified for married workers, as they had to provide for their often quite demanding husbands or *compañeros*. Some testimony suggests that despite the significant increase in family income, female work put a great strain on marriage. For temporary workers, the strains were greater as there were changes in shifts and during the *chacalín* season, many worked the night or midnight shift. As Gloria García recalls, "The guy would get ticked because his wife didn't have his food ready or his clothes washed because she was working. So he looked elsewhere ... men always look for el plato ajeno"[62] (a different meal – woman).

Union activism placed even greater strain on families. Gloria recounts that when she was elected to the SIP leadership, her husband posed an ultimatum: "Either the union or me and the kids!" She responded, "Well you can go but you'll leave the kids with me."[63] He moved out. Other marriages also broke up over female union activism. It is difficult to chart the relationship between the development of class consciousness among women and the rise of gendered forms of consciousness that led to individual resistance against male patriarchy. Yet, in the case of Gloria and other activists, there seems to be a clear correlation.

There were also sharp limits to the union's ability to accommodate the proto-feminist discourse that was emerging; no one challenged the notion that women had certain naturally endowed characteristics: more nimble hands to peel and sort shrimp and a predisposition to cook, clean, and

---

[60] The hose spraying usually occurred on the graveyard shift. Ibid., Los Angeles, 2016.
[61] Ibid.   [62] Ibid., Feb. 2015.
[63] Gloria García, interview with the author, Los Angeles, 2016.

FIGURE I.6 Gloria García with her sister, Concepción García and her sister's daughter
(courtesy Gloria García)

nurture her family.[64] No women operated or repaired machinery. Finally, as noted, the most important three positions of SIP General remained exclusively male.[65]

TROUBLE AT SEA

If SIP could overcome the effects of the gendered division of labor in the processing plants, they had much more trouble dealing with the machista lifestyle of the *marineros* (fishermen), rooted in the perils of work on the high seas. One former fisherman described that labor as like being in prison – others compared it to slavery.[66] Both metaphors indexed the

---

[64] See Carla Freeman, *High Tech and High Heels in the Global Economy: Women, Work and Pink Collar Identities in the Caribbean* (Durham, NC: Duke University Press, 2000), 37–40, for a useful summary of gendered notions on women's suitability for certain kinds of factory work. Curiously as we will see, men did cut off thousands of shrimp heads per voyage on the seas.

[65] Typically, those were secretary general, secretary of organization, and secretary of conflicts. SIP General had 10 members of the directorate.

[66] Amilcar Galileo, interview with the author, Puerto El Triunfo, July 2012. For a fine description of working and salary conditions for the fishermen, see Ana Eloisa Herrera

FIGURE 1.7 Shrimp fishing boat
(courtesy Mario Sáenz)

fishermen's absolute subservience to the captain and to their entrapment
in a world of hard labor for 12 days and nights at a stretch.

The boats usually plied the seas between 3 and 10 miles from the coast
(although they often infringed the three-mile limit imposed for ecological
reasons) and roughly 40 miles east and northwest from Puerto El Triunfo.
Most trips lasted 12 days and involved at the very least 16 and often
20 hours of work a day. On each boat, the three *marineros* (fishermen)
and the *extra* hand cast and hauled in the 65- to 75-foot nets on both sides
of the boat every four hours.[67] They emptied the nets onto the deck and
then they separated the fish, shrimp, and the *chacalines*. While two or
three of the fishermen cast the nets again, the third one (and occasionally
an "extra") had the time-sensitive task of cutting off the heads of thousands of shrimp and then tossed them into the brine tank.[68] A mechanic

Schlesinger's thesis, "Los trabajadores de la industria pesquera," presented for a doctor-
ate in law to the Facultad de Jurisprudencia y Ciencias Sociales, Universidad de El
Salvador, May 1980. The thesis does not cover the conflict between the unions or *la
movida*.

[67] Typically, each voyage had one or two extra hands. They essentially worked as unpaid
apprentices, though they usually received "tips" from the rest of the crew.

[68] No one questioned the masculine nature of this work despite its similarities to the labor of
female workers who cut off the heads of *chacalines*.

(who earned 50 percent more than the others) was in charge of the maintenance of the motors. In addition, he helped with the nets and spelled the captain at the wheel. One of the *marineros* doubled as a cook.

When the boat arrived back at the dock in the Bay of Jiquilisco, the crew had to wait. At times, the *marineros* helped the dockworkers unload the shrimp and fish and earned an extra two dollars. Regardless, the rest of the crew had to wait until the product was weighed on the docks: The water and ice stuck to the shrimp was discounted. They were also allotted 20–25 pounds of fish that they received upon completing the voyage. The captain designated one of the *marineros* to guard the boat for 24 hours, receiving two dollars for his time. The crew would be paid, between 6 and 24 hours after docking and then would have to be ready to disembark again within 48 hours.

A ground crew was in charge of unloading the shrimp and cleaning the brine tanks. They shoveled the shrimp into metal tubs and loaded them onto pick-up trucks that transported the catch to the plant, where the shrimp were weighed again. The laborers who worked on the pier and in the *varadero* represented between 10 and 15 percent of the plant labor force. Because they tended to have much contact with the fishermen, SIP and Sindicato Agua (the breakaway union founded in 1971) vied to recruit these workers into their ranks. The situation was complicated by the "*eventual*" status that the companies accorded to the *varadero* workers. Moreover, the divisions between the unions were not so clear. Thus, for example, SIP represented the 59 fishermen who worked for Mariscos de El Salvador (1980) and most of the 90 fishermen (including captains) who worked for Atarraya.[69] The large majority of the roughly 200 fishermen who worked for the seven companies affiliated with Pezca S.A. belonged to Sindicato Agua. Legally Pezca S.A. was only a processing plant, but its owners also possessed controlling shares in the fishing companies. That arrangement helped the company and its stockholders deal with tax liabilities. It also gave the company an advantage in labor relations because it further divided the labor force.

There was also straight-out competition between the unions. During the late 1970s, SIP made inroads into the base of Sindicato Agua, largely

---

[69] "Nómina de afiliados al sindicato de la industria pesquera subseccional por empresa Mariscos de El Salvador," 1980 (SIP General Archives); "Lista de salarios de los trabajadores de La Ballena S.A.," 1973 (SIP General Archives).

due to the latter's ineffectiveness in negotiation. In February 1976, for example, Molina Lara reported to the SIP assembly that 78 marinos had joined SIP because "el sindicato hermano" (brother union) refused to back up their demands.[70] The relations still seemed amicable as the "hermano" designation suggested. In December 1976, Molina Lara urged each of the 500 SIP members in attendance to help foster closer ties with Sindicato Agua. Similarly, another union official urged members to "make the fishermen conscious of the need for unity."[71]. Many plant workers and fishermen viewed Sindicato Agua as "patronalista" (pro company) and corrupt. Since its inception, Sindicato Agua relied on strong support from the captains linked to Pezca S.A. and, in turn, the clientelistic links between the captains and their crews.

Although the competition over membership was a source of discord between the unions, the machista lifestyle of the fishermen tended to especially alienate the female base of SIP, some of whom were married to or lived with *marineros*. In those family units, often the female belonged to SIP and the male to Sindicato Agua. Many fishermen rationalized their machista behavior in the port as a consequence of their work. The 12 days at sea, often harrowing and always exhausting, conditioned them to, as it were, fulfill the stereotypical image of fishermen in port. As one former *marinero* confessed: "[W]e were degenerates."[72] The epitome of this degeneracy in many port workers' memories was the frequent appearance of skiffs filled with prostitutes as the fishing boats entered the Bay of Jiquilisco just before arriving at the port. The prostitutes' payment in shrimp only adds flavor to the tale of corruption[73]. Port residents, including their *compañeras* and kin, viewed the fishermen as inveterate womanizers and alcoholics (binge drinkers in our parlance). "We often didn't even go home – we just went straight to the bars, the billiard parlors, and the whorehouses." Another commented, "We felt we were owed the release."[74] Such behavior was not well received by many

---

[70] "Acta 22," *Libro de actas,* Feb. 3, 1976 (SIP General Archives).

[71] The statement was made at the same time that the union reported that a considerable number of fishermen affiliated with Sindicato Agua had joined Sindicato Tierra. "Acta 24," *Libro de actas,* Feb. 1977 (SIP General Archives).

[72] Ruperto Torres, interview with the author, Puerto El Triunfo, May 2013.

[73] Virtually all interviewees including the fishermen, Torres, Pérez, and Escobar recounted this custom.

[74] Ruperto Torres, interview with the author, Puerto El Triunfo, 2013; Migdonio Pérez, interview with the author, Puerto El Triunfo, 2013; Ángel Escobar, interview with the author, Los Angeles, 2016.

female family members and plant workers. One former plant worker recalls with disdain: "Some captains kept four or five women."[75]

LA MOVIDA

The *patrones de barco* (captains) and the crew could indulge their vices due, in no small measure, to "la movida," that is illegal sales to "pirate merchants" on the high seas or deserted beaches. This practice allowed *marineros* to earn from US$400 to US$800 a month (at times much more) in addition to the US$100 a month that they usually garnered during the late 1970s. The captain's share reached US$2,000 on some voyages. This unique form of resistance arose as a form of "life insurance" in response to Pezca's failure to indemnify the families of 10 fishermen lost at sea in in the cyclone of May 1977. In the words of one fisherman, "We thought, 'if this is what our life is worth to the company, I'll take an advance on my insurance.'"[76]

For fishermen, there was a moral economic dimension, rooted in a sense of the asymmetry of risk and a calculus of economic justice. They risked their lives daily to fill up what had been "empty bins" when they set sail; the company only "risked" the cost of food and fuel.[77] Many fishermen justified the sales as a direct appropriation of the value of their labor and as a form of resistance against an inhumane and rapacious management.

Most fishermen claim that this form of resistance developed following the cyclone. Yet, Noé Quinteros and others stress that the practice originated before 1977. Archival evidence supports their argument. Artisanal fishermen known as *murrayeros* would come alongside the shrimp boats to receive gifts of *murraya,* or surplus fish of little value. Some *murrayeros* began to commercialize some of the shrimp catch. In June 1975, Leonel Chávez denounced the hiring of police agents, known as AVIC (Asociación de Vigilantes de Industria y Comercio) disguised as private security to deal with this very minor problem. In September 1975, Quinteros argued that the AVIC's 47 agents (for 39 boats) absorbed 400 colones per month per agent in addition to their food expenses. Rather than waste the money, "[T]he company should raise salaries for the workers

---

[75] Rolando Franco, interview with the author, Los Angeles, 2015. For a similar account: Ana Paniagua, interview with the author, Puerto El Triunfo, Aug. 2015.

[76] Ruperto Torres, interview with the author, Puerto El Triunfo, Feb. 2016.

[77] Migdonio Pérez, interview with the author, Puerto El Triunfo, 2013.

suffering from severe inflation."[78] For Quinteros, *la movida* became a generalized form of resistance in direct response to management repression.[79]

Regardless of the precise origin of *la movida*, in the words of Ruperto Torres, after the cyclone, "[T]here was an explosion of sales. Everyone wanted to shell shrimp."[80] Until the late 1970s, packinghouse workers and their union leadership grudgingly accepted the practice, in part because of the shared outrage toward Pezca management following the cyclone. The extra income provided to spouses and kin of the fishermen mollified any opposition. Many came to justify the sales as a form of direct appropriation of the value of their labor or as a form of resistance. In the words of one female packinghouse union activist: "Well, once they had filled up the storage tank for the company, they should get what they produced."[81] Yet there was clearly a darker dimension to "la movida." High-level military officers figured among the merchants. A clear example of military complicity in the illegal activities occurred when a colonel fired two National Guardsmen because they had arrested the employees of a major "pirate" operation.[82]

By the late 1970s, the companies began to urgently seek solutions to the problem of "la movida." On one flank, they launched a publicity campaign.[83] They blamed the rise in local prices on the robbery, which curiously they did not pin directly on the fishermen. Rather, the National Guard and Treasury Police agents went after the putative buyers, harassing the local artisanal fisher population, arguing that the

---

[78] His argument was that Pezca was wasting this money at precisely a moment of extraordinarily high production but also of heavy investment in the plant infrastructure and maintenance. They should not be investing in a level of surveillance, "(que) nunca se ha visto en todo el historial de la industria de la pezca." Union Minutes, Sept. 1975, no. 11, 27, set 75 (Subseccional Pezca Archives).

[79] According to Quinteros and others, subsequently the AVIC agents became part of *la movida*. Others were threatened into silence. Noé Quinteros, interview with the author, Houston, 2014.

[80] Ruperto Torres, interview with the author, Puerto El Triunfo, Feb. 2016.

[81] Virginia Reyes, interview with the author, Puerto El Triunfo, May 2012.

[82] Ruperto Torres, interview with the author, Puerto El Triunfo, 2013; Ovidio Granadeño, interview with the author, Puerto El Triunfo, 2014; Adela Amaya, interview with the author, Puerto El Triunfo, 2013.

[83] "Las empresas pesqueras enfrentan el robo continuo del camarón en sus mismas embarcaciones, robos que perjudican a las empresas y al público ya al país por aquello de que el Fisco deja de percibir impuestos." *Diario de Hoy*, Feb. 13, 1979.

pirate merchants came from that sector.[84] Artisanal fishermen denounced *"una verdadera cacería"* (a true hunt) against them. The agents not only arrested some artisanal fishermen caught with shrimp, but they also extorted others, demanding the shrimp or cash.[85]

The companies viewed the artisanal fishermen as a nuisance, especially when company fishing boats entered the prohibited three-mile fishing area reserved for artisanal fishermen or when they accidentally captured shrimp larvae in the mangrove estuaries of the Bay of Jiquilisco. The response of the artisanal fishermen to the repression eloquently announced an historical moment decidedly adverse to the owners. A group of fishermen arrived at an opposition daily, where they claimed that they represented 15,000 more who for generations had fished in the waters of Jiquilisco and off the coast. The "monopolies" along with the regime were intent on depriving them of their livelihood.

Who are the thieves? Those who believe that God created the sea and its products for all people or these businessmen who believe they have some kind of titles signed by who knows who that makes them the absolute owners of the sea.[86]

This discourse of natural law may well have existed for generations as a "hidden transcript" among sea-faring folk on the Bay of Jiquilisco. Yet, in the context of heightened class tensions in the port, these fishermen could publicly enunciate this anti-monopolist discourse. There was interaction and some overlap between artisanal fishermen who resided in hamlets surrounding the Bay of Jiquilisco and the fishermen and workers of Puerto El Triunfo. Some Pezca *marineros* also fished in Jiquilisco as *artesenales*. Thus, the labor struggles surely had an impact on the artisanal fishermen as did peasant struggles that were sweeping the department of Usulután. For the companies, these ragged *artesenales* with their radical rhetoric added yet another dimension of increasingly bitter class antagonism.

* * * * *

The consciousness and practice of the Puerto El Triunfo working class changed substantially between 1970 and 1977. First, the level of

---

[84] According to many informants, the practice did start with artisanal fishermen, known as *murralleros* but larger economic agents quickly stepped in. The *murralleros* would approach the fishing boat to receive a gift of the fish, without monetary value, known as *muralla*. *La Crónica*, Jan. 23, 1979.

[85] Ibid.   [86] Ibid.

participation in the unions increased dramatically, from less than 200 attendees at SIP General meeting to more than 500. Union local meetings witnessed analogous increases. The larger meetings naturally reflected the increase in the number of union members, primarily females, in the plants. Because Salvadoran law did not permit closed shops, increased union membership hinged on the persuasion of the unaffiliated.

The decade also witnessed a substantial increase in female activity in the unions. Indeed, women ascended to leadership positions especially in the locals and actively participated in union meetings, often pushing their male *compañeros* toward more militant positions. Victoriana Ventura, for example, exclaimed in a union meeting, "We have to be brave! Don't let the bosses get their way! Don't let them achieve their objectives!"[87] Their participation and militancy formed part of a process whereby female workers were able to articulate and win demands of particular concern to them like first aid dispensaries (for the *chacalín* peelers) and simultaneously exert growing control over the production process. Moreover, they were able to create democratic forms of sociability on the plant floor that gave them a daily glimpse of a different kind of society. Female workers, especially on the night shift, joked and played games. They exuded a new sense of power that kept management at a distance.

The sense of liberation did not translate into a full-scale transformation of the family. Husbands and fathers continued to exert strong patriarchal control and female workers often resisted those venerable chains, particularly around finances. Gender conflict reached a higher level of intensity with *marinero* spouses. Domestic violence occurred with some frequency.[88] A significant percentage of women either divorced or remained single, secure that their union wages and extended family would allow them and their families to survive with dignity.[89]

The transformation of consciousness also involved an increasingly salient political element, though one that was largely circumscribed by a strong notion of syndicalism. As we shall see in Chapter 2, the conceptual key to the transformation lay in the terms *interest* and *solidarity*. Over the course of the decade, plant workers expanded the meanings of those terms so that increasing numbers of workers viewed state or management

---

[87] "Acta 35," *Libro de actas,* Apr. 19, 1979 (Subseccional Pezca Archives).

[88] Ana Paniagua, interview with the author, Montreal, 2016.

[89] Unfortunately, there are no statistics for the period on single motherhood, broken down by municipality. Nationally only a minority of adult women were married but that does not tell us much about single mothers because there were many common law arrangements. Most informants suggest that a majority of mothers were single.

repression against unionized workers elsewhere in the country as an attack on their own self-interest. The contact of the union leadership with leftist organizations through their participation in the labor federation FENASTRAS spurred the broadening of those meanings. Moreover, they injected a militant syndicalist vocabulary into discussions among workers.

Deborah Levinson's analysis of the Guatemalan labor movement in the late 1970s is appropriate for this brief moment in Salvadoran working-class history right before labor's destiny became tied to the revolutionary movement. She writes:

Although they had no revolutionary program, trade unionists disclosed possibilities for exceptional, radical social being and action. They wanted to live beyond the real limits, and they pressed for the creation of a world of resistance that was no one else's project or property, a countersociety always busy with the details of thoughtfully combating the barbarism that threatened it.[90]

The struggles of the female port workers were similar to those in other countries in that they contributed dramatically to the defense of the union when under assault. As Greg Grandin writes, "In Guatemala, as elsewhere, during moments of crisis, the institutionalized segregation of the public from the private broke down and women carried what was often an aggressive defense of their communities."[91] Female leaders like Gloria stuck with the union until death stared them in the face.

The experiences of Puerto El Triunfo were reflective of broader transformations in Salvadoran society and thus allow us to recognize the process of labor mobilization and radicalization in other parts of the country. The classic narrative of state repression radicalizing popular organizations holds true, only to a limited extent in the port. No doubt there was a slight radicalizing impact of the National Guard assault on union headquarters during the screening of the Soviet film in 1977. Yet, this was an isolated incident until December 1980. Rather, the transformation of the union responded primarily to endogenous factors, in particular the labor-management struggle over wages, working conditions, and labor rights. At the same time, the transformation was extremely uneven as significant sectors of the port unions remained politically conservative, sympathetic to management, and hostile to notions of solidarity and

---

[90] Levenson-Estrada, *Trade Unionists against Terror*, 141.
[91] Greg Grandin, *The Last Colonial Massacre: Latin America in the Cold War* (Chicago: University of Chicago Press, 2011), 137.

equality. And, a key sector of the labor force, the fishermen, remained apathetic at best in relationship to the SIP demands for solidarity.

The successes of SIP, measured by a growth in real wages and improved working conditions and benefits, would have been inconceivable without the emergence of an insurgent leadership group in the early 1970s and their openness to a form of proto-feminism that circulated among some female workers. Yet, the success of those leaders entailed, as we saw, the creation of new dependent relations, if radically different than the prior union leader-client relations. That dependency, in turn, created a sense of ambivalence among the rank and file about ideas and actions that came from the top down. At the same time, however, female workers increasingly joined the ranks of leadership injecting new concerns and ideas into the union discourse.

As we shall see in Chapter 2, 1978 and 1979 would mark the highpoint of labor mobilization and militancy when, proportionately, El Salvador ranked only behind Brazil in Latin America in terms of strike activity. Moreover, as a distinct sign of their militancy, Salvadoran workers occupied more factories than anywhere else on the continent. And the port workers played a major role. The newly mobilized women and the insurgent leaders in Puerto El Triunfo would have their mettle tested as they were thrust into a violent and rapid cycle of state repression and popular resistance.

2

The Cost of Solidarity

The Salvadoran Labor Movement in Puerto El Triunfo and Greater San Salvador, 1979–1980

We each took shifts, some of us in charge of security, watching out for threats from the police or National Guard or death squads. I remember feeling a double sensation – it was so exciting to listen and sing along to the revolutionary music – all of the activists and workers socialized. There were kids running around. We were all full of joy. But we were also afraid, anxious . . . as death squads lurked everywhere.

Carmen Parada on her plant *toma*

I told them you know in the future if you guys win (FAPU) you'll always need workers and you'll treat us like workers.

Noé Quinteros

Inside every worker there is a syndicalist trying to get out.

Eric Hobsbawm

WORKING UNDER SIEGE

On November 10, 1977 some 1,500 Bloque Popular Revolucionario (BPR) activists gathered in the Mercado Central of San Salvador. The military regime had previously blocked their efforts to hold a demonstration in Cuscatlán Park in support of two textile worker strikes. Protected by the large crowds of people who shopped, worked, and congregated around the Mercado Central, the radical Left organization held a "lightning" demonstration and then marched to the Ministry of Labor several blocks away. They blocked off the street in front of the ministry and set up loudspeakers. When some militants saw that security agents were closing the iron doors, they rushed over to occupy the building. Although unarmed, they were able to take 100 employees hostage including the Minister of Labor and the Minister of Economy. They called upon the Minister of Labor to intervene in favor of the unions and to raise the minimum wage from 6.20 colones to 11 colones (US$4.40) a day. After 48 hours, following the minister's promise to intervene, the BPR activists left the building.[1] Across town, unionized workers occupied US-owned Eagle International, a glove manufacturer, in protest against low wages and anti-union repression. Union militants not aligned with the BPR held three US citizens hostage for 24 hours. The regime's response was immediate. In the words of an US embassy observer: "These two incidents (the occupations and strikes) were among the factors that caused the government to promulgate the Law of Defense and Guarantee of Public Order, which among other provisions outlawed strikes and demonstrations. Steadily growing pressure from the wealthy elite and the military were contributing factors ... Labor disturbances thus had been significant factors in the passage of the law."[2]

The state of siege continued until February 1979. Despite the prohibition on "disruptions of productive activity," workers carried out at least 29 strikes during 1978. The very illegality of the actions tended to push workers toward more militant forms of activity, including in many cases factory occupations. As the same labor observer in the US Embassy pointed out, "Whereas before the usual negotiating method for a union had been to present a list of demands which it would then discuss with management with the idea of reaching a compromise ... the tactics of certain unions involved with the BPR or FAPU was to state an initial negotiating position, stick to it, and engage in strikes ... (including) the direct takeover of factories and the holding of representatives of management as hostages."[3] BPR and FAPU activists, according to the same

---

[1] The BPR was founded in 1975, the result of a split from the Frente de Acción Popular Unificada (FAPU), founded in 1974. The BPR developed a much larger presence in the countryside; it included a peasant and rural workers' federations. *Diario de Hoy*, Nov. 22, 1977.

[2] US Embassy to State Department, "Annual Labor Report – Part II: El Salvador's Urban Union Movement since August 1977," airgram, May 11, 1979, ES00131, "El Salvador: The Making of U.S. Policy, 1977–1984" collection, p. 4 (Digital National Security Archive [DNSA], George Washington University, Washington, DC).

[3] Ibid., 6.

report, offered aid to strikers in unions not controlled by the Left and then promoted more militant tactics.

The leftist-led labor movement grew exponentially in 1979. Most of the strikes involved the defense of the right to organize and an effort to resist the 9 percent decline in real wages since 1975. Some 80 percent of the strikes involved a demand to rehire fired union militants or to dismiss anti-union management employees. The relative success of the unions created a demonstration effect, and by the end of the year workers had launched at least 103 strikes involving some 30,000 people and far more work stoppages involving greater numbers of workers.[4] Nearly 20 percent of manufacturing workers engaged in strike activity. An expansive "militant minority," to cite the labor historian David Montgomery, propelled the movement. Writing about the early-twentieth-century US labor movement, Montgomery argued:

Working-class activists, and some individuals from other social strata who had linked their aspirations to the workers' movement, persistently sought to foster a sense of unity and purposiveness among their fellow workers ... [they] shared analyses of society and paths to the "emancipation of labor" ... the "militant minority": the men and women who endeavored to weld their workmates and neighbors into a self-aware and purposeful working class.[5]

Although revolutionary activists played a far greater role in the Salvadoran movement than in the United States, Montgomery's notion of the militant minority captures some of the ethos and potentialities inherent in the former, particularly in the port. In Chapter 1, we examined the nucleus of the militant minority in the port. In this chapter we will take that exploration further and expand it to the metropolitan area.

Most leftist accounts during the period viewed the growth of the leftist labor movement as the result of the application of correct ideas to proletarian reality: courageous militants combat the forces of repression and management with successful tactics that reveal the structures of capitalism and imperialism at the same time as they win material gains for the unionized workers. This chapter will examine more closely the causes and qualities of the growth and radicalization of the labor movement. I will suggest that the new forms of consciousness that emerged in the urban working class were indeed radical, but they did not necessarily

---

[4] International Labor Organization (ILO), LABORSTA.ilo.org.
[5] The term originated among early-twentieth-century syndicalists. David Montgomery, *The Fall of the House of Labor: The Workplace, the State, and American Labor Activism, 1865–1925* (Cambridge: Cambridge University Press, 1987), 2.

conform to any preconceived ideological notions. Indeed, a close examination of the labor movement in the port and in greater San Salvador
presents a murky picture where the terms *class*, *class consciousness*, and
even *union* lose something of their coherence.[6]

The common ideological bond linking both the port labor and the San
Salvador movement was a rudimentary syndicalism that had no formal
expression either locally or nationally. Eric Hobsbawm, in assessing the
usefulness of the term to depict rank-and-file insurgency in Britain during
the 1970s, states that the main characteristics of early-twentieth-century
syndicalism included the following: a hostile attitude to management and
all bureaucracies, including political parties; a productivist ethos (giving
supreme value to those who produce goods); the importance of spontaneous militancy, using any available tactic to hurt the adversary; a strategy
that relied upon the spread of strikes, culminating in a general strike; and
a hope for workers' control over industries. The evidence presented in this
chapter suggests that the local and national movements in late 1970s
Salvador reflected some of the attitude, technique, and strategy, but not
necessarily the hope, of classic syndicalism. Yet, those ideological forms
remained as inchoate expressions. Moreover, the syndicalists of El Salvador labored under authoritarian and increasingly terroristic conditions
that would have been difficult to imagine for the founders of the tradition.
The arrests, tortures, and assassinations not only provoked militant
responses but also imposed the necessity for semi-clandestine action that
made the full implementation of rank-and-file democracy – a *sine qua non*
for syndicalism – extremely difficult to achieve.

The disjunctions between the syndicalist ethos and formal ideological
expressions in the port and in the capital had several consequences. They
did lead to misunderstandings and alienation between the different
groups. But at the same time, these various dialectical interplays between
formal and informal discourse, between rank and file and leadership, and
between the port and the metropole all played significant roles in the
militant rise and expansion of the labor movement. In his renowned
study, *Resistance and Integration*, Daniel James wrote:

The more formal, traditionally validated tenets of Peronism were clearly ... an
important presence in working class culture ... Rather than a separation, a rigid
operation, we are dealing with a tension, both explicit and implicit between the

---

[6] The elasticity of "union" refers to the role of the multiclass Organizaciones Populares (OP)
that often acted as unions during intense struggles. "OP" was the term commonly
employed to refer to the BPR, FAPU, and the smaller Ligas Populares 28 de Febrero.

two [formal and informal]. The tension was itself related to an ever-present tension between experienced reality, and the "practical consciousness" that it generated, and the particular tenets of formal ideology.[7]

This chapter will trace these tensions within the broader transformation of labor relations while presenting a detailed examination of the changes in the port unions, a quite distinct history from that of the metropolitan area that nevertheless reflected, influenced, and paralleled the national labor movement. Solidarity and discord marked both the local and national movements.

ON THE ROAD TO LAS MAQUILAS

Salvadoran industry underwent a sustained period of growth in the 1960s, spurred by the import substitution strategy tied to the Central American Common Market; industrial output rose from 13 to 18 percent of the country's GDP during the decade. Then, Salvadoran manufacturing suffered two blows that affected the development of the labor movement. First, the Central American Common Market unraveled following the Salvadoran-Honduran war of 1969. Similarly, the oil shock of 1973 also adversely affected industry, in particular the cost of industrial inputs rose. Yet US and East Asian companies increased their investments in Salvadoran industry, especially in the intermediate goods and maquila sectors. During the 1970s, US direct investment in Salvadoran industry was US$124 million, most of it in textiles, chemical products, electronics, and electric machinery; 75 percent of the new investment involved joint ventures with domestic partners.[8] The Salvadoran industrial leaders almost entirely came from the old agro-export elite. Although originally concentrated in coffee processing plants and sugar mills, this group diversified its investments in the 1960s and was poised to join forces with US investors in the 1970s. Although several scholars have rightly emphasized the political differences between the more progressive agro-industrialists and the more reactionary traditional agrarian elite, the former did not exhibit any particularly enlightened attitudes toward labor unions.[9]

---

[7] Daniel James, *Resistance and Integration: Peronism and the Argentine Working Class, 1946–1976* (Cambridge: Cambridge University Press, 1988), 94.

[8] Often this involved buying existing plants. The only fully Salvadoran dynamic sectors were beverages and cement.

[9] See Jeffrey Paige, *Coffee and Power: Revolution and the Rise of Democracy in Central America* (Cambridge, MA: Harvard University Press, 1998).

Following the decline of the Common Market, the Salvadoran government invested considerable funds into the creation of a *zona franca* (free
trade zone) San Bartolo, an industrial suburb a few miles east of the capital.
This new industrializing strategy did not succeed in significantly addressing
the perennial unemployment problem, exacerbated by the rural-urban
migrations caused by the massive increase in the landless population.
Some 40 percent of the urban population suffered from unemployment
or underemployment; this reserve army depressed wages and provided
companies with potential strikebreakers. In the *zona franca*, labor unions
faced tight security, hostile regulations, and even greater managerial power.
Thus, unions could only organize a few of the newest factories in San
Bartolo. They did, however, have a strong presence in other foreign-owned
maquila plants outside of the zone. The maquiladoras did not pay any
taxes on the imported equipment or raw materials and generally performed
the final assembly of the product. As they would find out during the latter
part of the year, due to the highly labor-intensive nature of the maquilas,
the owners could relocate their plants with relative ease.

THE VIEW FROM THE PORT

From October 1978 until February 1979, the 1,000-member shrimp
packinghouse workers' union in Puerto El Triunfo mobilized successfully
in favor of demands for higher wages, improved working conditions,
and the dismissal of oppressive supervisors.[10] As noted in Chapter 1,
sharp sectoral divisions in the labor force militated against union success.
Under the leadership of Alejandro Molina Lara, Sindicato de la Industria
Pesquera (SIP) devised an effective discourse to organize the largely
conservative workforce against the powerful, oligarchic-owned companies backed by the repressive apparatus of the military regime.

In October 1978, Molina Lara attended a seminar on trade unionism
in Costa Rica.[11] When he returned to Puerto El Triunfo, he was angry to
learn that SIP had signed an agreement with Pezca S.A. that extended
their contract for another year.[12] According to the Labor Code, the union

[10] The SIP reported national membership figures as 2,000 in 1980, a number that also
reflected union membership in the port of La Unión.
[11] Molina Lara was then the union's Secretary of Education.
[12] When he had left for the seminar, a union committee had been renegotiating the contract.
The previous year, Leonel Chávez, then the Secretary of Organization (Molina Lara was
in his third one-year term as Secretary General), had commented that he hoped inflation
wouldn't increase much because he felt that the union was committed to respect the

was able to renegotiate a two-year contract after one year, if economic circumstances had changed significantly: in fact, inflation rose to 13 percent in 1978.

Rather than continue the negotiations, the secretary general, Leonel Chávez obtained a commitment from the company to increase the amount of overtime work. That last point irritated Molina Lara and others even more because the company owed a year's worth of overtime pay to its workers, a point not mentioned at all by the company or by Chávez.

In October, Chávez received a promotion in Pezca to *auxiliar de jefe de producción* (assistant production manager), a management-level position that was considered to be an "empleado de confianza," a category that was not compatible with union office. The Junta Directiva therefore demanded and received his resignation.

Two weeks later, Alejandro Molina Lara won election to the vacated post of secretary general with a stunning victory of 500–4, announcing a new phase of labor mobilization in the port that would last through March 1979. The vote expressed approval of his previous three years in office (February 1975–February 1978) and signaled both a rejection of Chavez and his agreement with Pezca S.A. to extend the current contract.[13]

For Molina Lara, Noé Quinteros, and most union members the problems with Chávez were his weak negotiating skills (*no tenía madera*) and his failure to consult the rank and file.[14] Moreover, the coincidence of his job promotion and his negotiation failure was hard to overlook. A November 13 SIP bulletin stated: "For a pocketful of money, he sells us out." Molina Lara called him a "traitor to our cause" and a "hypocritical traitor" who signed the document "behind the backs of the workers."[15]

This language of honor and deceit formed an integral part of SIP's mobilizing discourse. Gloria García pointed out that Pezca's actions

---

two-year agreement. Yet, his hopes were dashed as the inflation rate was running 13 percent in 1978.

[13] It is difficult to gauge the percentage of the workforce who attended meetings, given that a fluctuating number of workers were "eventuales" or "supernumerarios" that is people who were occasional and not seasonal workers and who did not pay dues to the union. The workforce of permanent and seasonal plant and maintenance workers was probably 1,000–1,100 in all three establishments. That said, within a year there were close to a thousand attending SIP general meetings.

[14] Although Molina Lara was active in Federación Nacional Sindical de Trabajadores Salvadoreños (FENASTRAS), in turn allied with FAPU, a radical group very hostile to the PCS whom they considered to be "revisionists," no reference to Chávez's Communist political affiliation emerged in the union discussion.

[15] "Acta 28," *Libro de actas*, Nov. 13, 1978 (SIP General Archives, Puerto El Triunfo, Usulután, El Salvador).

and words combined "mockery and trickery" revealing an utter lack of respect for the unionized workers.[16] Their offer to increase overtime work came when the *chacalín* (the smallest and most abundant form of shrimp) season, the main source of overtime for the plant workers, was essentially over. In a report on the initial negotiations in San Salvador, another SIP representative recounted how the company representative, the general manager, Cuellar Morán offered a 5 centavo raise. And then he had the temerity to make fun of them: "And that was how we were gathering up more courage." Union representatives responded with a demand for a 2.40 colones a day (US$0.96) and more benefits, especially for sick pay. Another union representative then commented on how they had to fight extremely hard because "they had suffered mockery and humiliation even though they were defending their rights."[17] On December 14, the SIP team won a major victory: a 1.56 colones per day raise, expanded sick pay, the payment of six months of back overtime pay, and the disciplining of supervisory employees. In hailing the victory, one SIP activist referred to the "courage" of the committee.[18]

The emotion-laden language of honor and humiliation could sustain patriarchal hierarchy and familial oppression and, at the same time, motivate people to rebel.[19] In the port, this powerful trope infused the

[16] In recognition of her vigorous intervention around the Chávez issue and of her prior union activities, the Pezca Local membership voted her onto the negotiating committee, representing the packinghouse workers in Plant #2 (devoted to *chacalín*). "Acta 32," *Libro de actas*, Oct. 21, 1978 (Subseccional Pezca Archives, Puerto El Triunfo).

[17] One negotiator stated that the confrontation was so intense as to drive one of the male negotiators to have "tears in my eyes." "Acta 33," *Libro de actas*, Dec. 16, 1978 (Subseccional Pezca Archives).

[18] Ibid.; Gloria García, interview with the author, Los Angeles, 2015; ibid., 2016. She offers conflicting accounts about the negotiations. In one interview that I use in my film *Port Triumph*, she refers to negotiations with a different manager, Varela Cañas, who mocked them more seriously by referring to death squad members who awaited them outside of the Ministry of Labor. It is possible that she conflated negotiations that took place in 1980 when death squad activity was ubiquitous with those in which she participated – and also suffered humiliation – during December 1978. It is also likely Varela Cañas was present at the 1978 negotiations.

[19] See Steve J. Stern, *Secret History of Gender: Women, Men and Power in Late Colonial Mexico* (Chapel Hill: University of North Carolina Press, 1995); Arlene Diaz, *Female Citizens, Patriarchs, and the Law in Venezuela, 1786–1904* (Lincoln: University of Nebraska Press, 2004); Sueann Caulfield, Sarah Chambers, and Lara Putnam, eds., *Honor, Status, and Law in Modern Latin America* (Durham, NC: Duke University Press, 2005). I wrote on this theme in Jeffrey L. Gould and Aldo Lauria-Santiago, *To Rise in Darkness: Revolution, Repression, and Memory in El Salvador, 1920–1932* (Durham, NC: Duke University Press, 2008), ch. 5.

language of women and men as they faced the same perpetrator of humiliation. Although the meanings of honor and humiliation may have varied, at the very least, both Gloria and her fellow negotiators felt the sting of class arrogance and prejudice at the table. Moreover, they conveyed the experience of negotiation as a form of combat. At the table, they battled with words and resisted the linguistic/cultural power of the management team. They felt empowered because the mobilization was such that they could assume that the rank and file was prepared to strike if necessary. As one militant addressed the union local meeting of 295 Pezca workers: "it was you who made the decision to take the necessary measures."[20]

Significantly Molina Lara – with seven years of negotiating experience – was absent as he was advising striking quarry workers. Unlike the negotiation team, he exuded confidence rooted in a sense of embodying the power of the organized workers; he felt joy rather than humiliation at the table.[21] Yet, he did share the other workers' idiom of honor; recall how he repeatedly accused Leonel Chávez of betrayal of trust and Pezca management of trickery. He also denounced Pezca: "they have mocked the workers' interests."[22] The defense of honor had a gendered element, reflecting the daily experience of female plant workers who strove to maintain a modicum of dignity in a job in which they were often disrespected for the very nature of the work and for living in a town marked as promiscuous. Makeshift whorehouses on the edge of the mangrove swamps further created a stench of corruption in the community as accusations abounded that plant workers supplemented their pay in the huts. Even when free of such taint, as one worker put it, "[Y]ou went to work stinking, you spent the day stinking and you left stinking. But money stinks."[23]

The defense of rights formed another key node in packinghouse workers' mobilization. A political model based informally on the Mexican Partido Revolucionario Institucional (PRI) had extended rights to workers, enshrining them in the national Constitution and in the Labor Code: the right to organize; to decent wages and working conditions and to negotiate and renegotiate contracts; and to overtime pay, year-end

[20] "Acta 33," *Libro de actas*, Dec. 16, 1978 (Subseccional Pezca Archives).

[21] Alejandro Molina Lara, interview with the author, Los Angeles, Feb. 2015.

[22] "Acta 28," *Libro de actas*, Nov. 13, 1978 (SIP General Archives).

[23] Maura de Zelaya, interview with the author, Feb. 2013. See also, Barbara Weinstein, *For Social Peace in Brazil: Industrialists and the Remaking of the Working Class in São Paulo, 1920–1964* (Chapel Hill: University of North Carolina Press, 1996); Deborah Levenson-Estrada, *Trade Unionists against Terror: Guatemala City, 1954–1985* (Chapel Hill: University of North Carolina Press, 1994).

bonuses, and vacation pay.[24] Playing on the distance between official discourse and everyday reality, SIP articulated those basic rights within a populist idiom that pitted the workers against the elite and its government (military) allies.

One SIP declaration stated: "Not only the bosses and the state have the right to become rich off of our natural wealth."[25] The declaration continued, "We understand that we have to sacrifice a great deal and suffer repression and threats, but nothing will come down from heaven … This is the precise moment in which management should tremble because of the combativeness of the Labor Force, because the [management] employees will not be able to handle the production of shrimp … Everyone must defend our rights; united we will combat this exploitation."[26]

Here, we can see the outlines of the productivist ethos and practical ideology that most unionized workers shared: management was incapable of performing the workers' job. This phrase echoes the justification for *la movida*: "the fishing boats left port empty"[27] and it was the fishermen who filled them. In other words, the workers on the plant and on the sea were the key factor in production, and management could not function without them. The implication was that the inverse was not necessarily true.

In addition, unionized workers also consistently referred to the "defense of their interests." The themes of honor, interests, and rights were often interwoven. For example, one worker alluded to the "right to defend our interests." Occasionally rights and interests seem to have been used interchangeably, as, for example, when a union militant exclaimed that "the interests of the workers are irrevocable." In this case, the term *rights* would have fit better syntactically in the sentence.[28] Another lauded "the valor that the conscious workers displayed, recognizing that they were asking for just salary raises and that was how they combatively defended their own interests."[29]

The notion of interests referred to individual and sectoral identities. Indeed, a constant discursive challenge was to try to create a sense of unified interests among a highly segmented labor force in which logical

[24] Jorge Cáceres Prendes, "Estado, sociedad y política de un contexto de insurgencia popular: El Salvador 1980–1987," *Anuario de Estudios Centroamericano* 14, nos. 1–2 (1988).

[25] Junta Directiva, Nov. 13, 1978 (SIP General Archives).

[26] *Boletín Informativo, I,* Nov. 13, 1978 (SIP General Archives).

[27] Migdonio Pérez, interview with the author, Puerto El Triunfo, 2013.

[28] "Acta 33," *Libro de actas,* Dec. 16, 1978 (Subseccional Pezca Archives).

[29] "Acta 31," *Libro de actas,* 1974, Jan. 9, 1979 (SIP General Archives).

cases could be made for opposing sectoral ones. Thus, for example at a January 1979 SIP meeting, activists tried to mobilize support among the 461 members in attendance for an impending strike in Mariscos de El Salvador to achieve equal pay with the other plants. One militant urged: "We must struggle to be united so that there will not be divisions among the workers." The next speaker referred to the discontent eight Atarraya workers expressed because the union, after a brief strike, had won a raise and a leveling of salaries in that plant. These workers were "resentful" that other workers now earned what they did. One rank and filer stated, "[W]e should not be egotistical because then we will not win the struggle."[30]

In reference to the successful struggles in Atarraya in early January 1979, Molina Lara exclaimed that the union had defended the "interests" of the company's fishermen and won an 18 percent pay raise for them, "even though they had not supported us in the struggle. Union policy is to support workers regardless of their class."[31] Later Molina Lara commented, "What a shame that the compañero fishermen did not accompany us even though we were fighting for their interests."[32] The invocation of interests was particularly tricky ground because the interests of the fishermen – given their pursuit of direct appropriation through *la movida* – were not transparent. The Sindicato Agua's acceptance of *la movida* (a de facto wage policy) proved a strong attraction for the fishermen in Atarraya whose loyalties and affiliations shifted back and forth between the two unions. As we shall see, the notion of interests would become a terrain of *desencuentro* I.

Rhetoric was important in at least two regards. The language employed in negotiations was critical as SIP leaders who typically only had primary school educations had to engage in convincing dialogue with highly educated and powerful antagonists. In addition, the words had to persuade a politically conservative rank and file to prepare themselves for work stoppages and strikes. Molina Lara and his group extended the meaning of the key terms in part by bringing in speakers from other factories and from FENASTRAS. The speakers emphasized that rights and interests were collective and could only be defended through muscular solidarity.

SIP leaders deployed honor, interests, and rights, the three key terms of mobilization, and wove them together through an ethic of solidarity.

---

[30] Ibid.   [31] Ibid.
[32] "Acta 31," *Libro de actas, 1974,* Feb. 1, 1979 (SIP General Archives).

To achieve honor and respect, and defend rights and interests, packing-house workers had learned that unity and solidarity were absolutely essential. In early January, SIP leadership protested strongly against Pezca security agents, who, when registering the female workers for stolen shrimp at the end of their shift, "touched their most intimate parts."[33] In response to the union protest, the company ended the humiliating practice immediately.

In late January 1979, Molina Lara's father unexpectedly passed away. On February 1 before the SIP general assembly, the 35-year-old Molina Lara swore an oath before his father's corpse, "I will keep struggling for the working masses." And then he read a message from his mother: "Hijo now I know that your compañeros truly care for you and appreciate you because of the way they have treated you today with the death of your father. Now I know you are united."[34] His mother's endorsement of Alejandro's work ratified by the rank and file enacted a newly enhanced notion of class solidarity. The next speaker was a union representative of the striking workers from the nearby vegetable oil company PRONACSA, owned by the oligarchic Wright family, who also owned Pezca S.A. Explaining how the vegetable oil workers had to resist anti-union repression and management's refusal to negotiate a new contract, he thanked the SIP members for their donations to their strike fund. Following him, one SIP member after another gave speeches calling for a solidarity strike. Gloria García, for example, told people not to bother striking unless they did it "with all of their heart."

Signifying an endorsement of this expanding notion of solidarity, the assembly re-elected Molina Lara to serve a full term by 475–25 votes. He claimed that he only ran for a fourth term due to the extraordinary conjuncture of national labor struggle, vowing that he would not run again (a vow he felt compelled to break the following year).[35] In another dramatic gesture, Molina Lara changed the location of the swearing-in ceremony of the new Junta Directiva from the resort in Lago de Coatepeque to the occupied vegetable oil factory, PRONACSA.

Over the next few days, the SIP leadership continued to mobilize for a solidarity strike with the PRONACSA workers.[36] One worker penned a poem of solidarity: "Compañeros you are not alone; don't get weak;

---

[33] "Acta 31," *Libro de actas, 1974,* Jan. 9, 1979 (SIP General Archives).
[34] "Acta 31," *Libro de actas, 1974,* Feb. 1, 1979 (SIP General Archives).   [35] Ibid.
[36] Here I use *stoppage* and *strike* interchangeably although in the Salvadoran context a one-day solidarity strike was labeled as a *paro* (stoppage).

victory is always ours and we will win."[37] At a February 7 meeting, many SIP workers again rose to speak in support of the action. They recognized the common antagonist and how the company had tried to "trick" the PRONACSA workers just as they had done to those of Pezca. Gloria García urged her fellow workers to take the action seriously and not act like it's "un paseo" (an outing).

Nearly the entire packinghouse labor force in the three plants stopped work the next day. The public announcement of the solidarity strike, signed by two other FENASTRAS-affiliated unions based in the department of Usulután, slightly differed from the discussion in the assembly, without violating the sense of the membership. First, rather than simply express solidarity with PRONACSA, it announced that the action was also in support of striking bus drivers and textile workers in the capital. SIP and the other unions demanded "respect for the right to strike on the part of authorities and the businessmen, respect for human rights, and the cessation of repression against the workers' movement."[38] The introduction of human rights rhetoric was increasingly frequent in Salvadoran labor conflicts and in protests against repression and appealed, in effect, to Carter administration policy vis-à-vis the military regime.[39] Yet, despite the basic congruence between the message and the sense of the union meeting, the amplification of the specific recipient of solidarity was indicative of the uneasy fit between strictly local concerns and actions and national-level labor tactics, strategies, and meanings.

Following the solidarity strike, Atarraya and Mariscos, undoubtedly chastened by the recent strikes, ceded to the SIP demand for the day's wages.[40] Pezca S.A., however, refused to pay for the day, and instead filed a demand against SIP with the Labor Ministry. We have no special insight into the motives of Pezca S.A. However, the Wright family was politically aligned with the far right and perhaps more importantly wanted to impede the incipient unionization of its vegetable oil plant.

SIP responded to Pezca's refusal to pay for the strike day by prolonging the job action and escalating its militancy. Faced with the threat of

---

[37] "Compañeros no están solos; no vayan a desmayar; y la victoria siempre es nuestra; y siempre la ganaremos." *Pueblo,* Mar. 20, 1979.

[38] "A los trabajadores y al pueblo en general informamos," *La Crónica,* Feb. 8, 1979.

[39] In a February 1979 report to Congress, the State Department had placed El Salvador along with Somoza's Nicaragua as the worst human rights violator in Latin America, worse even than Pinochet's Chile or Argentina during the Dirty War.

[40] Payment for strike days was typically a demand. The Labor Code mandated such payment but only in the exceedingly rare legal strikes.

strikebreakers, company security agents, and the National Guard, the union leadership opted to occupy the plant. SIP broadened its list of demands beyond payment of the strike day to include the firing of the Varela Cañas, the *gerente de base* (plant manager), for anti-union practices and another employee for harassment of a female worker. SIP listed the firing of Varela Cañas as their primary demand. They also insisted on the reinstatement of fired union militants and announced a general port strike if their demands were not met.[41]

Sindicato Agua's response to the SIP strike was one of solidarity in large part provoked by their animus toward the company that had launched a full-scale campaign against "la movida."[42] As noted in Chapter 1, the company had begun to intensify surveillance and to search and arrest artisanal fishermen whom they mistakenly blamed as the pirate merchants.[43] Company spokesmen offended the honor of the fishermen by accusing them of *robbery*, and that slur undoubtedly spurred the unionized marineros to ally, however briefly and informally, with the packinghouse workers. The fishermen refused to break the strike by delivering their catch to facilities in the port of La Unión as they had done in past strikes. Instead, the boats came into Puerto El Triunfo with their catch of 150,000 pounds of shrimp. The catch immediately became a cause célèbre. For the two unions, the shrimp would be processed only if Pezca S.A. agreed to their demands. The company expressed its intransigent attitude – undoubtedly exacerbated both by the plant occupation and their anger at their former allies among the fishermen – by refusing to negotiate and blocking the refrigeration of the shrimp by the striking workers. After a week, the US $800,000 worth of shrimp was dumped into the ocean. Both unions then demanded payment for the harvesting and processing of the discarded shrimp, a demand the company rejected out of hand.[44]

---

[41] *La Crónica* states that they took over the installations, holding hostages. This is a version that some workers agree with, but others do not. It seems that there was an occupation but that management employees were free to leave. Varela Cañas was despised in particular for his treatment of the negotiating team in November and December 1978. *Diario de Hoy*, Feb. 15, 1979.

[42] *La Prensa Gráfica*, Feb. 13, 1979.

[43] The origins of the practice had to do with fishermen tossing noncommercial fish to artisanal fishermen. At least one of those families became involved in the illegal commercialization of shrimp. However, when the companies and government began to harass artisanal fishermen, the business had become far more formalized with high-level military officials at the top. *La Crónica*, Jan. 23, 1979. Ruperto Torres, interview with the author, Puerto El Triunfo, 2013; Migdonio Pérez, interview with the author, Puerto El Triunfo, 2013.

[44] *Diario de Hoy*, Mar. 5, 1979.

By mid-February, Sindicato Agua initiated a de facto solidarity strike.[45] Yet, it was a peculiar action insofar as the fishermen publicly claimed they were not on strike but rather the victims of a company lockout.[46] Sindicato Agua's public, vociferous denial that their members were on strike is significant in that it signaled a difference with SIP; it also sent an ambiguous message to its own rank and file. They were, and yet they were not, on strike. They practiced and received solidarity with SIP and at the same time distanced themselves from the packinghouse workers' union. Notwithstanding Sindicato Agua's ambiguous posture, they used the SIP strike to make demands on the company in particular for the salaries they had earned on the seas (in addition to the piece rate on the discarded shrimp). They added another demand on the SIP list for Pezca to cease its practice of sending fishing boats back out to sea within hours of docking instead of waiting the contractually stipulated 48 hours. Sindicato Agua also demanded with the aid of SIP a US$4,000 life insurance policy and payment to the 10 families of those lost at sea in the May 1977 cyclone.[47] Immediately, SIP offered solidarity to the strikers, especially food. SIP, in addition to relying on its own rapidly depleting strike funds, was receiving food aid from Atarraya and Mariscos workers who staged brief solidarity strikes. Indeed, the whole town contributed: SIP had established such a high level of legitimacy within the town that during the strike of February–March 1979, observers commented on the high degree of community support. FENASTRAS also contributed supplies for the strikers. At that moment, the leftist federation was embroiled in often-violent conflicts in the metropolitan area.

VIOLENCE AND SOLIDARITY

Molina Lara pushed for greater involvement with FENASTRAS just as the national labor dynamic of labor rebellion and repression was beginning to accelerate. FENASTRAS scored major victories during the first months of the year. On January 22, 1979, textile workers in San Salvador

---

[45] The solidarity action in Atarraya and Mariscos only lasted a few days, though the workers continued to offer material aid to the Pezca strikers.

[46] See full-page paid ads by SGTIPAC in *Diario de Hoy*, Mar. 2, 1979 and *La Prensa Gráfica*, Feb. 10, 1979.

[47] Sindicato Agua's demands were incorporated into SIP's official demands.

occupied the IMES textile plant and held four management employees hostage, including two Americans. The union won all its demands.[48]

The key strike, however, took place in the La Constancia and Tropical bottling plants. On February 23, a group of unionized workers in one sector of a plant declared a strike primarily to protest a change in work shifts that would let people out at 2:00 AM (the workers preferred the status quo, 6:00 AM). They also demanded the reinstatement of five union members and the firing of 11 management employees whom they considered to be anti-union.[49] In addition, they called for a 75 percent increase in the bonus for night work. By the following day, workers had occupied the adjoining plants. Nine management employees remained inside the facilities to observe the takeover and were subsequently taken hostage.[50] Declaring the strike illegal, the Ministry of Labor ordered workers to return to their jobs by March 10 or face dismissal. On the morning of March 10, security forces surrounded the plants, blocking the delivery of food to the strikers. By the afternoon, a large crowd of demonstrators organized by the BPR gathered "to express their moral and material solidarity."[51] Apparently unprovoked, the security forces attacked the demonstration killing 7 and wounding 15. In response, enraged workers threatened to burn down the plant. Monseñor Oscar Romero stepped in to negotiate, along with the head of the Red Cross. Underscoring the limits of the burgeoning movement, however, on the same day hundreds of workers, perhaps one-third of the workforce, expressed their opposition to the strike at the Ministry of Labor, demanding to be reinstated and paid for the strike days.[52] The day after the shootings, unionized workers at 27 plants walked off their jobs in solidarity with the La Constancia workers and more than 1,000 electrical power company workers staged

---

[48] National Security Agency documents, "El Salvador: The Making of U.S. Policy 1977–1984" collection (DNSA); US Embassy to State Department, "Chronology of Strike and Holding of U.S. Citizens Hostage in IMES Factory," airgram, Feb. 15, 1979, ES00096, "El Salvador: The Making of U.S. Policy, 1977–1984" collection (DNSA).

[49] La Constancia was the soft drink plant and the adjacent Tropical was the brewery, owned by the same people and represented by the same union. Here *La Constancia* refers to both. José Guillermo Rivas, "Viva la combativa huelga de los compañeros de La Constancia y Tropical" (Centro de Información, Documentación y Apoyo a la Investigación [CIDAI], Universidad Centroamericana [UCA], San Salvador, El Salvador).

[50] *La Prensa Gráfica*, Mar. 9, 1979.

[51] FENASTRAS, "Hacia la unidad del movimiento popular," 1981 (CIDAI, UCA).

[52] *La Prensa Gráfica*, Mar. 14, 1979. The rightist paper suggested there were 575 workers at the Labor Ministry.

two blackouts in the San Salvador metropolitan area and in 10 of the country's 14 departments in support of the La Constancia, Pezca, and PRONACSA workers.[53] This was the country's largest solidarity action since 1967. BPR militants occupied the national cathedral in support of the La Constancia strikers. On the night of the 13th, La Constancia management settled with the strikers acceding to nearly all their demands.

The solidarity strikes in the capital resounded in the port. To aid the cause of the workers in Puerto El Triunfo, STECEL (the power workers' union) members engaged in selective power outages that affected Pezca owner, Juan Wright's hacienda, *La Carrera,* as well as the freezers in the processing plants. The power outages and the solidarity strikes finally brought Pezca to the bargaining table where the company granted most of the two unions' demands, including 90 percent of the salaries that would have been earned for the processing of the decomposed shrimp and 75 percent of the strike days.[54] They also agreed to reorganize management in such a way that Varela Cañas, the *gerente de base,* would be ushered out. Sindicato Agua received a commitment to indemnify the lost fishermen's families and to finance life insurance policies worth 4,000 colones. Similarly, PRONACSA granted most of the union demands.

On March 19, thousands of electrical power workers walked off the job. Supported by FAPU militants, they shut off power to the nation for 23 hours to demand increased wages and benefits, improved working conditions, and an end to anti-union repression. They also protested the measures that would privatize the industry. Ignacio Ellacuría, a prominent Jesuit intellectual, used the successful STECEL strike as an example of the resurgent labor movement and to explore its broader implications. First, he reminded his readers that for one-third of the nation's population, the blackout was their permanent condition. But, "the situation was new for the powerful ... during the 23 hours of blackout the *powerful lost their power.*" Along with the poetic flourish, Ellacuría counseled caution. Reflecting on the expansion of the urban labor movement, he stated: "The working class has rediscovered its power; an important and real, but relative and limited power, a power that needs to be managed with prudence and realism." For Ellacuría, capital and its allies were much

[53] "President Threatens Measures to Cope with Strike," Paris AFP (Mar. 14, 1979), trans. Foreign Broadcast Information Service, FBIS Daily Report, Latin America, Mar. 15, 1979.
[54] *Pueblo,* Mar. 20, 1979.

stronger and therefore it was urgent to resist the "messianic" notion that "revolutionary conditions" now existed.[55]

Despite its decisive role in the labor victories, FENASTRAS became further embroiled in factional conflict between FAPU and the BPR.[56] Yet SIP was largely immune from the *desencuentros* II on the Left.[57] FENASTRAS leaders came to a SIP meeting at the end of March to congratulate the rank and file and remind them of their commitment to unity and solidarity. In the context of increasing death squad assassination of union militants, Bernabé Recinos, leader of STECEL and FAPU militant, lauded their courage and promised to "offer his life" if it was necessary for the cause.[58] Others singled out female workers for their bravery and unity. All mentioned the defense of rights and interests.

Several testimonies suggest that the union activists kept the Organizaciones Populares (OP) and the guerrilla Left at arm's length. For Pezca Local leader Noé Quinteros, the tactical issue was tied to a broader strategic and ideological concern. Referring to the guerrilla group, el Ejército Revolucionario del Pueblo (ERP), he stated:

The ERP came around and offered armed protection to the union during the strikes. Although we were being harassed by the authorities, we could foresee a massacre of the workers if they got involved so we declined the offer. It was the same with FAPU, we accepted their food aid, but didn't allow them to work our bases. I told them you know in the future if you guys win, you'll always need workers and you'll treat us like workers.[59]

The elaboration of this proto-syndicalist worldview was perhaps unique to Quinteros and to his immediate circle. Yet, his vision broadly reflected those of other port union activists. Their highly attuned sense of solidarity and all its ramifications did not extend to a sense of commitment to student revolutionaries whom they considered to occupy a

[55] "23 horas sin poder," Mar. 21, 1979 in *El Salvador entre el terror y la esperanza: los sucesos de 1979 y su impacto en el drama salvadoreño de los años siguientes*, ed. Rodolfo R. Campos (San Salvador: UCA Editores, 1982), 158–59.

[56] See BPR, "Las luchas de la clase obrera enero/marzo" (Centro Universitario de Documentación e Información, UCA). The BPR argued that the influence of "economicism," "pacificism," "revisionism," and "opportunism" caused several strikes to drag on. Specifically, the BPR argued that "despite the hermosa solidarity of the *pesqueras*, the strikes in 'Pezca' and 'PRONACSA' had to confront the deaf intransigence." In response, FAPU attacked the BPR for sectarianism.

[57] Although there were some members of the PCS and at least one member of the BPR in the union, no one seemed to care one way or another.

[58] "Acta 34," *Libro de actas, 1974*, Mar. 28, 1979 (SIP General Archives).

[59] Noé Quinteros, interview with the author, Houston, Oct. 2013.

distinct class position.[60] These unionists would support the rights of students to protest but would not ally themselves with the radical or revolutionary Left. Notwithstanding, their commitment to unrestricted labor solidarity earned them the enmity of both the regime and the right and eventually landed them on the death squad lists.

AN UNREMARKED HISTORIC VICTORY

The union achieved its greatest victory in August 1979, a blow against the neoliberal-inspired flexibilization of labor. However, the rampant violence throughout the country relegated the news to a minor story. Since the beginning of the decade, the union leadership had attempted to organize the temporary workers in the three plants – some 35–40 percent of the total workforce – and to meet their basic needs, primarily the acquisition of rights to benefits, including access to the national health system, pensions, vacation pay, and seniority rights. As Virginia Reyes commented, "It was a real serious problem. The company did not want to make the *eventuales* permanent, so they would fire people so they didn't have to pay benefits."[61]

The growth and increasing strength of SIP surely weighed on the management of the three companies. By mid-1979, despite its fissures, SIP had organized the large majority of temporary workers and white-collar employees as well as permanent blue-collar workers. The continued vitality of FENASTRAS, despite repression, also probably influenced the owners' decision to capitulate. Finally, August was the height of the *chacalín* season, a period of potentially high profits. Throughout the month, SIP engaged in contract negotiations and work stoppages to win those rights for the temporary workers.[62] SIP first won at Atarraya and Mariscos de El Salvador. Pezca S.A., which had an entire plant worked by seasonal *chacalín* workers, was harder to convince.

Following a one-day work stoppage and the threat of a general strike, the company caved in, granting permanent status to the 156 seasonal workers of Plant #2 with all the attendant benefits, including social security, vacation, and overtime pay. They committed to finding all the

---

[60] Still a small minority of the population, under 5 percent of age cohort.

[61] Virginia Reyes, interview with author and Carlos Henríquez Consalvi, Puerto El Triunfo, Feb. 2013.

[62] Gloria García recounts two episodes in which security forces or death squads attempted to attack her team meeting in San Salvador. Gloria García, interview with the author, Lake Elsinore, Feb. 2015.

FIGURE 2.1 Virginia Reyes holding photo of herself from 1970s

seasonal workers maintenance work during the off season. They also agreed to provide them with three pairs of boots and aprons per year. All three companies granted unprecedented 50 centavo (US$0.20) an hour raises, in some cases amounting to nearly a 30 percent raise. In addition, Pezca promised to install a health dispensary and to provide free day care. Pezca also agreed to fulfil its promise to build a cafeteria, which, as noted in Chapter 1, was a vitally important benefit. Overall, this resounding strike victory further strengthened the union as its ranks swelled and the level of participation, particularly among women, increased dramatically. Although there was no specifically feminist language in the movement, the victory overwhelmingly benefited female workers, both temporary and permanent.[63] In the words of Gloria

---

[63] By 1980, thanks to the union agenda, the gender wage differential had declined to under 5 percent.

FIGURE 2.2 Pezca workers
(courtesy Juan Raúl Alberto)

García, "It wasn't a question of feminist demands, but our conquests directly helped female workers."[64]

The August 1979 strike victory was quite remarkable as it came at a moment of intense anti-labor repression and represented a blow against the logic of capital, a halt in the advance of neoliberal-style management practices, rejecting the segmentation and marginalization of temporary workers. Yet, union discord put a damper on the celebration. An increase in union dues was a key source of dissent. Manuel Muñoz, the conservative former leader of SIP, led the group of dissidents who rejected the dues increase. Several argued that the decision was made after the bulk of the membership had left the union hall. Gloria García denied the charge and made it clear that those in the leadership earned nothing from the dues that instead allowed the union to win decisive battles, through strike funds and minimal per diem payments for negotiators. After some debate, the SIP leadership backed a measure lowering the amount from 2 percent of the salary to 1.5 percent. The debate about dues prompted Molina Lara and Quinteros to try to recast the understanding of the rank and file about the meaning of interests and solidarity. Molina Lara summarized

[64] Gloria García, interview with the author, Lake Elsinore, Feb. 2015.

the claim: "Here it is not a question of watching out ... for one's own interests ... here we see the problems of all workers in general."[65]

SIP staged a large victory celebration, with many invited speakers from FENASTRAS; Plant #2 workers received special certificates registering their permanent status. Molina Lara took the opportunity to offer a more thoroughgoing explanation of the meaning of syndicalism. First, in a rhetorical flourish, he claimed that the union would be necessary until its members no longer needed higher wages or houses (the lack of adequate housing was a major issue). Next, he exclaimed that despite their victories that were the result of hard-fought battles, the struggle was not over. As workers, they had to remember the rural workers who earned 4.20 colones a day (25 percent of SIP wages). Then he recast the previous day's theme: "we have to struggle for everyone not for the good of the individual, if we struggle united then we are functioning as a union."[66]

For even if union members had been brought up with the idea of solidarity, the notion of *intereses propios* had been integral to not only their own understandings but also to the public acceptability of union discourse. In other words, official discourse (however authoritarian its political structure) readily accepted the notion of the defense of personal interests in the same way as it promoted the defense of the family. In fact, that was a key discursive prop of the legitimacy of unions in Salvadoran society. The move, however, from individual interests to solidarity – "we have to struggle for everyone not just for individual interest" – was smooth for the SIP leadership and for a significant sector of the labor force, but not for all. The labor movement in the port achieved astonishing victories. Along the way, however, the expansion of meaning of the terms' rights and interests, infused with the emotional power of honor and shame, simultaneously enthralled many and alienated a minority of its membership.

Toward the end of Molina Lara's victory speech, he launched into a scathing criticism of Sindicato Agua, which had been recruiting SIP members since April, disenchanted with what they called the "politicization" of the union: "the leaders of the sindicato del sector agua are not worthy of being called compañeros." He underscored a key difference between the two unions. SIP did not discriminate against workers on any basis whatsoever, whereas implicitly he suggested that Sindicato Agua did so on ideological grounds, rooted in anti-communism. By the end of the

[65] "Acta 39," *Libro de actas, 1975,* Aug. 30, 1979 (Subseccional Pezca Archives).
[66] "Acta 40," *Libro de actas, 1975,* Aug. 31, 1979 (Subseccional Pezca Archives).

year, the split had reached dangerous proportions. In late November, Molina Lara denounced "la movida," what he called "piracy on the sea," and added that "we have not been able to stop the loss of shrimp ... we are turning in those who take the shrimp ... we are going to break their chains."[67] He subsequently had conversations with the *Marina Nacional* about the practice. Noé Quinteros believes that the price on Molina Lara's head was due, at least in part, to his denunciation of the illegal sales.[68]

In Puerto El Triunfo, late August was a time fraught with hope and anxiety. The historic victory of SIP, combined with that of March, signified a major shift in social and labor relations in the port, as workers began to exercise power over hiring and firing and reversing long-standing discriminatory policies toward temporary workers, as well as dramatically increasing wages and benefits. The victory not only enhanced the prestige of the Molina Lara group locally but also it added to the luster of FENASTRAS nationally. Yet the victory came with costs. As suggested previously, discursively Molina Lara and his group through their own reflections upon their collective practice extended the meanings of "interest" in such a way as to undermine any particularist understanding, that is limited to "propios intereses" (self-interest). Thus, for example, syndicalism now referred exclusively to the unity and solidarity necessary to defend collective interests that included the nation's rural and urban working classes. Given labor successes operating with these expansive meanings of interest and solidarity, it seems likely that much of the rank and file became conversant with or at least understood these broader meanings.[69]

SIP had become a powerful institution in the port, a symbol of a resurgent, increasingly radical national labor movement. Yet both the local and national movements suffered from severe, crippling obstacles – profound *desencuentros* – that were not clearly visible in the crest of the radical labor wave.

STATE REPRESSION AND THE RADICAL RESPONSE

The regime and rightist response to the labor upsurge of February and March dealt lethal blows to the BPR and FAPU. Human rights activists

---

[67] "Acta 39," *Libro de actas, 1974,* Nov. 26, 1979 (SIP General Archives).
[68] Noé Quinteros, phone interview with the author, Houston, Mar. 2013.
[69] It is hard to calculate how many of SIP members defected, but within Pezca it is doubtful that they represented more than 10 percent.

charged the Romero regime (June 1977–October 1979) with 461 executions and some 300 disappearances, a new tactic designed to instill fear and anxiety into the families of activists.[70] On April 29, security forces detained Facundo Guardado, Secretary-General of the BPR, and four other leaders of the group, causing alarm throughout the labor movement and the Left. After several days of fruitless efforts to locate their leaders, the BPR occupied the Costa Rican and French embassies, as well as the Metropolitan Cathedral of San Salvador. The regime responded by encircling the embassies with security forces. On May 7, workers throughout the metropolitan region staged a four-hour walkout demanding freedom for the captured BPR leaders; the solidarity action took place in 16 factories, including the bottling plants, many textile plants, metal workshops, and a furniture factory, in addition to the teachers' federation. On May 8, the BPR staged two marches that converged on the occupied cathedral. When the demonstrators approached the cathedral, security forces opened fire, killing 22 protesters; four bystanders and one policeman were also killed and 37 wounded.[71] One of the wounded, a young mechanic, commented, "They mowed us down like chickens."[72] Some of the demonstrators were armed with pistols. In a widely diffused video image, amidst a multitude of people trying to escape from the indiscriminate shooting while on the cathedral's steps, a demonstrator rolls over and points a small pistol in the direction of the torrent of bullets. The image seen round the world at once revealed the barbarity of the regime and the willingness of protesters to fight back, regardless of the odds. Despite government and national media efforts to attribute the violence to the BPR, the *Voice of America* as well as other foreign correspondents blamed the security forces for initiating the gunfire. Following the killings, workers in 10 plants staged protest walkouts.

On May 15, FAPU mobilized its supporters in repudiation of the state repression. Activists marched from factory gate to factory gate in the industrial suburb of Soyapango. One FAPU militant recounted the protest in front of the country's largest cookie and cracker manufacturer: "In DIANA ... the [female] workers closed the gates and gathered together in front of the factory in order to massively join our Frente's

[70] Paul Almeida, *Waves of Protest: Popular Struggle in El Salvador, 1925–2005* (Minneapolis: University of Minnesota Press, 2008).

[71] Even the *Voice of America* blamed the security forces for initiating the gunfire. "Un llamado más a la racionalidad," in *El Salvador: entre el terror y la esperanza*, 252.

[72] Alan Riding, "Militants in El Salvador Undeterred by the Death of 22," *New York Times*, May 10, 1979. Other reports list 19 deaths. Captured demonstrators were tortured.

mobilization."[73] They shouted slogans such as "Juicio a los Criminales de Guerra" and "Viva la Alianza Obrera-Campesina."[74] Then the police attacked; armed "brigadistas de propaganda" repelled the assault. The group then marched to a shoe factory: "As we walked along the main street of Soyapango, the people waited for us to arrive at ADOC [major shoe manufacturer], when suddenly two convoys of the enemy pounced on the workers." The security forces militarized the entire zone and attempted to block all exits for the demonstrators. The FAPU militants built barricades to stave off the attack and then found refuge in the local Catholic Church.[75]

The intensity of state repression and the armed self-defense by militants of the OP were creating a state of incipient class warfare. Under such conditions, it was becoming increasingly difficult for workers to stay on the sidelines in those factories with strong support for the OP. That same pressure to join the struggle contributed to *desencuentros* II among the rank and file, such as those that occurred in the port, between the rank and file and the leadership. In every strike and *toma* (plant occupation), a significant minority, in effect, defected to management by offering to work. Many of those potential strikebreakers feared or rejected the role of the OP.

By 1979, the PCS (Communist Party) had been displaced from the FENASTRAS leadership, due in large part to its ineffectiveness rooted in its dependence on the Ministry of Labor to resolve disputes; its weakness opened space for the BPR and FAPU, which wrestled for control over the federation and the expanding labor movement.[76] Although the two groups had different views on how to achieve revolutionary change – with FAPU searching for a multiclass coalition and the BPR adhering to a strategy of "prolonged people's war" – they shared certain tactics, especially the factory *toma* and the solidarity strike.

Both groups arguably stimulated rank-and-file democratic expressions. According to Kristina Pirker, sociologist at the Instituto Mora,

The politicization of the unions had different meanings: in the first place, break with the daily practices of unions, based in the delegation of powers to

[73] *Pueblo Internacional*, July 1979, 8.
[74] "Bring the War Criminals to Justice" and "Long Live the Worker-Peasant Alliance."
[75] Ibid., 11.
[76] Later in the year, the BPR later broke off from FENASTRAS to form its own federation, the Federación Sindical Revolucionaria.

representatives and to promote solidarity with other workers among rank and file union members.[77]

As Pirker also recognizes, this particular form of democratizing had its limits. In particular, the use of "vías de hecho" imposed a particular tactic that often involved marginalizing and, in effect, silencing minority voices.

The growing support for the radical Left corresponded to a strike wave that swept the metropolitan area. As employer intransigence delayed the resolution of strikes, funds provided by the OP were critical to their maintenance.[78] Such support allowed them vital contact with union members. The ranks of the OP grew. According to US State Department estimates, in a country of some 4.5 million inhabitants, the BPR could count on 60,000–80,000 militants (a majority of whom were peasants and rural workers); FAPU had between 10,000 and 20,000 militants; the Ligas Populares had some 5,000 militants, many of whom were peasants in the northeast.[79] The OP, in turn, had ties to guerrilla organizations. During the same month of May, the Fuerzas Populares de Liberación linked to the BPR contributed to the state of incipient civil war through kidnappings and 20 assassinations including the Minister of Education and the Swiss consul.[80] In late May, the regime declared another state of siege.

Notwithstanding the state of siege, the BPR and FENASTRAS continued to lead strikes. On June 18, more than 300 workers at IMES, the textile plant that had experienced the *toma* in late January, occupied the installations in protest against management plans to lay off 80 workers for 50 days.[81] By mid-July, workers at more than 12 other factories were on strike in solidarity with IMES workers and in support of their own demands for a cessation of anti-union repression and for salary hikes to

---

[77] Kristina Pirker, "Radicalización política y movilización social en El Salvador: los frentes de masas," *Observatorio Latinoamericano* 9 (Nov. 2012): 71.

[78] Presumably the funds would have been funneled from guerrilla groups who had acquired it in prior years through bank robberies and kidnappings.

[79] US Department of State, "Telegram from the Embassy in El Salvador to the Department of State, Subject: High Level Dialogue with GOES," May 29, 1979, in *Foreign Relations of the United States, 1977–1980, Vol. XV: Central America, 1977–1980* (Washington, DC: Government Publishing Office). The Embassy estimated 60,000 members of the BPR in May. Apparently internally, the BPR estimated 75,000 and the government estimated 130,000 members. Subsequent State Department estimates reached 80,000. The wide range in the case of FAPU probably was due to a difficulty to separate support for FENASTRAS from support for the OP.

[80] The number is culled from the chronology section of the document and includes what might be called combat deaths. BPR, "Los sucesos políticos de mayo," La alternativa para la liberación (NACLA Archive) microfilm, pp. 136–45, roll 7.

[81] *Pueblo Internacional*, July 1979, 17.

compensate for the 11 percent inflation rate. In two of the textile plants, US managers were held hostage.

Whereas earlier in the year, struggles centered on the defense of the right to organize and an improvement in wages, benefits, and working conditions, by midyear many labor struggles responded directly to layoffs or to the threat of plant closings. Partially in response to the growing power of the labor movement, domestic and foreign capital flight became a pressing concern. Approximately 25 percent of the strikes dealt with the threats of closure and layoffs (a plurality responded to anti-union repression).[82] On August 6, workers from IMES and two other plants occupied the Metropolitan Cathedral of San Salvador and 14 of them launched a hunger strike demanding, above all else, the reopening of the plants, all of which had suffered lockouts following strikes. The hunger strikers released the following declaration: "We are more than 1,500 families; for the past two and a half months we have been in a desperate situation thanks to the bosses and their accomplices in the Ministry of Labor."[83]

The US Embassy assessed the labor panorama: "If nothing else, the recent spate of labor disputes demonstrates growing influence of BPR in organized labor field."[84] In a subsequent communiqué, embassy observers stated that as soon as one strike was settled, the BPR would foment another one and, at that moment in late July, they were in control of five strikes where hostages were held.[85]

FENASTRAS (increasingly controlled by FAPU) also promoted *tomas*, which became common practice among the labor federation's 43 affiliated unions (including locals), justified as a defensive measure against police and military violence and the use of strikebreakers (called *negreros*).[86]

---

[82] Wages were the prime cause of 17 percent; poor working conditions 11.7 percent; demand for raw materials, 11.7 percent – based on an analysis of a sample of 14 strikes from July to October.

[83] The coordinator was named after a martyr and was the labor branch of the BPR. José Guillermo Rivas, *Boletín Obrero*, Aug. 1979, no. 5 (CIDAI, UCA).

[84] The embassy claimed heavy involvement in 8 of 12 strikes. US Embassy to Secretary of State, "Heavy BPR Involvement in Recent Labor Disturbances," Airgram, July 19, 1979, ES00176, "El Salvador: The Making of U.S. Policy, 1977–1984" collection (DNSA). The embassy claimed heavy involvement in 8 of 12 strikes.

[85] US Embassy to Secretary of State, "Teachers' Strike Ends; Strikes in Industrial Sector Continue," cable, July 30, 1979, ES00188, "El Salvador: The Making of U.S. Policy, 1977–1984" collection (DNSA). The message mentions five strikes influenced by the BPR where hostages were being held.

[86] All Puerto El Triunfo informants employ this term, which originally meant slave traders, but presumably those who facilitate slave drivers (e.g., strikebreakers who aid authoritarian bosses). I have yet to find its usage elsewhere.

During the first nine months of 1979, there were at least 46 such occupations.

The origins of the *tomas* were defensive, as security forces arrested strikers or at least forced the entrance of strikebreakers into the plants. Despite occasional attacks by the National Guard to end the occupations, in no cases were hostages harmed, suggesting the symbolic nature of labor violence. In other words, the fact of the occupations became evidence for their violence in the absence of actual harm against management hostages. This, in turn, supplied the justification for regime violence. According to a FAPU publication, in addition to its defensive use, the *tomas* had three primary effects. First, they allowed for a flowering of worker democracy and for a platform to denounce human rights and labor abuses. Second, they served to push management to negotiate seriously. Third, they occasionally ended in "partial defeats" (implying that without the *toma*, a total defeat would have ensued).[87]

As the analyst Salvador Samayoa pointed out at the time, the tactical conservatism of the traditional Left and centrist leadership of the labor movement, and the inoperativeness of the Labor Code combined with the extreme anti-union bias of most companies and harsh state repression pushed workers toward more militant tactics. The BPR had a distinctive style of action. On the one hand, they refused any form of tactical alliance with other sectors of the Left or the labor movement. On the other, they mobilized nonlabor sectors of their organization to actively aid *tomas:*

The presence of students, teachers, and peasants inside the factories on strike appears to bother the bosses a great deal as well as the political adversaries of the BPR. The inclusion of political demands in their list of demands also bothers them as do the repeated work stoppages in solidarity with striking workers.[88]

Samayoa distinguished the preceding BPR tactics from those of FAPU, whom they were eclipsing organizationally within the labor movement. FAPU does seem to have accepted a subsidiary role in strikes and unions where they had influence, as the Puerto experience suggests. The BPR's rapid ascent within the labor movement probably speaks to the success of the tactic of using militants from other sectors to bolster strike morale and deliver necessary supplies. The entrance of the nonworker BPR activists was apparently greeted with some enthusiasm by factory workers,

---

[87] *Pueblo Internacional*, July 1979.
[88] Salvador Samayoa and Guillermo Galván, "El movimiento obrero en El Salvador ¿Resurgimiento o agitación?" *Estudios Centroamericanos* 369–70 (July–Aug. 1979): 595.

breaking their sense of anxiety and isolation and allowing for the expression of a sense of power shared by ordinary people in the face of clear-cut adversaries – some of whom they held captive. The involvement of students, market women, and peasants in the *tomas*, according to some testimonies, had the effect of creating a festive tone to an otherwise serious affair.

Carmen Parada, a *maquiladora* worker and union activist, spoke of the joy of cooperative work during a FENASTRAS-led *toma* in the zona franca: "We sang. And then we did all work together equally. We cooked, cleaned and performed maintenance on the machinery."[89] A young laborer at a metal machinery plant, organized into the BPR, recalls joining the occupation at the textile plant, IMES:

We each took shifts, some of us in charge of security, watching out for threats from the police or National Guard or death squads. I remember feeling a double sensation – it was so exciting to listen and sing along to the revolutionary music – all of the activists and workers socialized. There were kids running around. We were all full of joy. But we were also afraid, anxious ... as death squads lurked everywhere.[90]

The qualities of occupations do not seem to have differed significantly under the influence of FAPU or the BPR. Regardless of leadership, the festival-like experience did not translate directly into any notion of workers' control over the productive process. Moreover, the *tomas* could not reach the growing numbers of disaffected workers, many who had lost their jobs or feared imminent factory closures.

ON THE RADICALIZATION OF THE LABOR MOVEMENT

Throughout 1979, large numbers of workers were becoming radicalized, formally or not. The qualities of that radicalization differed a great deal. Most organized workers recognized the harsh social-political reality and saw themselves as playing a vital role in its transformation. Put differently, what today seems quaint – the notion of class struggle had become a vivid reality in 1979 for tens of thousands of workers, as much as one-quarter of the urban working class. Different actors interpreted class struggle ranging from the proto-syndicalism of the Puerto El Triunfo leaders to those accepting the notion of the working class as

---

[89] Carmen Parada, interview with the author, Los Angeles, 2012.
[90] Fidel Campos, interview with the author, San Salvador, 2012.

vanguard of a popular revolution. Degrees and qualities of commitment to the cause varied among workers depending on factors such as age, labor experience, family biographies, and direct exposure to the BPR or FAPU.

Labor conflict in Puerto El Triunfo was different than in the rest of the country in part because of the union's "work place bargaining power" (as discussed in Chapter 1). The shrimp industry depended not on foreign capital and raw materials but rather on the expanding consumer market in the United States. The port unions took great advantage of the absence of a viable threat to the industry. They could advance in ways unavailable to their class brethren whose jobs were always on the line. SIP had the strength, through a mobilized female workforce to reverse the neoliberal inspired trend toward the flexibilization of labor. In this sense, the granting of permanent status to temporary workers was an historic achievement.

In the metropolitan area, the structure of industry posed a sharp limit to the movement's growth as the *maquila* sector moved their operations with relative ease. The increasingly frequent labor demand throughout the textile and clothing manufacturing sectors for more "raw material" was indicative of managerial responses to economic and labor pressures. The functioning of the factories hinged on raw materials from abroad. More significantly, in August 1979 four plants closed down alleging labor strife as the prime factor. The government and media directly pointed the accusatory finger at the radical Left for its "illegal" actions because in all four cases workers occupied the plants. By late September, more than 20 plants had shut down operations or were on the verge of doing so. As the Left grew, a significant minority of workers became disaffected from the labor movement due to the plant closure crisis. Indeed, despite the advances of the labor movement, at its peak in 1979 at most 20 percent of the urban working class was involved in union activity in one form or another (and the official statistics placed the figure under 10 percent).[91] The radical Left had no immediate solution to this overwhelmingly grave problem, at once obscured and exacerbated by the storm of labor and peasant protest.[92]

[91] Moreover, the construction workers' union, by far the largest with some 40,000 members, remained firmly under the control of a centrist leadership that only infrequently supported the left wing of the labor movement. See US Embassy to State Department, "Annual Labor Report – Part II: El Salvador's Urban Union Movement since August 1977," p. 4.

[92] For a useful summary of US policy during this period, see William Deane Stanley, *The Protection Racket State: Elite Politics, Military Extortion, and Civil War in El Salvador* (Philadelphia, PA: Temple University Press, 1996), 128–30.

As we will see in Chapter 3, however, the threats and realities of plant closures also pushed grassroots activists to exert pressure on the radical leftist leadership to take seriously the alternatives to classic Leninist approaches to the class struggle. In the explosive year of 1979 industrial workers confronted the state and management more so than ever before. They also challenged the limitations of the ideological categories with which their courageous leaders understood and acted upon the world.

3

The Last Chance

The Junta Revolucionaria de Gobierno and the Impending Civil War

> The ERP came and wanted us to organize a march to see whether the new government was revolutionary or not.
>
> Escolástico – militant of LP-28, Morazán, 2009

> You of the Salvadoran Right: you have defeated those who defend the people. But celebrate quickly, because the civil war is one step closer.
>
> Ignacio Ellacuría, December 1979

> The Salvadoran labor movement has had to become clandestine because it is the only manner that it can continue living since its union halls have been dynamited and its leaders jailed or executed.
>
> Jailed Salvadoran Labor Activists, July 1981

On October 15, 1979, junior officers carried out a bloodless coup. They entered into coalition with civilians of the moderate Left and formed the Junta Revolucionaria de Gobierno (JRG) that issued a proclamation promising structural (including agrarian) reforms, an end to human rights abuses, the abolition of the paramilitary group ORDEN (Organización Democrática Nacional), freedom for political prisoners, the protection and extension of union rights, and the democratization of society.[1] The subsequent failure of the JRG signaled a rapid descent toward a civil war that cost some 75,000 lives.

---

[1] Rafael Menjívar Ochoa, *Tiempos de locura: El Salvador, 1979–1981* (San Salvador: Facultad Latinoamericana de Ciencias Sociales [FLACSO], 2006), 157.

The failure of the first junta had immediate, dramatic repercussions throughout the country. In 1980, security forces eliminated an estimated 8,000–11,000 civilians. Most analysts and scholars have considered the JRG's project doomed from its inception, due to the implacable repression promoted by the military command, the Right, and the machinations of the US government.[2] This chapter offers an analysis that modifies such a deterministic view, suggesting that contingent factors, discursive limitations, and subjective choices played a substantial role during the first junta (October 15, 1979–January 3, 1980) and that therefore an alternative historical outcome was possible.

Most narrative accounts and analyses of the period diminish the importance of what I deem to be a critically significant time. From November 6 until mid-December, thanks to an informal truce between the Organizaciones Populares (OP) and the JRG, security forces for the first time in a decade refrained from attacking demonstrations or engaging in death squad activities. The truce period fits uneasily into the dominant narratives of the interval because a serious consideration of it compels a questioning of both the twin extremisms view, dominant in the US media that blamed the Far Left and Far Right in equal proportion, or a generally leftist view that assumes that the military and Far Right were fully and always capable and committed to squashing serious structural reform.[3] This chapter will describe and analyze this brief but decisive period. It also continues our discussion from Chapter 2 about the dialectical interplay between the categories of the revolutionary Left and the forms of consciousness that emerged within the rank and file of the increasingly radical labor movement.

Since the beginning of 1979, junior officers had been discussing the possibility of a reformist coup in large part to defuse the revolutionary threat. They engaged in dialogue with different sectors of the Left including the brilliant Jesuit scholar Ignacio Ellacuría and Archbishop Romero.

---

[2] Ibid., 135. For a discussion of the significant conservative US influence on JRG, see William M. LeoGrande, *Our Own Backyard: The United States in Central America, 1977–1992* (Chapel Hill: University of North Carolina Press, 1998), 41. Despite the title, "State Department Hand in El Salvador Coup," *Executive Intelligence Review* 6, no. 42 (Oct. 30–Nov. 5, 1979), the article only mentions US attempted influence on the composition of the Junta once it was being formed (e.g., October 15), to make sure only "desk officers" were included.

[3] William Deane Stanley, *The Protection Racket State: Elite Politics, Military Extortion, and Civil War in El Salvador* (Philadelphia, PA: Temple University Press, 1996); Adolfo Majano, *Una oportunidad perdida: 15 de octubre 1979* (San Salvador: Indole Editores, 2009).

Many junior officers involved in the plot were committed democrats who were ready to purge the military and to remake it as a nonrepressive force. On October 6, an assembly of junior officers voted to place another military officer on the proposed JRG in addition to the progressive Colonel Adolfo Majano. They gave the moderate leftist Lieutenant Colonel René Guerra y Guerra a majority with 17 votes out of 27. The next day, when Guerra y Guerra was meeting with Monseñor Romero, Colonel Jaime Abdul Gutiérrez convened the junior officers again and warned them about the leftist proclivities of the leading candidate. Again, Guerra y Guerra garnered 17 votes but the conservative Colonel Guillermo García won 14 votes. With neither candidate attaining a majority, Gutierrez was able to emerge as a compromise selection.[4] The role of Gutierrez both before and after the coup was decisive but not preordained. In the words of William Stanley, "It ... seems to have been an incredible stroke of bad luck for Guerra that he was absent from the 7 October meeting. Guerra had in the past defended himself against red-baiting, and he knew how to exploit the corrupt reputation of Gutierrez and the others to undercut support for them among idealistic junior officers."[5] If Guerra y Guerra had scheduled his visit with Monseñor Romero for the following day and thereby attended the meeting Gutierrez called, it is entirely possible that he would have formed part of the JRG, providing a majority vote for the Left, ensuring a different outcome for the new government.

As Rafael Menjívar Ochoa states: "The importance of the Proclamation was obvious both at the time and historically; there has never been a declaration of principles so advanced in terms of social sensibility and benefits for the majorities, or at least there has never been one issued by a government ready to fulfil them."[6] At once signaling a full-scale assault on oligarchic power and the possible removal of the military from political life, the Proclama bore the imprint of Ignacio Ellacuría.[7] He and Monseñor Romero offered support for the new government, conditional on meeting major human rights objectives and bringing military criminals to justice. Román Mayorga, a member of the left wing of the Christian

---

[4] On the seemingly fortuitous inclusion of Gutiérrez, see Stanley, *The Protection Racket State*, 44–45. Stanley found no evidence to suggest US involvement in promoting the second vote (p. 144). Also see, Rodrigo Guerra y Guerra, *Un golpe al amanecer: La verdadera historia de la proclama del 15 de octubre de 1979* (San Salvador: Indole Editores, 2009), 62–65; Menjívar Ochoa, *Tiempos de locura*, 136–41.

[5] Stanley, *The Protection Racket State*, 145.

[6] Menjívar Ochoa, *Tiempos de locura*, 157.   [7] Majano, *Una oportunidad perdida*, 74.

Democratic Party (PDC) and the rector of the Universidad Centroamericana (UCA) was picked as a civilian member of the JRG along with Guillermo Ungo, a UCA professor and leader of the social democratic Movimiento Nacional Revolucionario. Within days, the JRG declared a political amnesty and invited exiles to return.

The Left and Right entered this critical conjuncture both sharply divided and to some degree caught off guard. The Right was divided between those who sought a tightly controlled and limited reform program to stabilize the country and those who sought to overthrow the JRG, which they viewed as communist. In addition to the split between moderate leftists in the government (including the Partido Comunista Salvadoreño [PCS]) and the revolutionary Left, the latter was also divided over tactics and over the question of who would become the vanguard. Yet, the leftist groups all agreed that the United States was behind the coup and that the JRG promoted a counterinsurgent strategy. Moreover, the entire revolutionary Left designed actions that would unmask the reactionary character of the JRG.

The Ejercito Revolucionario del Pueblo (ERP) and its allied mass organization, the Ligas Populares 28 de Febrero (LP-28) immediately took a militant stance against the regime. In the words of LP-28 leader, César Martí:

We prepared the armed uprising throughout the night and at 5:30 am on the 16th, we had taken the peripheral cities in order to expose the imperialist maneuver and to at all costs avoid demobilization.[8]

The goal of the insurrectionary activity – which Ellacuría labeled "suicidal" – was political and not military, namely to "unmask" the new government. The ERP captured the mayors and took over the town halls. They also executed some members of ORDEN. The military responded with tanks and heavy arms. In the industrial suburb of San Marcos, the National Guard laid siege to the town hall. After five hours of battle, the military had killed 24 civilians and guerrillas and wounded 80. The brutality of the military response indicated either the continuity with the old regime or a failure on the part of the JRG to exert control over the military.

On the same day, protesters aligned with the Bloque Popular Revolucionario (BPR) staged a demonstration in front of the DIANA factory

---

[8] César Martí, "LP-28: Unidad revolucionaria y perspectivas de poder," in *El Salvador: Alianzas políticas y proceso revolucionario,* Cuadernos de Coyuntura, no. 5 (Mexico City: Sociedade de Economia Política Latinoamericana [SEPLA], 1979), 21.

(cookies), in support of workers who had occupied the plant the day before in protest against the presence of heavily armed private guards in the factory.[9] Security forces assaulted the demonstration, killing one person and then entered the factory where they arrested 70 workers and killed 4 more. They then proceeded to storm four other neighboring factories in the industrial suburb of Soyapango. In the course of their attacks on the factories, authorities killed five workers and arrested dozens. In a desperate response, workers reportedly attempted to burn down two of the factories.[10]

The JRG's strikingly contradictory positions, calling for the respect of union rights, on the one hand, and storming the occupied factories, on the other, symbolized the profound division at the core of this new reformist regime. The repression derived from the inability of the JRG to exercise its legal authority over the security forces.

The Left, with the notable exception of the PCS, unequivocally rejected the new government.[11] The OP-led protest demonstrations, always protected by self-defense brigades, emboldened the hard Right inside and outside of the military. On October 22, troops opened fire on a demonstration by Frente de Acción Popular Unificado (FAPU) causing several deaths. In response, its allied labor federation, Federación Nacional Sindical de Trabajadores Salvadoreños (FENASTRAS), withdrew from the *Foro Popular*, a coalition of political groups and unions that had been offering critical support of the JRG. On October 24, the BPR staged a demonstration that culminated in a takeover of the Ministry of Labor and the Ministry of Economy. Among the hostages was the Minister of Labor, a member of the PCS. The BPR demands echoed those of the Left and of the human rights community: for the freedom of political prisoners and

---

[9] The strike also included several demands including a union petition to stage a commemorative celebration of the union's founding that the company had denied. It is unclear how the workers occupied the plant with such a contingent of private guards (apparently former members of the National Guard). Leaflet, Oct. 16, 1979, signed by Sindicato de Dulces y Pastas Alimenticias (SIDPA) (Centro de Información, Documentación y Apoyo a la Investigación [CIDAI], Universidad Centroamericana [UCA], San Salvador, El Salvador).

[10] The factories included APEX, where the general manager, an American, Boorstein had been held hostage and that had been occupied for two months. "Informática El Salvador," Centro Intercultural de Documentación (CIDOC) (Oct.–Nov. 1979): 9.

[11] Curiously, on October 19 the ERP/LP-28 vacillated and recognized "progressive elements" in the JRG; they demanded representation in the new government. Reflecting the LP-28's confusion and disorientation, a few days later the organization, once again, denounced the JRG.

for an accounting of the disappeared. Most of the demands, however, directly addressed the immediate needs of the urban and rural working classes, including a 100 percent rise in wages; specific reductions in prices of basic necessities and of bus fares; and the provision of drinking water for the entire population.

On October 29, security forces opened fire on a *Ligas Populares* demonstration in support of the BPR occupation, killing 29 people, mostly peasants from the department of Morazán. Although the government and the right-wing press blamed the radical Left group for initiating the shooting, impartial observers witnessed the security forces opening fire first. That said, one LP-28 member from Morazán, Andrés Barrera, recalled,

We went to a demonstration to support the Bloque who had occupied the Ministry of Labor. We went around it twice, shouting slogans, and each time we passed by the National Police. It was like we were looking for something and we were: we were looking for trouble. The third time the police opened fire on us.[12]

Whether the LP-28 consciously provoked the repression (as they did on October 16), the violent military reaction was far out of proportion to the provocation. Once again, the JRG was incapable of reining in the security forces who remained so aggressive that the LP-28 militants had to bury their dead inside the church.

On October 31, Ellacuría reproached the Left for its constant, often-violent street demonstrations: "Why couldn't you give the Junta a month?"[13] We do not know if his public cry played any role in the negotiations between the BPR and the JRG or whether the agreement was primarily reached due to the continuing protests by the OP and the bloodshed on the streets. Regardless, on November 6, in the Nicaraguan Embassy, the BPR agreed to a one-month truce with the government that included the end of the occupations and a series of concessions by the JRG. FAPU and LP-28 also agreed informally to the truce. The JRG agreed to cut intercity bus rates by 50 percent and to intervene in two current labor conflicts. The JRG also committed to negotiate indemnification or the reopening of four other factories. The JRG also promised within the 30-day period to enact significant wage increases in the fields

---

[12] Andrés Barrera, interview with the author and Carlos Henríquez Consalvi, 2007; ibid., 2011.

[13] Ignacio Ellacuría, "Las organizaciones populares ante la nueva situación," in *El Salvador entre el terror y la esperanza: Los sucesos de 1979 y su impacto en el drama salvadoreño de los años siguientes*, ed. Rodolfo R. Campos (San Salvador: UCA Editores, 1982), 614.

and factories and to institute human rights policies, in particular to resolve the issues surrounding the disappearance of some 176 political prisoners.[14] On the same day, the JRG announced the dissolution of the 100,000-strong right-wing paramilitary group, ORDEN.[15]

On November 6, 12,000 people under the banners of the BPR began a march in support of the occupations. Workers staged a stoppage and walkout in 13 factories. According to the organizers, thousands joined the march en route to the ministries where the occupants filed out of the buildings. The BPR supporters then marched to the National University where they staged a victory celebration.[16] Per orders from the JRG, troops and security forces remained in their barracks. Two days later, 50 militants of the LP-28 filed out of the San Miguel Cathedral after a weeks-long protest against the "autogolpe fascista de la Junta."[17]

Although much has been written about the first JRG (October 15–January 3), the period of the truce remains remarkably unstudied, in part, perhaps because it fits uneasily in any dominant narrative. From November 6 until the end of the middle of December, security forces refrained from violently attacking demonstrations or strikes. November recorded a significantly lower level of arrests and street clashes; it also recorded very few urban executions. Indeed, nationwide, there were only 10 documented civilian deaths by far the lowest monthly total from 1979 to 1992.[18]

THE JRG IN NOVEMBER 1979

With the commencement of the November 6 truce, security forces ceased their repressive activities against the OP. According to a contemporary

[14] Earlier in the week, the government formed a commission to search for a total of 300 disappeared persons. BPR, *Combate Popular*, Nov. 15, 1979 (North American Congress on Latin America [NACLA] Archive) microfilm, pp. 590–92, roll 6; Tomás Guerra, *El Salvador, octubre sangriento: Itinerario y análisis del golpe militar del 15 de octubre de 1979* (San José: Centro Víctor Sanabria, 1979), 72–73; Stanley, *The Protection Racket State*, 157–58.

[15] "Government Junta Disbands ORDEN," Paris AFP (Nov. 7, 1979), trans. Foreign Broadcast Information Service, FBIS Daily Report, Latin America, Nov. 7, 1979.

[16] BPR, *Combate Popular*, Nov. 15, 1979 (NACLA Archive) microfilm, pp. 590–92, roll 6; Guerra, *El Salvador, octubre sangriento*, 72–3; Stanley, *The Protection Racket State*, 157–58.

[17] STECEL also engaged in an eight-hour strike to protest the killing of one of its militants. Guerra, *El Salvador, octubre sangriento*, 78.

[18] Indeed, contemporary analysts, such as Eugenio Anaya, suggested that the civilian deaths were caused by the guerrillas. See Stanley, *The Protection Racket State*, 166, for a figure of 10 deaths in November.

analyst connected to the UCA, they executed no one during the following six weeks, a remarkable departure from their previous lethal practices. According to the analyst,

The security forces adhered to the new guidelines and from that moment begins a more tranquil period, in which violent repression practically disappears and we are allowed a month of much tranquility. The *tomas* are negotiated and not responded to with force.[19]

There is little doubt that from October 15 to October 31, the security forces had acted against the stated policies of the JRG. Perhaps the killings at the October 29 LP-28 demonstration and at the BPR demonstration on October 31 tipped the internal balance and pushed the JRG toward a more forceful policy of reining in the security forces. That the government was then able to stop violent repression for a month suggests that at least within the JRG (as opposed to the military) a majority strove for a peaceful response to political and social protest. At the same time, the JRG pushed forward, albeit slowly, toward the fulfilment of the Proclama. During its first weeks, the JRG was stunned by its realization that all the political prisoners had been executed. Even the conservative military member, Abdul Gutiérrez, was deeply moved by the mothers of the disappeared and remained speechless when listening to their testimonies. The JRG formed a commission that moved quickly to gather evidence against the former presidents Romero and Molina and their security chiefs and to search for the remains of the disappeared.[20] By the end of the month, the commission had uncovered corpses in clandestine prisons and issued a call for indictments. On December 3, the JRG formally issued an order for a pretrial investigation of Molina and Romero.

Throughout November and December, the JRG tried to mobilize its own bases of support for its program of structural reform. Rubén Zamora, Presidential Minister of the JRG, addressed some 5,000 peasants who were attending a congress of the reformist Unión Comunal Salvadoreña (UCS). The peasant organization, originally financed by the US Agency for International Development (USAID) and the American Institute for Free Labor Development (AIFLD), strongly endorsed Zamora's

[19] Eugenio Anaya, "Crónica del mes," *Estudios Centroamericanos* 34, no. 374 (Nov.–Dec. 1979).
[20] "Junta Commission to Investigate Missing Prisoners Issue," Panama City ACAN (Nov. 2, 1979), trans. Foreign Broadcast Information Service, FBIS Daily Report, Latin America, Nov. 6, 1979.

call for land reform.[21] On December 14, more than 10,000 urban labor members of the Foro Popular attended a demonstration in San Salvador that called for a 40 percent wage increase, a 30 percent reduction in rents, and union rights in the countryside. The demonstrators also demanded the extradition of Romero, Molina, and a host of other human rights violators from the previous regimes. Despite the nature of the protest demands, evidence of its radicalization, the Foro Popular remained a pillar of support for the JRG.[22]

The government also depended to some degree on the Christian Democrats (PDC). During the last week of October, a crowd of 30,000–50,000 people welcomed José Napoléon Duarte as he returned from seven years of exile in Venezuela.[23] The size of the demonstration signified the PDC's continued strength. As *Radio Ysax* (Ellacuría) pointed out: "There is no doubt that only [Duarte] can mobilize so many people – more than the Bloque, FAPU, and the LP-28. They told us that the people, educated by the OP were convinced that Duarte and his party were useless ... this shows how fooled the OP can be in their judgments."[24] That error in calculation was certainly a symptom of revolutionary triumphalism.

The JRG could count on PDC support up to a point. Yet Duarte and his team were unsteady allies. They pushed for elections before carrying out structural reforms, a position also endorsed by the Right (who simply wished to block the reforms). Moreover, Duarte and other PDC leaders

[21] *El Independiente*, Nov. 27, 1979.

[22] "La semana fue así (Del 8 al 15 de diciembre de 1979)," Dec. 15, 1979 in *El Salvador entre el terror y la esperanza*, 734. *Radio YSAX* noted that this demonstration, essentially blacked out by the rightist media, could not be attended by rural workers and peasants due to the harvest. Despite the withdrawal of FENASTRAS, most Foro organizations were labor unions. "Three Demonstrations Held in Support of Various Demands," Panama City ACAN (Dec. 15, 1979), trans. Foreign Broadcast Information Service, FBIS Daily Report, Latin America, Dec. 17, 1979. See *El Independiente*, Dec. 12, 1979. Fourteen groups, including FENASTRAS and other labor federations, came together earlier in the year to oppose the Romero regime. As noted previously, FENASTRAS withdrew in protest against JRG repression.

[23] *Latin American Weekly Report*, Nov. 2, 1979, reported that 30,000 people greeted Duarte.

[24] "La semana fue así (Del 20 al 27 de octubre de 1979)," Oct. 27, 1979 in *El Salvador entre el terror y la esperanza: Los sucesos de 1979 y su impacto en el drama salvadoreño de los años siguientes*, 606.

engaged in backroom negotiations with the military and with the US Embassy as they eyed a major role in a new junta.[25]

Despite wavering and dissension within its ranks, the JRG did implement key parts of its reform program. The government dramatically raised the minimum rural wage for the harvests as it froze prices on the "canasta básica."[26] On November 14, it decreed a minimum daily wage in the coffee harvest of US$5.70.[27] In early December, it took its first step toward implementing agrarian reform by blocking sales of land more than 100 hectares (retroactive to October 15). At the same time, Enrique Alvarez, the Minister of Agriculture, instituted a major reduction in land rent, bringing rents down from at times 1,000 colones a manzana to a maximum of 200 colones and as low as 25 colones (US$10). In a televised address, Alvarez presented shocking statistics that justified the reforms, including that 73 percent of campesino children suffered from malnutrition, and 40 percent of the rural population lacked access to land.[28] Later in the month, the JRG nationalized the coffee and sugar export trade. It also froze urban rents and offered a package of more than US$50 million to attend to the needs of those living in marginal communities.[29]

On the international stage, the JRG completely reversed policy and opened relations with the Sandinista government and Cuba and broke relations with South Africa. Until mid-December then, in extremely tense and unusual circumstances, the JRG, with a potentially strong base of support, behaved like a center-left government struggling to fulfil its program and to neutralize its opponents.

Throughout November and into December, the JRG engaged in some dialogue with the popular organizations. Although the details of those conversations are murky, it does seem that FAPU and elements of the BPR

---

[25] Majano, *La oportunidad perdida*, 178.

[26] An estimate of the cost of basic food items necessary for a minimal level of subsistence.

[27] "Foreign Minister Says Talks with Honduran Counterpart Suspended," Panama City ACAN (Nov. 14, 1979), trans. Foreign Broadcast Information Service, FBIS Daily Report, Latin America, Nov. 15, 1979.

[28] Other statistics included: 37 percent lack of access to drinking water. Seven-tenths of 1 percent of landowners possessed 40 percent of the land – the most fertile land. US Embassy to Secretary of State, "Presentation of Agrarian Reform by Minister of Agriculture," cable, Dec. 17, 1979, E00322, "El Salvador: The Making of U.S. Policy, 1977–1984" collection (Digital National Security Archive [DNSA], George Washington University, Washington, DC).

[29] "Marginal": in effect slum communities with little or no infrastructure. Eugenio Anaya, "Crónica del mes," 1090–91; US Embassy to Secretary of State, "Presentation on Agrarian Reform by Minister of Agriculture," cable, Dec. 17, 1979, E00322, "El Salvador: The Making of U.S. Policy, 1977–1984" collection (DNSA).

were ready to play the role of a more or less loyal opposition, pushing the JRG to meet its demands in favor of workers and peasants.

Under the Carter administration, US foreign policy shifted toward limited opposition to state repression in Central America. The triumph of the Sandinista Revolution pushed US policy in the direction of containment of the region's revolutionary movements, while still maintaining harsh critiques of the military regimes. The State Department policy in El Salvador clearly reflected the two-pronged strategy. Although Ambassador Frank Devine recognized the threat from the Right, his greatest preoccupation was the growth of the armed Left and the weakness of the military. He was profoundly hostile to the OP. The revolutionary Left, in turn, consistently claimed that the Carter administration and the CIA were behind the coup. Although there is some evidence that the CIA had worked with Colonel Abdul Gutiérrez before the coup, the Carter administration's hostility to the Romero regime due to its human rights abuses had a strongly negative impact on US relations with the armed forces.[30] The coup remedied that situation and it is likely that the CIA and the Embassy then developed close ties with Minister of Defense García and with Abdul Gutiérrez. Nevertheless, a report prepared by the Embassy staff on November 8 rejected a repressive strategy in favor of "firm restraint coupled with a coherent political strategy to discredit the extreme left."[31]

At the same time, Devine and his advisors were acutely aware of the limitations of their capacity for intervention. The November 8 report included the following recommendation:

At this delicate stage in the Junta's life, the USG's role is very important but requires political understanding and sensitivity to local realities . . . Moderate but still politically shaky it [JRG] is seeking to establish a broad political base by

---

[30] As late as October 4, the United States was unaware of and uninvolved in the coup plotting. See US State Department to Viron Vaky, "US Policy to El Salvador," memorandum, Oct. 4, 1979, EL00624, "El Salvador: War, Peace, and Human Rights, 1980–1994" collection, pp. 1–6 (DNSA).

[31] US Embassy to Secretary of State, "Analysis of Salvadoran Situation (Redistributed by Department of State on 8 November 1979, to U.S. Embassies in Central America)," cable, Nov. 6, 1979, EL00645, "El Salvador: War, Peace, and Human Rights, 1980–1994" collection, p. 9 (DNSA).

reaching out to an ideologically diverse political constituency part of which would resist or even oppose a close, overt relationship with the US.[32]

Without mentioning names, the report referred to the PCS (and its front group the Unión Democrática Nacional – UDN) and to those labor unions who had remained in the Foro Popular. For a brief moment, it appeared that Embassy officials peered outside of their Cold War blinders.

By early December, the Embassy began to watch the countryside apprehensively as the OP took advantage of the withdrawal of security forces to promote as many as 50 occupations of coffee plantations and 25 cotton plantations. By this time, the Embassy feared the growth of the radical Left more so than the rightist reaction.[33] By mid-December, the US Embassy and presumably the CIA were pushing the JRG to come down hard on the "implacable enemy," the "extreme left." The Embassy worried that "time may be running out," and they tried to stress that urgency to the JRG, and to García.[34]

The United States played a key role in the strengthening of the military within the JRG. Yet, there is no indication that they wished to eliminate Ungo or Mayorga or provoke the mass resignations that the military hard line engendered in early January. In short, despite an eagerness to harness or crush the OP and their allied guerrilla organizations, there is little evidence of decisive intervention during this conjuncture: the United States could not dictate JRG behavior nor was there any hint of military intervention in this period. Ironically, by May 1980 the Carter administration recognized that the chief threat to US interests came from the very rightists in the military whom the United States had bolstered at the end of the previous year.[35]

[32] Ibid., 10.
[33] US Embassy to Secretary of State, "General Uneasiness of Salvadoran Political Scene: An Assessment," cable, Dec. 4, 1979, E00307, "El Salvador: The Making of U.S. Policy, 1977–1984" collection (DNSA).
[34] US Embassy to Secretary of State, "Survivability of Revolutionary Governing Junta (JRG)," cable, Dec. 19, 1979, EL00646, "El Salvador: War, Peace, and Human Rights, 1980–1994" collection (DNSA).
[35] US Department of State, "Telegram from the Embassy in El Salvador to the Department of State, 'Updating our Strategy for El Salvador,'" May 26, 1980, in *Foreign Relations of the United States, 1977–1980, Vol. XV: Central America, 1977–1980* (Washington, DC: Government Publishing Office). The document states that within the military, officers voted 60 percent–40 percent to support Gutierrez over Majano (whom the United States wished to support). The document also recognizes the strength and terrorism of the Far Right, connected to sectors of the security apparatus.

THE RIGHT AND THE MILITARY

The Right was caught off guard by the coup. Although strongly hostile to the JRG, the radical Right within the agrarian oligarchy and sectors of the military had a difficult time designing a coherent strategy. In the words of the November 8 Embassy report, "The most immediate threat from the right appears to stem from a potential combination of two groups: a reactionary element in the private sector which was engaged in rightist terrorism under Romero and disgruntled segments of the armed forces."[36] The report emphasized the military fear of a loss of discipline caused by the disruption of the chain of command, through the "discarding of some fifty senior officers and massive personnel shifts."[37] A Southern Command representative had the opportunity to "inspect Salvadoran military units in the field ... [with] alarming results."[38]

Strategically aligned with the Right, the armed forces had been in control of the government since 1931, and now they were technically subordinate to the JRG. In early November, the Right within the military, prompted by the extreme Right, plotted a countercoup but those plans could not immediately solidify, especially as the PCS denounced them.[39]

On November 15, the establishment of the democratically elected Consejo Permanente de la Fuerza Armada (COPEFA), a new military organization, signaled that the progressive junior officers remained committed to the Proclama and that the military Right was under dire threat. COPEFA's express goal was to ensure that the military and the JRG carried out the structural reforms and ended repression against the Left. Similarly, the JRG abolition of ORDEN also disoriented the Right, though the paramilitary organization's leaders pledged to continue their lethal work under a new name.

---

[36] US Embassy to Secretary of State, "Analysis of Salvadoran Situation (Redistributed by Department of State on 8 November 1979, to U.S. Embassies in Central America)," cable, Nov. 6, 1979, EL00645, "El Salvador: War, Peace, and Human Rights, 1980–1994" collection, p. 7 (DNSA).

[37] Ibid., 4.

[38] The United States wanted to push the JRG to accept its aid in the face of the crisis, but still needed to allow the JRG to "impose limitations, if any, if it feels it must." US Embassy to Secretary of State, "The Military of El Salvador in Its Moment of Crisis," cable, Dec. 11, 1979, E00314, "El Salvador: The Making of U.S. Policy, 1977–1984" collection, p. 2 (DNSA).

[39] "Junta Calls Countercoup 'Suicidal,'" Panama City ACAN (Nov. 2, 1979), trans. Foreign Broadcast Information Service, FBIS Daily Report, Latin America, Nov. 5, 1979; "Right May Launch a Coup in El Salvador," *Latin American Weekly Report*, Nov. 9, 1979.

Although the Right within the military remained hesitant and on the defensive, following the November 6 agreements, the conservative civilian reaction began to mobilize. The newly founded Movimiento Nacionalista Salvadoreño (to be discussed in Chapter 5) supported such tactics while attempting to foster another *coup d'état*.[40] A protest strike (lockout), organized by Consejo Nacional de Entidades Agropecuarios, made up of eastern plantation owners and ranchers aimed directly at the "structural reforms" and the new minimum wage for rural workers.

The first sign that the Right's pressure (and perhaps that of the Embassy) was beginning to work occurred with the eviction of strikers from the Entre Rios cotton mill on December 4. Yet, even that move lacked the violence characteristic of the preceding months and years. More significantly, the Right promoted three mass demonstrations. On December 10, Asociación Nacional de la Empresa Privada (ANEP, a private enterprise organization) financed an 8,000- to 10,000-women-strong march officially for Paz y Trabajo (Peace and Jobs) but primarily directed against "communism." ANEP declared a lockout and urged its employees to attend.[41]

ANEP also promoted two subsequent demonstrations directly in support of Guillermo García. Since mid-November, the Minister of Defense stood out within the government for his reluctant endorsement of structural reforms and for his pro-repression stance.

As the JRG pushed forward to institute the reforms, the Right inside and outside of the military began to cohere in opposition. There is no doubt that the majority of senior National Guard officers opposed the JRG removal of 50–60 of their own.[42] They also opposed the land and financial reforms. Moreover, as the commissions advanced in their work and the JRG issued its first orders against Molina and Romero those same officers, most of whom had served in the repressive apparatus, became increasingly anxious about their own survival. García recognized that he had strong support to move against the reforms and against the OP. Hence, by mid-December he had the political strength to unleash

---

[40] Its leaders would eventually form the core of Alianza Republicana Nacionalista (ARENA), the main rightist opposition party during the 1980s and the governing party, 1989–2009.

[41] "Paz y trabajo," Dec. 11, 1979 in *El Salvador entre el terror y la esperanza*, 713.

[42] The State Department reported 50 dismissals. "60 Guardsmen Dismissed from Security Corps," Paris AFP (Nov. 11, 1979), trans. FBIS Daily Report, Latin America, Nov. 14, 1979.

repression reminiscent of the old regimes. The Embassy was, of course, encouraged by the new, hard line against the Left.

THE ORGANIZACIONES POPULARES AND THE JUNTA REVOLUCIONARIA DE GOBIERNO

The OP also took advantage of this unique moment that commenced on November 6; they continued to take to the streets, albeit in a less aggressive fashion, corresponding to the withdrawal of the security forces back to their barracks.

On November 28, FENASTRAS called for a one-day walkout and demonstration in protest against the government for its failure to fulfil its promises. At least 5,000 workers joined the mid-week march. Sindicato de la Industria Pesquera (SIP) represented one of the largest contingents of strikers/protesters, wearing their work *gabachas* (aprons) to belie press distortions that nonlabor elements formed the mainstay of the march. FENASTRAS and FAPU provided busses, and close to a thousand packinghouse workers from all three companies in the port participated in the march.[43] The protesters demanded across-the-board raises, the extradition and arrest of "los criminales del pueblo," and the demilitarization of numerous factories that had been taken over by security forces since October 15.[44] In addition, FENASTRAS called for the confiscation of goods by past officials linked to human rights abuses. Unlike most of the Left, FENASTRAS did not directly impugn the legitimacy of the JRG.

In the countryside, the rural workers' movement exploded with similar force to that of the urban labor movement that had erupted on the national scene earlier in the year, with a militancy and scope unmatched in the country's history.[45] The rural popular movement had always faced brutal repression as *hacendados* could easily mobilize ORDEN or the National Guard to imprison or execute union organizers. The Federación de Trabajadores del Campo (FTC – affiliated with BPR) and the LP-28

---

[43] Alejandro Molina Lara, interview with the author, Los Angeles, 2015; Ovidio Granadeño, interview with the author, Puerto El Triunfo, 2013.

[44] "Grandiosa movilización de la FENASTRAS," Nov. 28, 1979 (CIDAI, UCA).

[45] The day of the truce 15 members of the Comité de Madres de Presos y Desaparecidos Políticos occupied an office in the Ministry of Justice and declared a hunger strike, demanding an immediate response by the commission, rather than the 60 days ordered by the JRG. The hunger strike ended a week later, when the protesters argued that the GN intimidated them; the commission did release findings before the end of November.

took advantage of the opening provided by the JRG.[46] A *Radio Ysax* commentary summarized the new situation:

The land occupations occur spontaneously as repression lessons in the country-side. The inhumane conditions that reign in the countryside make it so that the campesinos can only be kept silent, peaceful, and tranquil through increasingly brutal repression. When the repression stops, thus arises campesino demands, combative actions, and revolutionary spirit.[47]

The promise of land reform and the establishment of relatively high minimum wages (especially for coffee workers) conditioned the rapid expansion of the movement. Moreover, recently proletarianized peasants made up the bulk of the rural union activists.[48] These campesinos were more inclined to rebel than other rural folk as they often combined a protest against (past) land expropriation with a demand for higher wages.[49] On November 27, rural workers, organized by the Federación de Trabajadores del Campo (FTC; BPR- affiliated) launched a strike on 17 haciendas and plantations in demand for higher salaries, more and higher quality food, better sanitation, and improved treatment in the fields, among other demands. The movement spread to other parts of the country. Along the coastal plain, workers occupied some 30 cotton plantations.[50] In some cases, the FTC demanded that the owners meet the JRG-stipulated minimum wage. On other haciendas, the union demanded that the owners raise the wages to the recently decreed official minimum in the coffee sector. The JRG decrees in favor of the rural poor, rather than put a brake on the rural Left, accelerated the movement.

---

[46] Immediately following the truce, for example, the coffee plant workers ended the occupation of six mills after receiving a US$2.00 per day raise.

[47] "Las tomas de tierra," Dec. 4, 1979 in *El Salvador entre el terror y la esperanza*, 695.

[48] See Jeffrey L. Gould, *To Die in This Way: Nicaraguan Indians and the Myth of Mestizaje, 1880–1965* (Durham, NC: Duke University Press, 1998), 231–38, on primitive accumulation; Carlos Cabarrús, *Génesis de una revolución: análisis del surgimiento y desarrollo de la organización campesina en El Salvador* (Mexico City: Centro de Investigaciones y Estudios Superiores de Antropología Social, 1983).

[49] Cabarrús, *Génesis de una revolución*. In this classic study, this Jesuit intellectual argues, with ample evidence from Aguilares, El Salvador, that semi-proletarians (e.g., minifundistas who worked for wages) were the most likely to join the OP. I would add the memory of land loss; also see Jeffrey L. Gould and Aldo Lauria Santiago, *To Rise in Darkness: Revolution, Repression, and Memory in El Salvador, 1920–1932* (Durham, NC: Duke University Press, 2008). Also see Jeffrey L. Gould, *To Lead as Equals: Rural Protest and Political Consciousness in Chinandega, Nicaragua, 1912–1979* (Chapel Hill: University of North Carolina Press, 1990).

[50] "Army Evicts BPR Peasants from Cotton Plantation," Paris AFP (Dec. 4, 1979), trans. Foreign Broadcast Information Service, FBIS Daily Report, Latin America, Dec. 6, 1979.

The US Embassy was strongly concerned about such forms of militancy, reporting that an "agricultural group" had denounced that "extremist fanatics ... had attacked over 90 properties."[51] Even more ominous from the point of view of the agrarian elite, rural union activists began to operate some plantations under their own management. An Embassy report cited the following:

In some cases, occupiers have taken over complete de facto management of farms, with reports of varying efficiency in operation. Occupation of cotton processing plant at Entre Rios by reported 1500 peasants led the Cotton-Growers Association to halt any acceptance of cotton harvest.[52]

On December 4, a noted previously, the JRG sent in army units using tear gas to evict the strikers at Entre Rios (near Zacatecoluca). The eviction represented the first repressive move by the JRG since November 6, and it is noteworthy that the security forces did not harm any strikers during this action.[53]

On December 12, in response to the owners' intransigence, the BPR converted some strikes into occupations. The next day, the BPR called out on strike some 3,000 workers in 13 factories in the metropolitan area to support the rural workers and their own demands.[54] On December 17, the owners of 17 sugar plantations in the Aguilares area and Cabañas made major concessions to the FTC. They raised the daily wage by a colón and increased the piece-rate pay for cane cutters. They also promised higher quality food, a first aid station, and better treatment by foremen. Finally, they agreed to permit union organizing on their plantations and haciendas.[55]

On the same day as this major victory for rural workers, 100 miles east, on a coffee plantation in Berlín, Usulatán, a group of more than

---

[51] US Embassy to Secretary of State, "General Uneasiness on Salvadoran Political Scene: An Assessment," cable, Dec. 4, 1979, E00307, "El Salvador: The Making of U.S. Policy, 1977–1984" collection, p. 3 (DNSA).

[52] Ibid.

[53] "Army evicts BPR peasants from cotton plantation," Paris AFP, Dec. 4, 1979; An Embassy observer wrote: "[I]t is the first time in recent history security forces have successfully intervened against extremist occupiers without excessive violence and bloodshed." US Embassy to Secretary of State, "Troubles in Agricultural Areas: Incidents and Agrarian Reform," cable, Dec. 6, 1979, E00309, "El Salvador: The Making of U.S. Policy, 1977–1984" collection (DNSA).

[54] "Strikers Demand Immediate Solution to Factory Problems," San José Radio Reloj (Dec. 13, 1979), trans. Foreign Broadcast Information Service, FBIS Daily Report, Latin America, Dec. 14, 1979.

[55] *El Independiente,* Dec. 19, 1979.

200 workers occupied the offices of the owner in protest over the plantation's failure to pay a week's wage. The LP-28 had organized the coffee pickers; many of them hailed from Morazán where they had initially participated in Christian Base Communities (CBCs; as had many of the Aguilares campesinos). At 7:00 PM, a combined force of the National Guard and the police attacked the strikers with automatic weapons. Caifás, recently affiliated with LP-28, recalls:

We took over the offices. We were just protesting to get the wages we were owed and the *aguinaldo*. Then suddenly the Guardia arrives and opens fire. Some of us had a few pistols but they were useless against automatic fire. So, we had to flee.[56]

The security forces killed at least 1 coffee picker, wounded 5, and captured 25. This was the first death at the hands of security forces since November 6.[57]

The day after the attack on the farmworkers in Berlín, the National Guard attacked LP-28 organized farmworkers who had occupied the large coffee hacienda, *El Porvenir*, located 50 kilometers northwest of the capital, in demand for higher wages, benefits, and better work conditions. According to an official communique from the armed forces: "in the absence of negotiations between the farm owner and the strikers the government decided to force out the laborers." After claiming that the strikers fired on them, a four-hour battle ensued. Troops killed some 25 farmworkers, wounded 10, and captured 16 others.[58] The troops sustained no injuries or fatalities.[59]

Ignacio Ellacuría, the rector of the Jesuit Universidad Centroamericana who had previously offered critical support to the JRG, commented about the military:

---

[56] Caifás (a nom de guerre), interview with the author and Carlos Henríquez Consalvi, Morazán, 2009.

[57] In the words of Ellacuría, "Llevábamos mes y medio sin que la Fuerza Armada y los cuerpos de seguridad derramaron sangre," in "De nuevo sangre sobre El Salvador," Dec. 19, 1979 in *El Salvador entre el terror y la esperanza*, 743. The number of deaths in Berlín was hotly disputed by the LP-28. A participant recalled five deaths. Caifás, interview with the author, Morazán, 2009.

[58] "More on Farmworkers' Clash with Police in El Congo," Paris AFP (Dec. 19, 1979), trans. Foreign Broadcast Information Service, FBIS Daily Report, Latin America, Dec. 20, 1979, reported: 'These strike actions coincided with the rural workers' victorious strikes in 17 haciendas and sugar plantations, that had begun on November 27." See *El Independiente*, Dec. 19, 1979.

[59] "More on Farmworkers' Clash with Police in El Congo," Paris AFP (Dec. 19, 1979), trans. Foreign Broadcast Information Service, FBIS Daily Report, Latin America, Dec. 20, 1979.

They have been deceived, once again, by listening only to the voices of the oligarchy. Neither in Congo nor in Berlín did they face guerrillas ... they killed 25 and did not find more than a small number of arms; they have killed, then, unarmed people.[60]

Ellacuría and other analysts recognized that a fundamental change had transpired within the JRG. One analyst wrote of a "contragolpe" on December 18. The following week, Ellacuría presaged the departure of the moderate Left elements from the JRG, when he ironically congratulated the Right on its success in placing the military once again under its control: "You of the Salvadoran Right: you have defeated those who defend the people. But celebrate quickly, because the civil war is one step closer."[61]

Colonels García and Abdul Gutiérrez and their allies in the military had gained control, thanks in no small part to the massive propaganda campaign in the newspapers, the mobilization of the Right, and some monetary corruption of officers. Yet, despite the rightist triumph that was akin to a silent coup against the progressive elements of the JRG, García and Abdul Gutiérrez still needed to carry through some elements of a reform program. Thus, at the very moment, when the repressive apparatus unleashed its violence for the first time in six weeks – security forces killed some 40 people during the last two weeks of 1979 – the government announced the nationalization of exports and promised to continue forward with the land reform. Analysts at the time baptized the strategy "reform with repression," a phrase that would characterize the regime's practice in 1980. In short, the oligarchic Right had dethroned the center-left government but was unable to completely take control so as to promote its agenda.

At a meeting on December 27, Eugenio Vides Casanova, Vice-Minister of Defense, addressed the civilian members of the JRG and exclaimed: "We put you there and we can remove you when we wish."[62] The next day, 22 cabinet members accused García of needlessly ordering violent repression.[63] On January 3, the progressive members of the JRG and the

---

[60] The week before the army had attacked a cotton plantation arresting an undetermined number of workers. "De nuevo sangre sobre El Salvador," Dec. 19, 1979 in *El Salvador entre el terror y la esperanza*, 744.

[61] "Rumores de golpe de estado," Dec. 20, 1979 in *El Salvador entre el terror y la esperanza*, 746.

[62] Majano, *La oportunidad perdida*, 176. Majano also recounts serious efforts to bribe him to push him to the Right and toward full-scale repression against the OP (pp. 172–74).

[63] The same group had urged the JRG to remove Mario Andino, business representative on the governing body, for pushing the government to the "Right." *Latin American Weekly Report*, Jan. 4, 1980.

cabinet resigned to be replaced by a new junta that incorporated José Napoleón Duarte and the PDC.

RHETORIC AND REALITY ON THE REVOLUTIONARY LEFT

The period of mobilization in peace came to an end with little recognition by the Left. Recall that the entire revolutionary Left had denounced the JRG from its inception: all groups referred to the government as the Junta Contrarevolucionaria de Gobierno. In their view, the JRG's entire *raison d'être* was to demobilize the Left and the popular movements and thus to impede a revolutionary outcome. When the BPR achieved several of its objectives in negotiations on November 6, it claimed victory against the now unmasked, pro-imperialist protector of the "rich exploiters."[64] Notwithstanding, for three weeks the OP-led demonstrations and occupations were peaceful and met no repression. Yet protesters repeatedly denounced the JRG for continuing to "capture, torture, disappear, and assassinate people."[65]

On November 27, the LP-28 held the closing events of its congress, attended by some 3,000 militants. Ana Guadalupe Martínez, the guerrilla leader who had endured months of torture in clandestine jails, made a surprise appearance, which she underscored was not the result of a concession by the JRG but rather the result of popular struggle against the "Creole oligarchy, military fascism and Yankee imperialism."[66] She also denounced the JRG for delaying measures that allowed the escape of the major violators of human rights from the prior regimes. The LP-28 declared that its principal objective was the overthrow of the Junta Contrarevolucionaria de Gobierno, and "the establishment of a popular government that would lead to a socialist society."[67]

[64] BPR, *Combate Popular*, Nov. 15, 1979 (NACLA Archive) microfilm, pp. 590–92, roll 6.
[65] Quoted in Guerra, *El Salvador, octubre sangriento*, 87.
[66] "La clausura del Congreso de las Ligas Populares," Nov. 28, 1979 in *El Salvador entre el terror y la esperanza: Los sucesos de 1979 y su impacto en el drama salvadoreño de los años siguientes*, 680; US Embassy to Secretary of State, "LP-28 National Congress Brings Indication of Unity Move with BPR," cable, Nov. 29, 1979, ES00300, "El Salvador: The Making of U.S. Policy, 1977–1984" collection (DNSA).
[67] "Declaración del Primer Congreso de las Ligas Populares 28 de Febrero, 'Irma Elena Contreras.'" Juan Chacón, the leader of the BPR, attended the event along with a small delegation and called for unity. FAPU militants did not attend the congress. There was still bad blood from ERP execution of Roque Dalton, noted poet and comrade of the founders of FAPU.

Although the guerrilla leader's presence at the closing event had been announced previously, the congress was held without incident, thus symbolizing the gap between leftist rhetoric and everyday reality during the truce.

Even as it publicly continued to denounce the government as counterrevolutionary, the FAPU enunciated a more nuanced position than the other OP. A FAPU leader commented that the existence of a progressive sector in the military and in the JRG meant that "there is now the possibility for the revolutionary and popular groups to advance since it is not the same to fight a fascist dictatorship ... as it is to face a regime that can cede (with the organized popular struggle) an opening."[68] The BPR's analyses of the JRG, however, evinced difficulty allowing for such an "opening." Rather, Rafael Menjívar, a major theoretician of the group, recognized a shift in the "model of domination ... [the JRG] definitively tries to limit the freedom of action [*mediatizar*] and to repress the revolutionary movement."[69] Yet similar to FAPU, the BPR engaged in conversations with the JRG and urged it to push through the reforms rapidly.[70]

Although the OP all avoided violence in their demonstrations during the truce period, the Fuerzas Populares de Liberación (the FPL, a guerrilla group aligned with the BPR) did not follow suit and continued to attack ORDEN in the countryside and engage in kidnapping and selective terrorism. UCA analysts blamed them for the 10 civilian deaths that occurred during the six weeks of the truce. Some of the executions of ORDEN militants may well have been local revenge killings. The kidnappings of the South African ambassador and of an elite *cafetalero* clearly responded to decisions made at the top. These military actions raise the question: if the BPR scrupulously abided by the truce why didn't the FPL? Although we have no access to FPL decision making at this juncture, Ignacio Ellacuria offers an important insight.

Ellacuría was the main, if not the only, public figure who focused on the distinction between the OP and guerrilla practices in November as an example of the former's autonomy:

---

[68] *Pueblo*, Oct. 28–Nov. 3, 1979: 13.
[69] *El Salvador: Alianzas políticas y proceso revolucionario.* Cuadernos de Coyuntura, no. 5 (Mexico City: SEPLA, 1979).
[70] Ignacio Ellacuría, *Veinte años de historia en El Salvador (1969–1989), tomo II, escritos políticos* (San Salvador: UCA Editores, 1991), 768.

In order to understand the guerilla problem ..., it is necessary to drastically separate the guerrilla groups, FPL, FARN, and the ERP from their mass organizations, the BPR, FAPU, and the Ligas. There are connections between the political fronts and the guerrilla groups, but they are distinct.[71]

For the Jesuit intellectual, the distinction was fundamental for the JRG to understand, so as not to repress the OP, whom he hailed as the key to the "process of liberation."[72] Moreover, he hoped that the autonomy (and their unity) would deepen.[73] He proposed that the guerrillas' *raison d'être* would begin to dissipate when the protection of strikes and demonstrations was no longer necessary. Moreover, as broad sectors of the public accepted some form of socialism, its imposition by force would lose any possible justification.

For some former militants, the distinction was illusory in that most BPR leaders were also FPL militants.[74] Yet, Ellacuría's point was valid in that the OP and the guerrillas had different organizational needs and thus divergent tactics. Notwithstanding, the truce could not hold in large part because the OP and the moderate Left members of the JRG, despite shared fundamental goals and some behind-the-scenes dialogue, could not form an alliance, however informal. This impossibility in turn hinged on their different understandings regarding how fundamental political and social change could be achieved and the role of the OP in such transformations. There was a fundamental *desencuentro* I about the meaning of structural reforms, and their changed meanings depending on their method of implementation. This *desencuentro* impeded a potential alliance between the radical Left and the "moderate" sector, grouped primarily in the Foro Popular, which was smaller but in the process of radicalization. Such an alliance might not have prevented the civil war, as the military Right would not have ceded power without a fight.[75] Yet, some junior officers allied with Majano and working with Rubén Zamora (presidential minister) and Ramón Mayorga planned a coup to remove

---

[71] "Las acciones guerrilleras," Nov. 12, 1979, in *El Salvador entre el terror y la esperanza*, 643.

[72] Ellacuría, "Las organizaciones populares ante la nueva situación," 771.

[73] Rafael Menjívar in *El Salvador: Alianzas políticas y proceso revolucionario* (Mexico City: SEPLA), 17; reprinted in Rafael Menjívar Larín, *El Salvador: El eslabón más pequeño* (San José: Editorial Universitaria Centroamericana [EDUCA], 1980), 93–94.

[74] Miguel Huezo Mixco, personal communication with the author, Nov. 2017.

[75] See Jeffrey L. Gould, "Ignacio Ellacuría and the Salvadorean Revolution," *Journal of Latin American Studies* 47, no. 2 (May 2015).

García and Abdul Gutiérrez.[76] Majano refused to participate. His decision sealed the fate of the JRG.

The revolutionary Left could not be considered a potential ally for the second coup because it never ceased to condemn the entire JRG. Their blanket condemnation – even when the government began to carry out its program of structural reforms and military transformation – was problematic. The relationship of the OP leadership to the rank and file hinged on the ability of the former to deliver material gains to its base. In this sense, even if strategically the JRG sought to impede a revolutionary insurrection by curtailing repression and carrying out a land reform, during this period the OP rank and file benefited materially and gained greater quotas of real power.

The rhetorical limitations of the OP – that is the categories with which they operated – seemed to block an adequate understanding of the political moment. Despite the absence of repression in November, the BPR and the LP-28 continued to depict the JRG as "fascistic" and counterrevolutionary. And here, the "acceleration" time characteristic of revolutionary moments surely played a powerful role. As Greg Grandin noted, "The speeding up of felt time, corresponded to, and was driven by, an acceleration of the state's capacity to repress. For untold numbers of Latin Americans living through revolutionary times meant living part of a life in which political violence and terror were the stuff of everyday existence."[77] The repression of the first two weeks following the coup had been brutal, radicalizing the already radicalized.[78] For many within the OP, it was impossible to absolve the JRG from responsibility for the massacres and their anger was so intense they could not recognize the change in JRG actions. In the words of a peasant from Morazán, a militant of the LP-28, "[W]e marched to see if the JRG was truly revolutionary or not."[79] The massacre of the Morazán campesinos on October 29 made the answer clear. Thus, it was relatively simple to maintain the public posture that the JRG was in its essence "anti-popular."

[76] Menjívar Ochoa in *Tiempos de locura,* 202–3, quotes Rubén Zamora as stating that a young military officer came to see him on behalf of Ellacuría, to involve him in the conspiracy to replace Gutierrez and García. Three of Ellacuría closest confidantes, Rodolfo Cardenal, S.J., Jon Sobrino, S.J., and Hector Samur all deny that Ellacuría was involved.

[77] Greg Grandin, "Living in Revolutionary Time," in Greg Grandin and Gil Joseph, *A Century of Revolution: Insurgent and Counterinsurgent Violence during Latin America's Long Cold War* (Durham, NC: Duke University Press, 2010), 2.

[78] Miguel Huezo Mixco, personal communication with the author, Nov. 2017.

[79] Escolástico, interview with the author and Carlos Henríquez Consalvi, Morazán, 2007.

The six weeks without violent repression and the positive consequences for the rural and urban labor movements could not fit within the dominant narratives of the revolutionary Left, with the limited exception of the FAPU. In the weeks following the collapse of the first Junta, Rafael Menjívar of the BPR wrote: "From October 15 until the end of '79 the level of repression increased, while political time was lost in the impotence of introducing structural reforms … In December, rightist pressure on the army led to an increase in repression."[80] Despite the high level of sophistication of this revolutionary intellectual, we can see his difficulty in dealing with the period. He first highlights the entire two and half months as a period of increased repression, and then he underscores the last month as one of even greater repression. Strikingly silenced from this near-contemporary account are the six weeks with no violent repression.

Notwithstanding the silence of the revolutionary Left, the JRG's positions on rural wages, unionization, and land reform along with the withdrawal of security forces conditioned one of the proportionally largest and most militant rural labor movements in recent Latin American history. Leftist militants imagined the wave of strikes in the fields as the fruit of their organizing efforts and a harbinger of a revolutionary triumph. Certainly, the *tomas* of cotton and coffee plants and the ensuing workers' control over production was quite extraordinary, going beyond what the radical labor movement had imagined or achieved. Yet, the firestorm in the fields seemed to blind the Left.

The development of consciousness among the *campesinos* was highly uneven. A group of coffee workers, for example, wrote to a FAPU affiliate in mid-December, asking if they could send an "investigative commission" to report on the horrendous working conditions on the plantation, where water was even rationed. The group of coffee pickers exclaimed, "You are our only hope."[81] With 900 workers, the plantation was in the heart of coffee country, revealing a large pocket of underdevelopment on the revolutionary landscape. Moreover, relatively well-known recent Latin American history might have led rural activists to a different stance vis-à-vis the JRG. The Guatemalan land reform of 1952 spurred a year of intense *campesino* mobilization. The Brazilian Goulart administration's promotion of rural unionization and the promise of major land reform spurred massive *campesino* mobilization. Finally, both the Frei and

---

[80] Rafael Menjívar Larín, *El Salvador: El eslabón más pequeño*, 109. He was the father of the late Rafael Menjívar who wrote *Tiempos de Locura*, cited previously.

[81] *El Independiente*, Dec. 20, 1979.

Allende administrations in Chile, with their land reform policies, conditioned the explosive growth of rural labor and peasant organizations. US-backed military staged coups in all three countries at least partially in response to the rural movements, and this may have dulled any possible revolutionary interest in working with reformist governments. Yet, unlike in most other Latin American countries, in El Salvador potentially the Left could count on the support of a sector of the military.

The breadth and depth of support and rage at the postcoup violent repression shaped leftist thought. When the JRG began to exercise control over the repressive apparatus and move toward carrying out its reformist program, the OP could not find the discursive range to interpret the moment that they were experiencing. They could not move beyond the almost ritualized denunciations of the JRG as counterrevolutionary despite the reality that the Right inside and outside of the military was at its weakest point since 1932. Most significantly, under the Carter administration, the empire was not ready to strike. On those grounds alone, to use the phrase of Colonel Majano, this was a "lost opportunity."

The interregnum from early November to mid-December 1979 witnessed an unprecedented upsurge in agricultural worker and peasant mobilization that outlined the possibility of a radical restructuring of rural society. The withdrawal of the security forces also allowed for intense synergy of radical Christian and Marxist consciousness – most notably when people seized plantations and ran them, however briefly, as cooperatives. The real activity of subaltern movements thus escaped inherited categories.

A YEAR OF LIVING DANGEROUSLY: MOLINA LARA AND FENASTRAS UNDER SIEGE

On December 12, 1979, Alejandro Molina Lara, was riding in a pickup with Bernabé Recinos, Secretary General of FENASTRAS. Five workers accompanied them on their way to an organizing meeting in the port of La Unión. Molina Lara, recently elected secretary of organization of the leftist labor federation, had been working with the port authority union, which was demanding a 75 percent pay raise and an increase in the budget for social benefits for its members. As they approached the city of San Miguel, they spotted a National Police roadblock ahead: Recinos exclaimed, "a la gran puta ... we're cooked. We've got pistols. So, either we shoot it out or they're going to arrest us and God knows what will happen." After a brief discussion, they decided not to fight back.

The police found the guns and immediately arrested them as *guerrilleros*. Molina Lara tried to play on their common working-class origins, "Look we're union organizers and sometimes the boss sends goons after us. So we have to carry pistols."[82] Perhaps in response, the police treated them decently. Recinos was able to call STECEL (the electrical power workers' union that he had led for years). The union notified the National Police that if the FENASTRAS leaders were not freed immediately they would shut down power throughout the country (as they had done during the March strike wave). After four hours, they were set free.[83]

In 1980, Molina made a return organizing trip to La Unión, this time to help organize shrimp workers and once again was arrested. "They let me go with a warning: 'Get going and don't come back!' They made it clear that they'd kill me if I came back to the port."[84] Molina Lara's experiences of arrest and release in 1980 reflected the growing tension between the thin veneer of legality that the Military-Christian Democratic Junta maintained and the reality of increasing repression. Shortly after the new junta was sworn in, the OP sought to unify and incorporate those on the Left who had supported the JRG. They formed the Coordinadora Revolucionaria de Masas. The new coalition called for a march on January 22 to symbolize that newfound unity. The largest demonstration in Salvadoran history, an estimated 150,000–250,000 people marched through the streets of the capital. Monseñor Romero noted in his diary: "From the heights of the National Palace, sniper fire broke up this precious demonstration that was a popular fiesta."[85] Military snipers opened fire on the marchers, killing between 22 and 50 people. The next day, troops surrounded at least 40,000 demonstrators who had sought refuge on the campus of the Universidad de El Salvador. As the troops prepared to enter the campus on the pretext that the protesters had arms, Monseñor Romero interceded and prevented an even greater massacre.

---

[82] Molina Lara, interview with the author, Los Angeles, Jan. 2015.

[83] FENASTRAS used the arrest as an organizing tool as they put pressure on the Port Authority to grant the demands. The union organized a march on December 20 calling for a "quick granting of the demands of the port workers and in protest for the capture of [Recinos and Molina Lara]." Another FENASTRAS flyer denounced the arrest as a "provocation against consequential unionism that once again confirms the repressive attitudes of the security bodies." "Gran movilización en La Unión," flyer, Dec. 17, 1979 (CIDAI, UCA).

[84] Molina Lara, interview with the author, Los Angeles, Jan. 2015.

[85] Óscar A. Romero, *Archbishop Oscar Romero: A Shepherd's Diary*, trans. Irene B. Hodgson (Cincinnati, OH: St. Anthony Messenger Press, 1993).

FIGURE 3.1 Outskirts of San Salvador: buses taking people to January 22, 1980 march
(photo by Laurent Vogel; courtesy of Museo de la Palabra y la Imágen)

More than 1,000 packinghouse workers, a substantial majority of the Puerto El Triunfo labor force, attended the march in their work uniforms.

Although Molina Lara had become aligned with FAPU, he envisioned the protest march of January 22, not as a demonstration of the revolutionary Left, but rather "It was the expression of workers' power, the power of the organized working class."[86] That analysis reflected Molina Lara's desire to maintain a sharp division between the union and the revolutionary movement, nurturing the hope for a politics to emerge from the working class that was not directed by middle-class radicals.

The tension between revolutionary goals and immediate interests, as we have seen, permeated the Left labor movement in the cities and in the countryside. Both the BPR and FAPU – outside of Puerto El Triunfo – were able to conduct economic struggles effectively following a classic Leninist approach, pushing unionized workers toward "higher political consciousness." And yet, it was not a one-way street. The militants' desire to address the immediate needs of their rank and file led to an important ideological shift away from a Leninist formulation.

On January 21, FENASTRAS issued a statement denouncing the maneuvers of "la patronal imperialista" to weaken the labor movement by

---

[86] Molina Lara, interview with the author, Los Angeles, Sept. 2012.

FIGURE 3.2 Rallying people in market to join January 22 march
(photo by Laurent Vogel; courtesy of Museo de la Palabra y la Imágen)

closing factories and by creating an artificial scarcity of goods such as sugar and vegetable oil to blame the labor movement. The labor federation capitalized its response: *"OUR RESPONSE TO THE COMPANIES' ECONOMIC AND POLITICAL MEASURES WILL BE TO PROMOTE THE AUTOGESTION OF THE CLOSED FACTORIES SO THAT THEY WILL BE NATIONALIZED."*[87]

The call for autogestion (workers' self-management) – a distinctly non-Leninist demand/strategy – was not a mere rhetorical gesture. Rather, Recinos and another FENASTRAS leader went to the US Embassy and engaged in serious discussions, trying to urge the State Department to intervene and persuade the companies to either reopen or to facilitate workers' management of the plants. The Embassy negotiator pointed out that FENASTRAS was partially to blame for the departure of the US companies and doubted that they could help remedy the situation.[88]

---

[87] FENASTRAS, "Con la unidad hacia la liberación definitiva," Jan. 21, 1980 (CIDAI, UCA).

[88] Bernabé Recinos argued that Beckman essentially was opposed to unionization and that FENASTRAS would guarantee stable labor conditions if they were given the opportunity to operate under the management of Salvadoran workers and technicians. The Embassy officials lent a sympathetic ear but claimed they could not intervene. US Embassy to Secretary of State, "FAPU and FENASTRAS Make Offer in Factory Closing; Express

FIGURE 3.3 Protesters gathering in San Salvador for January 22 march
(photo by Laurent Vogel; courtesy of Museo de la Palabra y la Imágen)

On February 15, the labor branch of the BPR occupied the Instituto Salvadoreño de Comercio. The primary goal of the takeover was to compel the government to address the growing problem of factory closures; 12 had closed in recent months. During the first three months of 1980, factory closings threw some 11,000 workers out of work, roughly 7 percent of the industrial labor force. The agreement committed the government to explore all alternatives to reopen the factories. If those proved unsuccessful, it would compel the companies to indemnify the workers.[89]

The case of the Aplar factory in the free-trade zone of San Bartolo is particularly instructive. This high-tech company produced potentiometers (a sophisticated device to measure and divide voltage in joysticks), liquid crystal displays, and plastic molded integrated circuits. In September 1979, a small guerrilla group kidnapped the company manager and a visiting technician. In early November, after agreeing to the demands the

Concern over Loss of Employment," Jan. 28, 1980, ES00397, "El Salvador: The Making of U.S. Policy, 1977–1984" collection (DNSA).

[89] BPR, *Combate Popular*, Feb. 1980, NACLA Archive, microfilm, p. 600, roll 6; Also see "Las Tomas Pacíficas: Una alternativa obrera frente a los cierres de las fábricas, Federación Sindical Revolucionaria," Apr. 1980.

hostages were released.[90] The parent company, Beckman Instruments, decided to cease operations on the new integrated circuit transistor line because it necessitated sending US technicians to El Salvador. Rumors of the impending layoff of 200 workers (one-third of the total) led to a union takeover of the plant on December 11.[91] The company then agreed that they would discuss the union demands; the occupation ended the same day. Over the Christmas holiday, Beckman decided to end its entire US$3 million operation at Aplar and began to dismantle the machinery. Advised of the situation by "honest guards," the workers once again occupied the plant, refusing to allow the transfer of machinery.[92]

After suffering violent repression in January, the Aplar workers continued their occupation through February when, under FENASTRAS supervision, they formed a cooperative.

They sent a delegation to Los Angeles to negotiate with Beckman Instruments who agreed to allow for the production of potentiometers.[93] Financed by union members' severance pay, the cooperative started its production in March.[94] By the end of the year, however, citing insufficient market demand, Beckman broke the agreement. Notwithstanding, the FENASTRAS-backed labor experiment was a highly significant departure from Leninist propositions on class struggle for two reasons. First, it proffered an alliance between capital and labor over the means of production whereby workers would manage production while leaving

---

[90] The demands of the Partido Revolucionario de Trabajadores Centroamericanos included widespread publication of a manifesto and an undisclosed amount of cash. Arnold Thackray and Minor Myers Jr., *Arnold O. Beckman: One Hundred Years of Excellence* (Philadelphia, PA: Chemical Heritage Foundation, 2000), 315–16.

[91] "FENASTRAS ante la clase obrera y pueblo en general," Jan. 3, 1980, Labor Collection (CIDAI, UCA).

[92] One American executive had been kidnapped by a small guerrilla group in September. He was released after the company paid ransom. FENASTRAS aided a brief occupation in early December to demand back pay to 600 production workers and improved safety conditions. The company agreed to the demands but then secretly planned to close the factory and remove the machinery necessary for continued production elsewhere. Mark Kantor, Michael D. Nolan, and Karl P. Sauvant, *Reports of Overseas Private Investment Corporation Determinations* (Oxford: Oxford University Press, 2011); *La Crónica*, Jan. 4, 1980; American Arbitration Association Commercial Arbitration Tribunal, "Award in the Matter of the Arbitration between Beckman Instruments, Inc. and Overseas Private Investment Corporation," *American Society of International Law*, 27, no. 5 (Sept. 1988): 1265.

[93] Kantor et al., *Reports of Overseas Private Investment Corporation Determinations*.

[94] "Award in the Matter of the Arbitration between Beckman Instruments and Overseas Private Investment Corporation," 1265.

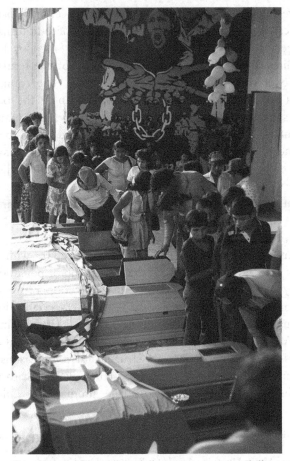

FIGURE 3.4 Searching for loved ones following January 22 killings
(photo by Laurent Vogel; courtesy of Museo de la Palabra y la Imágen)

ownership squarely in the control of the company. Second, Marxist-
Leninists typically had scoffed at cooperatives as palliatives to workers
that undermined the class struggle.

In Puerto El Triunfo, as we saw in Chapter 2, and at the national level,
we can discern the spontaneous emergence of rank-and-file discourse that
contested existing economic and political power relations. In the case
of the port, the outlines of a proto-syndicalist ideology that emphasized
class solidarity were visible. Nationally, faced with the wave of factory
closures, Leninists began to break with a view of the revolutionary
process that conceived of workers' control over production in a capitalist

system as an ideological deviation.[95] These incipient ideologies were the product of the sustained urban and rural working-class struggles in 1979 to defend the right to union organization, to decent working conditions, and to employment. Rank-and-file workers often initiated the *tomas*; they announced the possibility of a new form of labor politics in El Salvador, rooted in the praxis of a significant minority of the urban and rural working class. Notwithstanding, the paramilitary right and its government allies had no interest in letting such a politics develop.

Death Knell in the Port

Whether viewed as the high point of the labor movement or as the zenith of the revolutionary movement, January 22, 1980 represented yet another moment of rupture in relations between the leftist unions and the state. In the port, the events caused a minor slippage of support for Molina Lara and SIP. A few members defected to Sindicato Agua in part in protest against the limited coercion employed by SIP and in part due to the political implications of January 22. The union compelled the companies to dock workers a day's pay if they didn't participate.[96] Despite the dissent, however, Molina Lara's group maintained a firm grip on power and countered criticism of its radical leanings with a coherent discourse. He argued to an assembly of 470, days before the demonstration, that the state was assassinating FENASTRAS labor activists who were defending collective worker interests, and therefore "We can't stand by and do nothing."[97] Similarly, he linked the demonstration to the collective need to "win more benefits from the bosses." Molina Lara in effect argued for identification with FENASTRAS as necessary for the individual and collective interests of the SIP rank and file.

A female worker from Puerto El Triunfo was among those killed by snipers on January 22. Molina Lara accompanied her casket back to the

---

[95] Most of the OP leadership subscribed to some form of Marxism-Leninism.

[96] The union compelled the companies to dock workers a day's pay if they didn't participate. Molina Lara retrospectively calculates that close to one-half of the participants might not have journeyed to the capital without the symbolic coercion. In the past, rarely more than a hundred union activists had attended marches in the capital. See Carmen Minero, interview with the author, Puerto El Triunfo, 2014; Molina Lara, interview with the author, Puerto El Triunfo, 2015. Others believed that the union would get them fired if they did not participate. Adela Amaya, interview with the author, Puerto El Triunfo, 2013. Amaya left SIP and later became a leader of SGTIPAC.

[97] "Acta 41," *Libro de actas*, Jan. 17, 1980 (SIP General Archives, in the possession of the author).

port. Her vigil was in the SIP headquarters. On February 4, more than 800 people attended a SIP meeting. Molina Lara offered a eulogy for the martyred Lidia Cortez. He recalls the deep responsibility he felt for her death and his relief when he realized that the rank and file did not seem to blame him. Following the speech that underscored the links between local and national repression of the labor movement, the union held their annual elections. Despite having promised the previous year that it would be his last term, Molina Lara ran again for the position of secretary general, winning 600–213.[98] Molina Lara and his group believed that the stakes were so high, with the country on the verge of civil war, that he was indispensable to the labor movement because of his highly developed skills as a negotiator, level of legitimacy among the rank and file, and high position in FENASTRAS.

A few months later, Molina Lara was driving to the Puerto after a family visit in Usulután. As he was leaving the city, two pickups with armed men surged ahead to block his path. He managed to swerve into a gas station and then gunned the engine. The car that FENASTRAS had lent him operated with a souped-up motor specifically designed to evade death squads. He was able to elude the pickups and speed past them, outracing them to the port.

Molina Lara reflected on his precarious circumstances. By then he had survived two ambushes and three arrests. Yet, he didn't see any turning back; he continued to devote his energies to SIP and FENASTRAS. He did not want to die, and yet he saw little chance of a peaceful solution to the mounting, violent, class strife. He knew he possessed a strong survival instinct and skills, and he would count on those attributes to navigate the perils of the death squads.[99]

The Coordinadora Revolucionaria de Masas (the CRM – organized expression of left unity of whom FENASTRAS formed the largest contingent) called for a national general strike on March 17 against firings, layoffs, and plant closures. The successful strike was overshadowed by the assassination of Archbishop Romero on March 24. The CRM declared another general strike for June 24 in demand for higher wages and end to repression. Notwithstanding the military's stern warnings and threats against strike participation, SIP members joined an estimated 150,000 urban workers and 100,000 rural laborers in a national general

---

[98] Cortez had a son who was active in the radical left. "Acta 43," *Libro de actas*, Feb. 4, 1980 (SIP General Archives).

[99] Molina Lara, interview with the author, Los Angeles, Jan. 2015.

strike. Foreign observers calculated that some 90 percent of the workforce joined the strike in the metropolitan area.[100] In Puerto el Triunfo, workers occupied the three processing plants to support the general strike and protect the installations. SIP did not call out its fishermen on strike due to the logistical difficulties of such a move. Despite the close ties of management with the oligarchy and the regime, no repression took place either directly or indirectly; the companies even paid for one of the strike days.[101]

The day after the general strike, a foreign correspondent reported:

Some 500 heavily armed government troops, supported by armoured cars stormed the headquarters of the Coordinadora Revolucionaria de Masas (CRM) in the university and the surrounding la Fosa barrio. More than 50 people were killed ... the army is still occupying the university ... at the time of the attack the CRM were holding a meeting to consider the results of the strike.[102]

The military's brutal, unprecedented action perhaps was a compensatory response for its inability to halt the general strike.

In mid-August 1980, the CRM once again called for a general strike, conceived as a potential dress rehearsal for a popular insurrection. Only 60 percent of the metropolitan area working class participated, due to the intense levels of repression and perhaps to apathy induced by the growing threat and reality of factory closures. Archbishop Rivera y Damas (who replaced the martyred Archbishop Romero), however, considered the action to be a plebiscite, due to the participation of the majority of the labor force in clear repudiation of the regime.[103] Death squad activity intensified against union activists. Sixteen rank-and-file members of STECEL were gunned down during the strike. In response, the union, led by Recinos, occupied all the power plants and, in a desperate move to thwart the repression, threatened to blow up the stations if attacked.[104] The government crushed the strike, eliminated the union, and imprisoned its leadership.[105] Soon, the government forces and death squads drove the

---

[100] Menjivar Ochoa, *Tiempos de locura*, 297.

[101] Molina Lara, interview with the author, Los Angeles, Feb. 2016.

[102] *Latin American Weekly Report*, July 4, 1980.

[103] Cited in Oscar A. Morales Velado, *La resistencia no violenta ante los regímenes salvadoreños que han utilizado el terror institucionalizado en el período 1972–1987* (San Salvador: UCA Editores, 1988), 62.

[104] Menjivar Ochoa, *Tiempos de locura*, 267–68.

[105] William Bollinger, "El Salvador," in *Latin American Labor Organizations*, ed. Gerald Greenfield and Sheldon Maram (New York: Greenwood Press, 1987), 319.

rest of FENASTRAS underground, though Molina Lara continued to operate above ground, however cautiously.

The reign of terror that killed some 8,000–11,000 civilians in 1980 largely spared Puerto El Triunfo, in part, because of the hegemony of SIP and its tactic of including ORDEN members (connected to the GN and death squads) among its leadership. An incident recounted by Noé Quinteros illustrates SIP's legitimacy even during the evil times. Late in 1980 he heard a knock on his door. When he opened it, he froze in panic: it was a well-known death squad assassin. "Sorry to bother you," he said, "but I have a problem at work. They're trying to fire me so I'm hoping the union can help me out." The next day Noé went to see the man's supervisor at Pezca S.A. and brought up the case. The supervisor exclaimed, "Are you crazy, don't you know who he is?" Noé responded, "That may be the case, but he is still a union member." The next evening, the death squad member knocked on his door again. With less trepidation than the night the before, Noé opened the door. "I wanted to thank you for helping me out. I have to tell you – and this could get me killed – but you are top on the list. You have to be out of the country in 24 hours or you're a dead man."[106] This incident reveals a great deal about the legitimacy of SIP throughout the Puerto El Triunfo working class; it also signals how relatively simple it was for the Right at this juncture to cripple the unions, at the very moment when they were on the verge of fundamentally transforming the lives of their members.

Despite the growing violence, SIP and the shrimp companies continued to behave as if in "normal times." Notwithstanding the terror, the SIP leadership still brought out large numbers of members to its meetings. In June 1980, more than 500 workers attended a meeting of the Pezca S.A. Local and in August, more than 1,000 attended a general SIP meeting. As late as November 1980, shortly after the military had unleashed a massive scorched earth campaign to stamp out an incipient guerrilla movement in Morazán, the Pezca S.A. Local won a 2 colones per day increase, retroactive to August.[107] The established pattern of demands, negotiations in the Ministry of Labor, and strike threats continued throughout that blood-soaked year.

In December, however, the terror reached the port. According to a FENASTRAS report:

---

[106] Noé Quinteros, interview with the author, Houston, Oct. 2013. All translations by author.

[107] "Acta 44," *Libro de actas,* Nov. 4, 1980 (Subseccional Pezca Archives); FENASTRAS, *FENASTRAS Combate,* newsletter, Dec. 1980 (CIDAI, UCA).

Manuel Rivera [a member of the SIP leadership] was detained at 10:30 pm on Tuesday, December 10 in "La Taberna" Puerto el Triunfo, by security forces, dressed in civilian clothes; José Margarito Reyes [concierge of SIP] was captured on Friday December 5 at 4:30 pm in Usulatán, by agents dressed in civilian clothes and was taken directly to the command post [of the armed forces].[108]

Ovidio Granadeño, SIP militant, recalls that he had begged Manuel Rivera not to go out that night after a union meeting. Neither of the two union activists were ever found. Granadeño describes the disappearances as the beginning of an era in the port of "very brutal repression."[109]

Early in the morning, on January 15, 1981, Molina Lara awoke in the FENASTRAS office in San Salvador. Plainclothes agents barged in, tied him up, and blindfolded him.[110] For three hours they waited for the arrival of other FENASTRAS militants. They captured two more; a small tank then pulled up to the office to carry them off. They were placed in a basement cell at the headquarters of the National Police. For six days, Molina Lara was blindfolded, beaten, and given electric shock torture; the interrogators constantly demanded that he turn over names to save his own life and those of his family. Finally, the Red Cross arrived at the prison and the torture ceased. After another two weeks, he was transferred to La Mariona prison. After nearly six months he was released and went into exile in the United States.

Early in August 1981, Gloria García, with her union *compañeros*, wandered in the bush outside of the village of Tierra Blanca. They had been tipped off that there they might find the remains of Juana Páez, a union activist who had been missing for two weeks. Soon after they set off down a muddy path they saw her head on a post. On the ground nearby was her corpse. A stake entered her vagina and exited through her neck. Scholars have studied rape as a strategy and an opportunistic practice of war that strikes fear into "adversary" and undermines male self-worth.[111] The Salvadoran military and death squads did practice rape most notably in the massacre of El Mozote and the rape and execution of the three American nuns and religious lay worker. The Salvadoran death squad

[108] Ibid.
[109] Ovidio Granadeño, interview with the author, Puerto El Triunfo, Feb. 2012. It is hard to arrive at an exact number of killings or disappearances of port union activists. My estimate is between five and seven.
[110] The arrest occurred a few days after a bombing in the FENASTRAS building. Bollinger, *El Salvador*, 357; Molina Lara, interview with the author, Los Angeles, 2012.
[111] Elisabeth Wood, "Conflict-Related Sexual Violence and the Policy Implications of Recent Research," *International Review of the Red Cross* 96, no. 894(Sept. 2015): 457–78.

likely raped Juana, but they also created a spectacle of mutilation through rage or by design. Here in the bush – with no real audience except the buzzards – they attacked the body of their antagonist in a way that defiled her identity as a female labor militant. Ten years later another death squad would carve out the brains of Ignacio Ellacuría and other leading Jesuit intellectuals. Salvadoran counterinsurgent violence identified its enemies and mutilated them accordingly. In horror, Gloria and her friends gathered up what they could of Juana's corpse and carried her off to the port for burial.

Later that evening, shaken to her core, Gloria García managed to drift off to sleep. She awoke to loud pounding, shouts, and curses. She glanced at the clock – it was 2:00 AM. Panicked, she warily walked out of her bedroom. Dozens of uniformed masked men stormed into her house. She watched in terror, as they burned all her photos and papers and ripped open their couch and beds. They screamed at her "puta guerrillera!" After moments of terror, they departed. Gloria García was the last SIP militant to flee into exile. Despite the ties of the shrimp company owners to the Far Right, no labor activists at the time or subsequently believed that they were in any direct way responsible for ordering the hits. Rather the death squad actions in the port were part of the national campaign of terror that eliminated an estimated 5,000 urban and rural union members between 1979 and 1983.

In July 1981, jailed labor activists penned the following and slipped it to a Dutch journalist: "The Salvadoran labor movement has had to become clandestine because it is the only manner that it can continue living since its union halls have been dynamited and its leaders jailed or executed." Then, commenting on their own situation: "[H]ere there are compañeros who have been burned with acid, tortured with electrical shocks ... and then the persecution and execution of our family members who visit us in prison increases every day with the object of isolating us from the people."[112]

We can read this brief history of labor insurgency and violent repression as evidence for Greg Grandin's argument about counterrevolutionary violence as the midwife of neoliberalism. He writes, "Repression severed alliances between reforming elites and popular classes, disaggregated powerful collective movements into individual survival strategies, extracted leaders from their communities, and redefined the relationship between

---

[112] "La situación de la clase obrera en El Salvador," Kooster Collection (International Institute of Social Studies, Amsterdam).

human beings and society."[113] Nevertheless, the labor movements in the port and San Salvador would reemerge forcefully in the mid-1980s in the context of a brutal civil war that cost 75,000 lives. However valiantly the workers battled employers and the government under unimaginably difficult conditions, the wave of violent repression of 1980 had largely denuded the emancipatory potential of the movements.

The labor insurgency that provoked so much bloody rightist resistance was not solely a creature of the revolutionary Left, either organizationally or ideologically. Buried within the discourse and practice of the radical labor movement lay the efforts and expressions of rank and filers to achieve a secure and dignified life within a convulsed and highly stratified society. Often the distance between radical discourse and workers' consciousness led to *desencuentros* I, thus weakening the movement. Yet, at the same time, the rank and file pushed its radical Left leadership toward a razor-sharp attention to their needs and toward acceptance of experiments in workers' self-management that were anathema to classic Leninism.

The period immediately following the October 15 coup may well have represented an historic missed opportunity for a peaceful solution to the class conflicts that were wrenching apart Salvadoran society. *Desencuentros* II debilitated the workers' movement in the port and throughout the country. Had the radical Left remained consistently open to a practical dialogue with the JRG, they might have posed a more effective challenge to the homicidal Right who deliberately set out to annihilate all forms of resistance within the popular classes.[114] The transition to neoliberalism in El Salvador may have been inevitable, but government-backed death squads need not have been its midwives.

---

[113] Greg Grandin, *The Last Colonial Massacre: Latin America in the Cold War* (Chicago: University of Chicago Press, 2004), 196. Also see Deborah Levinson-Estrada, *Trade Unionists against Terror: Guatemala City, 1954–1985* (Chapel Hill: University of North Carolina Press, 1994).

[114] Moreover, had the US government remained truer to its commitment to human rights, it might have promoted, or at least accepted, such an alliance. US Embassy to Secretary of State, "Troubles in Agricultural Areas: Incidents and Agrarian Reform," cable, Dec. 6, 1979, E00309, "El Salvador: The Making of U.S. Policy, 1977–1984" collection (DNSA).

4

Labor Conflicts in Puerto El Triunfo,
El Salvador, 1985

Every day forms of resistance make no headlines. But just as millions of anthozoan polyps create willy-nilly coral reefs, so do the multiple acts of peasant insubordination and evasion create barrier reefs of their own. And it is largely in this fashion that the peasantry makes its political presence felt.

James Scott, *Weapons of the Weak*

By virtue of the fact that we are hard-working men, all of the Pezca workers have agreed to constitute a cooperative in Puerto El Triunfo.

Mauricio Benítez and José Luis Grande Preza
in message to the Legislative Assembly 1985

Something Stinks in Puerto El Triunfo
Headline, *El Diario de Hoy*, July 1985

Ovidio Granadeño knew about repression before he arrived in Puerto El Triunfo. In 1974, in the cathedral of San Vicente, he had voiced a statement of protest against the removal of the Liberation Theology–inspired priest, David Rodriguez, from his parish. From that moment on, Ovidio faced harassment and discrimination from local landlords who viewed him as a subversive. He had an increasingly difficult time obtaining work as a farm laborer. Gradually, his sympathy with Liberation Theology, his prior experience in the Bakers' Union in San Salvador, and the landlord reaction pushed him toward activism in the Bloque Popular Revolucionario (BPR) and the Federación de Trabajadores de Campo (FTC).

FIGURE 4.1 Ovidio Granadeño, in Pezca S.A. packaging shrimp
(courtesy Ovidio Granadeño)

Ovidio had access to a manzana (1.7 acres) of land that his family still possessed on which he grew corn and some vegetables. He helped form a large cooperative in which each family kept its own land and production, but they all helped each other with the labor. They also purchased fertilizer and supplies together.

In 1977, Ovidio participated in a *toma* of the hacienda *Las Moras* located 10 miles east of his home, near Tecoluca. The FTC had organized the *toma* and set out to collectivize the occupied land. Ovidio eagerly participated in the collectivized labor. After six months, the Guardia evicted the FTC activists. When he returned home, he reflected on his experience. Although he remained a committed socialist, he felt that the collective was a failure. "Some people just got lazy even though we all belonged to the FTC. And that caused dissension in the ranks. I always

insisted on everyone working equally."[1] Some years later, he would push
his fellow plant workers to work hard and to take care of the machinery.
They would call him a "negrero" (slave driver). He responded, "Cayetano Carpio [former Baker's Union leader and founder of the Fuerzas
Populares de Liberación] taught me that!"[2]

Subsequently, Ovidio returned home to his hamlet near Tecoluca,
eking out a bare subsistence on the family's plot, while attempting to
reanimate the cooperative. In March 1979, he received word that the
security forces were looking for him. He hid in the bush as the army
ransacked his home. Then, with his clothes in a bag, he set off along trails
toward the coast. He had no prior plans, but he did have a sister who
worked at Pezca, so he headed toward the port and arrived during the tail
end of the strike.

Ovidio recalls that he knew no one connected to the union. That
changed, when during a strike demonstration he got up and sang "Carabina
30–30," a Mexican Revolutionary war ballad. Bernabé Recinos, the Federación Nacional Sindical de Trabajadores Salvadoreños (FENASTRAS)
leader in attendance, then sought him out and he became a Sindicato Tierra
(SIP) activist. For three months in 1981, the Guardia Nacional kept watch
on his house. They only withdrew the guards when Ovidio got the Capitán
del Puerto and a high-level Pezca manager to intervene on his behalf. There
was at least one Guardia raid at the plant. He remembers someone handing
him a pistol and asking him to hide it. He buried it in a barrel of ice.

After 1981, however, the town was largely spared armed conflict. The
civil war that raged in the country from 1980 to 1992, nonetheless, did
frame events in Puerto El Triunfo. Most importantly, the threats and
actions of death squads were, as we saw in Chapter 3, decisive in driving
the SIP leadership underground or into exile in 1980 and 1981. Immediately following this repressive period, the two shrimp industry unions,
SIP and Sindicato Agua (SGTIPAC), began to reemerge. Although many
SIP leaders were still aligned with the Left, as the union regrouped
following the repression of the early 1980s, they dramatically restricted
their militancy and their visible commitment to the national-level labor
movement. Ovidio played a unique role. Although he served on SIP's

---

[1] Ovidio Granadeño, interview with the author, Puerto El Triunfo, 2016.

[2] Ovidio had worked with Carpio in the union during the late 1960s and participated in
strikes under Carpio's leadership. At the time Carpio was a PCS leader but broke with the
party to found the guerrilla group. Ovidio would collaborate with the FPL/FMLN during
the 1980s, primarily arranging rest and medical treatment for guerrillas who were fighting
in the region. Ibid.

junta directiva he did not wish to assume a higher leadership role because he had begun to work clandestinely with the FMLN, providing some logistical support. This chapter charts Sindicato Tierra's transition from a violently repressed shell of its former self into a relatively successful bread-and-butter union.

Sindicato Agua had been founded in 1971, in effect as a company union. Fishermen from the era tend to believe that it did nothing to further their cause (as opposed to the captains or *patrones del barco*). This chapter also narrates and analyzes the meteoric resurgence of the union in the mid-1980s. With 300–500 members at its height, consisting primarily of male fishermen, the union became increasingly aligned with the Christian Democratic Party, in power from 1984 to 1989. We will focus on Sindicato Agua's growth and the radical quality of its demands, and also explore its anti-communist populism. Although elements of this radical populism tended to converge with the basic tenets shared by the leftist leadership of SIP, both Cold War pressures, in particular from AIFLD and Duarte, and gender relations drove the two unions apart throughout much of the decade. In particular, Sindicato Agua militants often evinced scorn for women and practiced stereotypical levels of womanizing. Indeed, the leaders of Sindicato Agua viewed Sindicato Tierra as complicit with the shrimp companies. That attack reflected some reality, but it also derived from their view of Sindicato Tierra as "feminized," and therefore lacking in militancy. More strikingly, they viewed that complicity as a reflection of a broader alliance between the FMLN and the oligarchic Right. Eventually, as we shall see in Chapter 7, the division between the two unions facilitated the local triumph of neoliberalism with devastating consequences.

LA MOVIDA IN THE 1980S

In Chapter 1, we saw how male fishermen developed a machista lifestyle, nurtured in the arduousness and danger of their work, that negatively affected family stability. When fishermen arrived in port they typically engaged in gambling, womanizing, and drinking. Such behaviors did not sit well with their spouses and partners, and numerous conflicts ensued. At times, they were violent. Ana Alvarenga recalled that when her husband learned that she had been elected to the union leadership in 1986, "He beat me violently and he left me looking like a monster."[3]

---

[3] Ana Alvarenga, interview with the author, Puerto El Triunfo, 2015.

The unions and the company immediately sympathized with her. "They were going to arrest him, but I told the police I just wanted him thrown out of town. He was working in Acajutla so he had to stay there."[4] The power of female trade unionists in SIP acted as a brake on domestic violence and all forms of sexual harassment on the job.

As noted in Chapter 1, *la movida*, whereby fishermen sold part of their catch to "pirate merchants," subsidized the fishermen's lifestyle. When Alfredo Mena Lagos, a prominent right-wing activist in his early thirties, became president of Pezca S.A. in 1982, he saw curtailing sales as his main task: "I found a serious liquidity problem. They were simply stealing too much shrimp."[5] His system of incentives also had penalties: "any crew who went under a limit, we got rid of, gone."[6] Starting in 1984, crews received prizes, including refrigerators and televisions, if they delivered a certain quota. The fishermen's response was to accept the new system and appropriate the shrimp above the cutoff. Angel Escobar, a fisherman and Sindicato Agua activist, stated that, on each voyage, the fishermen calculated the necessary catch for the incentive payments and then appropriated the rest. As Escobar recalled, regardless of official company incentives, "we thought of *la movida* as our own incentive."[7]

Until the mid-1980s, packinghouse workers and their union leadership grudgingly accepted *la movida*, even though part of their pay depended on production quotas. The extra income provided to spouses and kin of the fishermen mollified the opposition. Moreover, Sindicato Tierra could claim no moral high ground as fishermen organized in SIP in the other two companies also engaged in illegal sales, albeit at less egregious levels.[8]

The public and private silence about *la movida* and its material consequences, however, created a serious *desencuentro* II in Puerto el Triunfo. To cite one poignant example, in 1984, SIP militants tried in vain to prevail upon fishermen who belonged to their union and worked for Mariscos de El Salvador to stop the practice.[9] When, later that year, the

[4] Ibid., Montreal, 2016.
[5] Alfredo Mena Lagos, interview with the author, San Salvador, Feb. 2016.
[6] In addition to the incentives, Mena Lagos instituted other policies, such as the advanced purchase of spare parts; he attributes the 37 percent rise of production to these new policies. Ibid.
[7] Ángel Escobar, interview with the author, Los Angeles, Jan. 2016.
[8] The levels were low enough for Molina Lara to joke about with the SIP fishermen, e.g., "So did you get your paycheck early?"
[9] Ovidio Granadeño, interview with the author, Puerto El Triunfo, 2012; ibid., 2014.

company shut down due to financial insolvency, the Sindicato Tierra militants blamed the fishermen. Yet, *la movida* continued unabated.[10]

A form of labor market coercion prevailed against captains who did not permit the illegal sales.[11] During the 1980s, a typical conversation about a captain would include the question: "El vende?" (Does he sell?) A negative reply would lead a fisherman to look for an opening in another crew.

A US Embassy report from 1986 underscores the important role of the captains in the illegal trade.

Half the captains are selling shrimp to small fishermen who arrive in cayucos. The small fishermen in turn sell to a new processing plant set up with government cooperation to serve cooperatives and small fishermen. They also often sell (illegal exports) to plants in Honduras and Guatemala. The boat captains receive payments inside and outside the country... And the sales end up in companies owned by reputed drug lords in Miami.[12]

Alfredo Mena Lagos, the president of Pezca S.A. from 1982 to 1985 echoes this claim of an interconnection between the drug and shrimp trades.[13] Although the drug connection remains unclear, the Embassy report does underscore the infrastructure of corruption:

There is a widespread belief in the industry that the Marina [navy] is involved in the corruption. According to source, informants are afraid to say who is involved in payoffs for fear of being killed. Effective action could be taken by the Marina if there was a will to do so. For example, other companies with high military officers as stockholders [e.g., Atarraya] receive protection when bothered by picketers or other obstruction.[14]

In addition to high-level military officers, even company management employees became involved in the illegal sales; one in particular became quite wealthy by local standards.

There is no doubt that by the mid-1980s *la movida* was causing serious financial distress for the companies. No fisherman wanted to ruin the

---

[10] Ruperto Torres a former *maquinista* and leader of Sindicato Agua commented: "I don't remember anyone who resisted the temptation."
[11] Ruperto Torres, interview with the author, Puerto El Triunfo, Feb. 2017.
[12] US Embassy to Secretary of State, "Crisis in the Shrimp Industry," Mar. 22, 1985, San Salvador, 6659, r221606z, no. 6659, case (obtained under the Freedom of Information Act from US Department of State, Washington, DC).
[13] Alfredo Mena Lagos, interview with the author, San Salvador, 2016.
[14] US Embassy to Secretary of State, "Crisis in the Shrimp Industry," Mar. 22, 1985, San Salvador, 6659, r221606z, no. 6659, case (obtained under the Freedom of Information Act from US Department of State, Washington, DC).

shrimp companies. Rather, as suggested in the preceding text, they adhered to a moral economic calculus of assessment of risk and sense of economic justice, including a fundamental right to direct appropriation of a portion of their production. For many fishermen, this sense of moral economic justice persisted until the end, regardless of changes in the trade network or in the perception by other port residents.

The *marineros* employed a moral economic understanding to promote and legitimate what James Scott calls a "weapon of the weak." Scott's related concept of hidden transcripts is also relevant to Puerto El Triunfo. Fishermen had wide access to a space for creating hidden transcripts, that is discussion and expression away from public view. Yet it was not an egalitarian space. During down time at sea, discussions involved the *patrón del barco* (ship's captain) who represented both a union brother and a superior, with absolute authority; he was fully complicit in and a beneficiary of *la movida*. In fact, the captain received five times more than a *marinero* in the illegal trade whereas he only earned 2 to 2.5 times more in legal income from the company. Captains often became quite wealthy, as a result of the practice. Former female workers recall captains with particular scorn: "They would come back and say "I got 10,000 [colones]"[15] (US$2,000).

The practice contributed to the emergence of a local class fraction: the captains became wealthy petit-bourgeois. Their emerging class status had significant implications for the union and the companies. The plans to develop a subcontracting system in 1987 would find allies among the *patrones de barco*, as their potentially new status as "management" would be congruent with their new class position.

The wealth of the *patrones de barco* and the involvement of high-level military and drug dealers point to a thorny question: when did this everyday form of resistance, accepted if not applauded by much of the port working class in its early stages, become an antisocial activity? This question is relevant to our story because it mattered how plant workers and fishermen understood *la movida*. The ways in which plant workers viewed the practice conditioned how they would respond to the fishermen as a social group and as a union. For fishermen, *la movida* affected their own social consciousness and their union activity.

The mere act of selling on the sea, of course, was illegal. Initially, very few port workers or fishermen objected to the practice on moral grounds.

---

[15] Adela Amaya, interview with the author and Carlos Henríquez Consalvi, Puerto El Triunfo, May 2013.

On the contrary, they viewed it as a justifiable act of resistance. Since the 1977 cyclone, when it became a widespread social practice (previously there had been far fewer cases), until the mid-1980s, *la movida* became part of a highly organized network. Port residents knew that military officers and especially the navy were key players. The artisanal fishermen (known as *muralleros* for the excess fish – *muralla* – that the *marineros* gave away) to whom the shrimp was directly sold became nothing more than hired help for the entrepreneurs. Similarly, the ostentatious wealth of some captains belied the notion that the fishermen were simply paying themselves a "just" salary. Finally, the line between resistance and criminality appeared to have been crossed when the companies began to shut down or financially reel from the impact of *la movida*. Put differently, when the practice caused plant workers to be laid off, its antisocial character became quite visible.

The impact of *la movida* was highly consequential for the companies and the packinghouse workers. It had a significant impact on the companies' liquidity. For the packinghouse workers, not only did the practice affect their livelihoods but also it bred a deep mistrust between the primarily female labor force and the fishermen whose machista lifestyles exacerbated the differences. From an acceptable mode of resistance, *la movida* had become at once the enabler and the expression of fishermen's behavior that profoundly disturbed and alienated many female workers.

SINDICATO TIERRA AND DUARTE'S OPENING TO LABOR

As we shall see in Chapter 5, the owners and managers of Pezca were linked to the Right. Nevertheless, there is no evidence that they directly encouraged the arrest or assassination of SIP activists. Pezca S.A., took advantage of the opening. Ana Alvarenga recalls that during and immediately after the repression, management again became "despots towards us."[16] René Cuellar Morán, *gerente general*, opened up the anti-union offensive in May 1981. Without notifying the union, he dismissed 200 workers, offering them inadequate severance pay.[17] The state of siege eliminated any option to strike. SIP was powerless to stop management.

---

[16] Ana Alvarenga, interview with the author and Carlos Henríquez Consalvi, Puerto El Triunfo, 2015.

[17] The severance pay was not in accord with the seniority of the dismissed employees. The union also denounced him for not deducting union dues for SIP affiliates on the fishing fleets. "Acta 57," *Libro de actas*, May 3, 1981 (Subseccional Pezca Archives, Puerto el Triunfo, Usulután, El Salvador).

Their appeals for aid from FENASTRAS were also useless, as the regime had closed down the federation headquarters and jailed their leaders. (including Molina Lara, as we saw in Chapter 3).[18] Finally, shortly after the firings, the National Guard searched and ransacked the SIP headquarters. With repression on the rise, the union opted to close its headquarters in Puerto El Triunfo.

When Molina Lara had become secretary of organization of FENASTRAS, in 1979, he began to groom a successor. He had noticed how Ricardo Jovel, a fisherman at Mariscos de El Salvador showed his mettle by standing up for his fellow workers on the job and at meetings. He presented Jovel with the idea of taking over the union leadership with one caveat: he had to quit drinking. Jovel protested: "no hay un marinero que no tome!" ("There are no fishermen who don't drink.") After some agonizing, he agreed, in part because he shared Molino Lara's leftist political and union vision and in part because he was tiring of the fisherman's life. Molina Lara got him permission to take some union courses in San Salvador and then persuaded the SIP local leaderships to support Jovel in the general election.

Dread, anxiety, and exhaustion filled Ricardo Jovel's first years as a union leader. Although loosely aligned with the revolutionary Left, he kept his contacts down to a minimum.[19] Despite violent attacks against its leaders and their families, FENASTRAS did pay him a subsistence salary and allowed him to use a small office in San Salvador.[20] There he met with the port leadership and FENASTRAS militants. He also met and later became partners with Febe Velasquez who would become secretary-general from 1986 until 1989 when she died along with nine others, victims of the terrorist bombing of FENASTRAS headquarters. Jovel also traveled at least monthly to Puerto el Triunfo where he met with members, trying to keep in touch with the rank and file. What seemed necessary to him for his own survival was not, however, acceptable to the other port union leaders and some of the rank and file who pushed him to return to the port full time, especially once they were able to reopen union headquarters.

---

[18] The junta jailed the leadership of STECEL; Bernabé Recinos was leader of both STECEL and FENASTRAS. Alejandro Molina spent much of 1982 on a solidarity tour in the United States on behalf of his jailed comrades.

[19] He was affiliated with Frente de Acción Popular Unificado (FAPU) and through them with the Resistencia Nacional (RN), a guerrilla group within the FMLN. Jovel did not participate in any guerrilla activities. Ricardo Jovel, interview with the author, San Salvador, 2014.

[20] Death squads executed the wife and daughter of the jailed FENASTRAS leader, Bernabé Recinos.

In April 1984, Jovel gathered up nine members of the *junta directiva* of Sindicato Tierra (including four women) and met in Usulután, the departmental capital. They decided to send a commission to petition the Capitanía del Puerto to reopen the union hall. The port's naval commander granted permission contingent on their pledge that the union and its locale would be apolitical and that they employ a secretary of his choosing whose job would be, in part, to monitor their activities. The local leaders felt they had no choice but to accept the deal. The collection of union dues was at an all-time low. Many workers had simply stopped paying dues; many others had been fired or laid off. To make matters worse, in a fit of pique, annoyed by union demands and by *la movida*, the oligarch Angel Guirola had shut down Mariscos de El Salvador, thus eliminating several hundred dues-paying members.[21]

The timing of the reopening of union headquarters was not fortuitous. José Napoleón Duarte was elected president the previous month, with large-scale backing from the labor movement that saw his election as the key to survival. Devastated by state terror, the Left had little presence in the peasant or labor movement from 1981 until 1983. Thus, the "center" had fertile terrain on which to organize. The UPD (Popular Democratic Unity) was a labor and peasant federation broadly aligned with the Christian Democratic Party. Founded in 1980 with major support from AIFLD and from the Central Latinoamericano de Trabajadores (CLAT), the UPD had its main base of support from the country's historically largest union, a 40,000-member construction union and among the cooperativist beneficiaries of the land reform. The land reform of 1980, rejected by the Left as counterinsurgent, eventually benefitted some 300,000 people, mostly organized in cooperatives. Those peasants, however, had to wage constant battle with the government for economic support (e.g., fertilizer, implements) and legalization of titles, but most belonged to organizations that supported the government. From those organizations, the UPD gained its large constituency.

The UPD signed a pre-electoral "social pact" with Duarte that guaranteed full respect for union rights and an end to the wage freeze, in effect since 1981. Moreover, the pact promised a deepening and broadening of the agrarian reform, a commitment to have UPD representatives in key posts in the government, and a pledge to open negotiations to end the civil

---

[21] Although SIP was not in good financial shape, it donated US$15,000 colones (out of US $26,000 in its accounts) to the workers of Mariscos del El Salvador who had just lost their jobs.

war. There is little doubt that Duarte's electoral victory over the rightist Roberto D'Aubuisson (with 53 percent) owed much to the activism of the UPD, which, despite its support for the Christian Democrats, was open to the Left as underscored by its unrestricted support for union rights and unconditional peace negotiations. Most labor activists greeted his victory with optimism, believing that the long night of anti-labor repression was finally coming to an end.

Despite the national note of optimism, in Puerto El Triunfo only 95 members attended the first SIP meeting at the reopened headquarters in May 1984, representing the lowest union meeting attendance in nearly 20 years. The union minutes stated that, during the meeting, "We analyzed the doubts about the union shared by many workers." Jovel stated, "We agreed to organize in the companies to overcome the impasse."[22] Ricardo Jovel urged his fellow union members to recruit others for the next meeting and to remind them that the meetings had the blessing of the Capitán del Puerto.[23]

Mena Lagos, despite his right-wing ideological convictions, was interested in establishing harmonious relations with SIP. The company was inclined to make concessions in the contract negotiations of 1984, as the industry was rebounding; that year it increased production by 37 percent.[24] Pezca agreed to a one colon daily raise; the raise came close to keeping pace with the rate of inflation (an average of 15 percent a year since 1980), but previous increases had been woefully inadequate due to a national wage freeze. Mena Lagos ceded ground, in part, because he considered the SIP leadership to be "responsible," notwithstanding their leftist identification.

The union had, as it were, shown its responsibility, by successfully lobbying the National Assembly to retract a *veda* (closed season) that had been announced for shrimp to combat overfishing. Understandably, the union, weak and on the defensive, saw an opportunity to "defend" the short-term interests of the workforce. The companies took advantage of the union initiative doing additional damage to the long-term needs of the shrimp industry.[25]

---

[22] "Acta 52," *Libro de actas*, n.d., p. 160 (SIP General Archives, Puerto El Triunfo).

[23] "Acta 54," *Libro de actas*, May 26, 1984 (SIP General Archives).

[24] The increase did correspond to the first increase in the minimum wage since 1980. Mario Lungo, *El Salvador in the Eighties: Counterinsurgency and Revolution*, trans. Amelia Shogun (Philadelphia, PA: Temple University Press, 1996), 95.

[25] The highest price *camarón blanco* (white shrimp) was in drastic decline (Archivo de la Asamblea Legislativa [AAL], San Salvador).

By 1985, SIP had rebounded in terms of active membership and was winning significant concessions from Atarraya (the other remaining plant in Puerto El Triunfo) and Pezca S.A. Counting two plants in the department of La Unión, it reported 1,745 members, down only slightly from 2,000 in 1980. There were several reasons for its relative success. First, there was continuity in the leadership and a recognition of the need for tactical change.[26] Second, and most importantly, when the leadership began to emerge from clandestine activity they opted to eschew strikes in favor of brief work stoppages in particular units of the plant and work slowdowns.[27]

Former union leaders look back with pride on their achievements in the midst of the civil war. Many of the achievements involved reinstituting those benefits that the company had stripped away during the years of repression. Ovidio Granadeño, who collaborated with the FMLN throughout the Civil War, remembers how his union attained scholarships for the children of union members, access to a health clinic, and a *botiquín* (first aid dispensary).[28] There were also victories ranging from special rights for pregnant temporary workers to the (re)creation of a cafeteria for workers with subsidized prices.[29] They also won the restoration of benefits for *eventuales* (seasonal workers). Moreover, the wage increases they obtained from 1984 to 1986 managed to keep up with the rate of inflation. In 1985, semiskilled workers earned more than twice the minimum industrial wage. Moreover, in the 1985 contract negotiation with Atarraya, SIP gained a 75 percent increase in rates for the fishermen affiliated with its union.[30]

---

[26] Pedro Henriquez Peña, Ovidio Granadeño, Rafael Antonio Vigil, and others were in the Junta Directivas during the mid- to late 1970s and during the mid-1980s. There were other ways in which SIP regained legitimacy such as the sponsorship of a soccer team.

[27] Yet, despite the overt attempts to project a nonsubversive image, SIP meetings also began with a "minute of silence for the fallen who struggled to conquer benefits for the members." "Acta 45," *Libro de actas*, May 24, 1986 (Subseccional Pezca Archives); "Acta 52," *Libro de actas*, Aug. 12, 1990 (Subseccional Pezca Archives). Rolando Franco reflected the state of paranoia "when I brought the band, 'El Indio' who sang protest songs, I was sharply criticized by many of the union members." Interview, Los Angeles, 2015.

[28] There were also more mundane victories such as a second roll of toilet paper per week. Granadeño was conflating some of the victories from the late 1970s that had been suspended and then reinstated in the mid-1980s. "Acta del Comité de Relaciones Obreros Patronales," Apr. 29, 1987 (Subseccional Pezca Archives).

[29] It seems that the previous cafeteria had fallen into disrepair during the period of repression.

[30] FENASTRAS, *Memoria anual de labores*, FENASTRAS, Nov. 1985, p. 15 (CIDAI, UCA, San Salvador).

Beyond their success at the negotiating table, there was another reason that they held on to most of their base despite what would become intense competition from Sindicato Agua. Although Ricardo Jovel, Granadeño and other leaders remained aligned with the Left, they toned down the radicalism of their public declarations. When the union headquarters reopened, for the first time in more than a decade every meeting was preceded by the singing of the national anthem.[31]

SIP was not the same union as it was in the 1970s. Although it remained within FENASTRAS, at most a few dozen leaders and rank and filers participated in May Day celebrations or protest marches in the mid- to late 1980s.[32] In this new atmosphere of ideological neutrality and cooperation, several union leaders became corrupt, succumbing to management enticements.[33]

SINDICATO AGUA

Sindicato Agua (SGTIPAC) did not immediately benefit from the weakness and corruption of SIP during the early 1980s. At the start of the decade, its leadership was also mired in corruption. In 1982, union members elected Mauricio Ascencio Benítez, who ran as an anti-corruption outsider. One-half of the 150 members abstained from the vote. Former militants recall that those who had profited most from *la movida*, the *patrones de barco* (captains), and had dominated the union since its inception in 1971 promoted the abstention option. Benítez was a *marinero eventual* (not permanent, often seasonal fisherman), a position that placed him low on the hierarchy of fishermen. Moreover, he was a recovering alcoholic – who had lived for years at the extreme margins of port society. After a decade dominated by *patrones de barcos*, his contested election marked a visible change.

The new leadership faced several structural problems. The *patrones de barco* complicated the union panorama. In all the companies, they

---

[31] See Government of El Salvador, *Memoria del Ministerio de Trabajo, 1985–86*; "Tabla de Salario," Nov. 1985 (Subseccional Pezca Archives).

[32] International Labor Organization, interim report, Nov. 1984, case 1258, no. 236 (ILO, Geneva, Switzerland). He was released with 10 other STECEL members. Also see, Chris Hedges, "Salvador Curbs Unions – Claps Leaders in Jail," *Christian Science Monitor*, Oct. 3, 1983. Recinos's wife and daughters were "disappeared."

[33] Jovel later came under suspicion of corruption but in effect the only charge was that he got small allotments of shrimp and fish from the companies – for personal consumption. Ana Alvarenga, interview with the author, Montreal, 2016; Rolando Franco, interview with the author, Los Angeles, 2015.

fulfilled three roles: employee and union member, company representative, and unquestioned authority on the vessel. Their joint role as management representatives and union leaders had limited Sindicato Agua's ability to achieve decent salaries, benefits, and working conditions for its rank-and-file membership.

The role of *eventuales* posed an additional structural issue. As discussed in Chapter 3, SIP agitated and launched a series of strikes with the goal of converting the status of the seasonal "chacalín" packinghouse workers (some 35–40 percent of the labor force) into that of permanent workers with full benefits. Their victory in 1979 marks one of the great achievements of the Salvadoran labor movement, reversing the global trend toward the casualization of labor. Although it also had a seasonal dimension, the problem of *eventuales* for the *marineros* was substantially different. Companies imposed five-member crew limits and national laws (influenced by US AID studies) limited the total number of shrimp boats to 73.[34] Over the years, fishermen pushed unsuccessfully to expand the crews, in part because the demands of cutting the heads off all the shrimp (except *chacalín*) and sorting them made the overall expenditure of labor that much more demanding. The captains often brought on board one or two "extras" whom the other fishermen paid a fraction of their own earnings. They joined the growing ranks of the *eventuales*.

In January 1983, shortly after Benítez assumed control, the union vehemently protested discrimination against fishermen over the age of 40 and against the failure of Pezca S.A. to make *aguinaldo* (end-of-year bonus) and vacation payments. Mauro Granados, the general manager, threatened the union with attacks by the air force due to its "subversion." The use of "subversive" as an epithet, usually reserved for the Left, was dangerous and often amounted to a death sentence. Intensifying the reigning paranoia, in 1982, Roberto D'Aubuisson, the infamous rightist (accused as the mastermind of the plot to assassinate Msr. Oscar Arnulfo Romero in March 1980) had become owner of a small fishing fleet in Puerto El Triunfo. As we shall see in Chapter 5, throughout the decade the board of directors of his fishing company, Mariscos Tazumal, included other death squad heads. During those dark days, Benítez felt under siege from both management and from the Right. Jovel recalls that he was eager to take advantage of Sindicato Tierra's tactical advice and

---

[34] Starting in the mid-1980s, the government seems to have lost control over the number of fishing boats, though due to decapitalization many remained *varado*.

minor forms of assistance. Benítez's fraternal attitude began to change with Duarte's election in 1984.[35]

At a July 1984 meeting, Benítez spoke to the union membership about several issues ranging from faulty scales used by Pezca S.A. allegedly to defraud them of their newly instituted incentive pay to the anti-union practices of three *jefes*.[36] He argued that the *sub gerente de operaciones*, José Rolando Villatoro, had stated that he did not "approve of simple fishermen without university degrees earning such high wages."[37] The union leader also denounced stagnant wages (due to a three-year wage freeze) and lack of any benefits for workers on the docks, workshops, and shipyard whom Pezca S.A. considered to be *eventuales*.[38] Benítez also attacked nepotistic hiring and food purchasing practices.[39]

The 33-year-old union leader's speech responded sharply to symbolic and real abuses of power and, in so doing, revealed facets of union ideology and practice. He made it clear that despite his own background as a *marinero eventual*, he sought to protect older, permanent workers from discrimination and firing.[40] Yet, as SIP leaders would later point out, his unwavering base of support was among the *eventuales* whom he hoped would achieve some form of permanent status.

Following the meeting, Benítez sent a letter to the Ministry of Labor. The union lodged a complaint against three *jefes* for anti-union practices and for nepotism, including one who had been a *patrón de barco*. Former Sindicato Tierra militants alleged that the animosity had to do with the *jefes'* attempts to contain the "piratería"; the former captain, Remberto Alemán, certainly would have known intimate details about the practice. Yet former Sindicato Agua militants charge that Alemán was utterly corrupt, demanding under-the-table payment in shrimp and cash in return for turning a blind eye to *la movida*.

---

[35] There is no direct indication that AIFLD played an early role in supporting Benitez, but there is no doubt that they backed Grande Preza who recruited the Sindicato Agua leader so that the union joined the CGT. Ricardo Jovel, interview with the author, San Salvador, 2014; ibid., Puerto El Triunfo, 2015.

[36] Minutes, June 1984 (digitized SGTIPAC Archives, in possession of the author). These minutes were submitted to the Labor Ministry. As with SIP "archive" no such formal archive exists but a digital archive will be created.

[37] Ibid., 7.

[38] Sindicato Agua calculated that fishermen earned far less than the minimum wage, roughly US$0.20 an hour.

[39] Mauricio Ascencio Benítez to Jonathan Liss, letter, Apr. 10, 1985, p. 6 (SGTIPAC Archives).

[40] This is the interpretation of Ricardo Jovel, former *marinero*, and Secretary General of SIP, 1981–87.

In response to the complaint, the Ministry of Labor sent two inspectors to Puerto El Triunfo who investigated for four days. In addition to management and Sindicato Agua leaders, the inspectors claimed to have talked with 200 workers inside and outside of the plant, including 40 fishermen. Their report dismissed many of the union's allegations. Moreover, they claimed that the 1,000 workers inside the plant did not favor removing the three *jefes*. They rejected the accusations of nepotism and favoritism. Although Pezca argued that the workers on the *varadero* (dry dock) were all *eventuales*, the inspectors agreed with the union that the company did owe them some vacation and *aguinaldo* (13th month bonus) pay.

Benítez accused the inspectors of drinking with management employees and presenting specious data. Their claim was patently absurd that more than 1,000 workers in the plant supported the three *jefes* because, at the time, fewer than 600 plant workers labored in Pezca S.A. Benítez also charged the company with blatant dishonesty. He alleged that management purposefully avoided paying the incentives by duplicitous means ranging from rigging the scales on the dock to contaminating the product with diesel fuel. Although it is impossible to ascertain the validity of these charges, they do reveal the depth of misunderstanding and suspicion between Sindicato Agua and the company.

La movida was at the root of the suspicion. As noted previously, Alfredo Mena Lagos instituted a system of incentives to curtail the illegal sales. Sindicato Agua responded to the company initiatives by demanding an increase in incentive pay. The company's response underscores the discursive gulf between labor and management. While ignoring the charge of contamination and scale fixing, in regard to the request for incentive increases a Pezca spokesmen declared to the Labor Ministry:

The incentive pay is not an additional "benefit" [prestación] rather a program created by the companies through their own initiative. Its primordial aim is to ensure that a greater amount of the catch arrives at the plant. In other words, it is a desperate effort by the companies to maintain employment for the people who work in the processing plant. We are not paying for more captured shrimp but rather for that product to arrive in the plant.[41]

For the union, this line of reasoning was at once unacceptable and impossible to address directly because the issue of the illegal sales by definition had to be silenced.

---

[41] Dirección General de Trabajo, statement by Pezca management, Dec. 11, 1984 (AAL, San Salvador).

THE STRIKE OF 1985

Following Duarte's election, Benítez began to distance himself from Jovel and the local SIP leaders. At the same time that Sindicato Agua launched its protest with the Labor Ministry, the union joined the Confederación General de Trabajo (CGT), a small Christian Democratic–controlled labor federation.[42] This move enabled Benítez and his leadership group to receive the guidance of José Luis Grande Preza who had been trained by AIFLD. Grande Preza straddled the ideological fence between the Cold War imperatives of AIFLD and the Christian-inflected democratic socialism of the Central Latinoamericana de Trabajadores. Grande Preza had started out as a rank-and-file member of the bus drivers' union and had gradually climbed the ranks of the CGT during the reign of anti-labor terror.[43]

As we shall see in Chapter 6, Duarte and his US allies did everything they could to marginalize the growing left wing of the labor movement without resorting to the violence characteristic of the early years of the decade. The resurgence of the labor movement and the desire of the Duarte administration to control it had immediate effects in the port. Throughout December 1984 and January of 1985, Labor Ministry officials tried in vain to resolve the grievances. The conflict intensified as the company responded to the aggressive union rhetoric with restrictions on the mobility of the Sindicato Agua leadership. Moreover, management remained unyielding on issues of hiring and firing.

On January 15, 1985, the company fired a refrigeration mechanic who belonged to Sindicato Agua. The union alleged that he was fired for asking for the same salary as another mechanic who performed the same tasks. The union placed his rehiring at the head of a list of demands that included the removal of the three mid-level managers whom they deemed guilty of anti-union practices, and a seven-hour work day for the dock and *varadero* (boat maintenance) workers with full benefits. On the 16th, the union demanded satisfaction of their petition within 24 hours or they would launch a strike. On the 17th, they delivered the warning to the

---

[42] In mid-1984, SGTIPAC quit the labor federation FUSS (generally controlled by the underground Communist Party since the 1960s) and affiliated with the CGT (Christian Democratic and pro-government). This change, in keeping with the traditional anti-Left orientation of the union (which makes the FUSS affiliation incomprehensible) was motivated by Duarte's victory.

[43] Grande Preza, interview with the author, San Salvador, 2014.

Labor Ministry stating in a note signed by 70 workers that they would stop work the following day at 10 AM.

At 7:00 AM, on January 18 – according to a company report:

> without waiting for this deadline, Sr. Benítez urged the workers on the varadero and on the dock to go out on strike … Due to the initial confusion and to the repeated exhortations and pressures of Sr. Benítez, the personnel of the processing plant joined the strike action beginning at 10 am. Following discussions with their union leadership [SIP] they rectified their initial attitude and by 3:00 pm had returned to work.[44]

The company claimed that 70 workers were on strike and that 550 continued to labor. Yet spokesmen admitted that due to the strategic nature of the dock, the strike could affect everyone despite the fact that it was about "minor matters."

Minor matters or not, this was no ordinary strike; it was a complex affair involving Sindicato Tierra, the Duarte administration, Sindicato Agua, and the Pezca management. Sindicato Agua's demands focused primarily on issues related to non-fishermen, especially the *varadero* and dock workers, clearly revealing their intention to expand their base beyond the fishermen.[45] In keeping with the CGT/AIFLD agenda, one of their goals was to displace the putatively leftist Sindicato Tierra and to establish their own control.

Benítez called in the fishing boats and with them 80,000 pounds of shrimp, augmenting the number of striking workers by another few hundred (including *eventuales*). Sindicato Agua assumed that the US $320,000 worth of shrimp that they brought on board their boats would be a decisive bargaining chip in obtaining victory. Over the next weeks, however, the shrimp in the holds of the fishing boats turned into the central issue. The company wanted it processed and then stored until after the conflict. If that solution was not acceptable, the shrimp would be given to charities, the armed forces, or to the war displaced but with the proviso that the company would not pay any salaries. The union wanted to sell the shrimp unprocessed on the local market; the proceeds would go to a joint account until after the conflict. Although never explicit, it seems likely that the union did not want the shrimp processed because the

---

[44] "Posición de Pezca S.A. frente a la huelga ilegal promovida por el Sr. Mauricio Ascencio Benítez," Jan. 21, 1985 (AAL).

[45] Moreover, they both sought to protect the seniority rights of permanent workers while attempting to broaden the rights and benefits of *eventuales*. The defense of seniority was particularly important for Benítez due to his own status as a *marinero eventual*.

packinghouse workers would have less reason to join the strike or to break ranks with SIP. Within a few weeks, the shrimp rotted. A dispute then ensued about who should be in charge of dumping it in the ocean.

The pro-Duarte CGT's support that reinforced its bona fides as a labor federation prompted Benítez and his fellow Sindicato Agua leaders to keep pushing hard against Pezca. The union remained intransigent, as did management. Several months later, a reporter for the rightist *El Diario de Hoy* wrote, "The stench that emanates from nearly 80,000 pounds of decomposed shrimp in the hulls of the fishing boats stuck in Puerto el Triunfo is something more than a repugnant olfactory experience. It has become the symbol of corruption of the principles of free unionism."[46] The article suggested that the strike was merely a ploy for the Christian Democratic–backed union to expel Sindicato Tierra from the plant. The irony of a far right newspaper in effect defending a leftist-led union was a source of some mirth among SIP members.

Despite sharp opposition from the board of directors, Mena Lagos, the president of Pezca, continued to pay the plant workers. The payment was a conscious strike-breaking tactic, aiming to exacerbate the division between the unions. After meeting the payroll for the first three months of the strike, faced with a liquidity crisis, Pezca stopped further payments and laid off 172 plant workers.

SIP then attacked the company and the incompetence of the Labor Ministry, offering "unlimited solidarity" to the strikers. The communiqué of April 18 stated: "SIP and the federation fully support the demands of the compañeros of sector agua. We belong to the same class but government and company interests have tried to keep us apart making us easy victims of management intrigues." The SIP declaration, referring to the dock and *varadero* workers, specifically emphasized the need to "[g]ive definitive contracts to the casual laborers because this is the most brutal way to repress through hunger the union aspirations of the compañeros."[47] Despite a critical understanding of Benítez's intentions, plant workers offered solidarity both formally and informally throughout the strike. Members of the two unions shared food donated by various organizations (including through AIFLD cash donations) and in various

---

[46] *Diario de Hoy,* July 26, 1985.

[47] Somewhat demagogically, both unions called for 100 percent wage hikes. During contract negotiations that had been interrupted by the strike, Sindicato Tierra had demanded a 50 percent wage hike. "FENASTRAS y SIP comunican al pueblo salvadoreño," paid advertisement, Apr. 18, 1985 (CIDAI, UCA).

ways expressed mutual solidarity, including when Pezca continued to pay plant workers.

Responding to some pressure from its base, the Sindicato Agua leadership agreed to meet with the leaders of SIP in their headquarters to coordinate a joint struggle. The head of the CGT, José Luis Grande Preza, joined the meeting as well. According to a SIP document, the meeting achieved nothing,

in the first place because the Secretary General of ESGTIPAC [*sic*], Mauricio Ascension Benítez only tried to attack our leaders singling them out for their supposed ties to the FMLN and that our union belonged to the [revolutionary mass organization] FAPU and that they were the same thing. In synthesis, we didn't get anywhere and they rejected our participation in the conflict.[48]

Not surprisingly given its goal to take over representation of the plant, Sindicato Agua did not reciprocate let alone acknowledge the solidarity. Presumably, AIFLD's support of Sindicato Agua's strike hinged on the expectation that a "democratic union" would supplant a "leftist" union. The removal of SIP was congruent with the goals and practices of the CGT and AIFLD. It would have represented a coup for the Duarte administration, despite the fact that SIP's politics had been subdued for some time.

In a statement to *El Mundo* that responded to accusations that the strike was primarily about taking control of Pezca from SIP, Grande Preza stated that they were not interested in affecting the "stability of the labor movement." In defense of the charge that Benítez was operating in effect as a *caudillo*, he stated, "[T]he strike was not decreed by compañero Mauricio Ascencio Benítez, it was decreed by the rank and file of SGTI-PAC [Sindicato Agua], whose eminently humanist ideology contrasts abysmally with the ideology of Sindicato Tierra [SIP]."[49]

This was the modus operandi of both the CGT and AIFLD during the period: through nonviolent measures, remove leftist union militants from control over unions or persuade (allegedly, at times, bribe) them to move into the "democratic" camp. Although Benítez despised the death squads and the oligarchic Right, he had no compunction about using the epithet "subversive" to attack the leaders of Sindicato Tierra. Notwithstanding

---

[48] In some ways, the declaration suggests Benítez's lack of seriousness. FAPU virtually had ceased to exist – given their ties to the RN in the FMLN. FENASTRAS, *Memoria anual de labores, FENASTRAS, 1984–1985*, Nov. 7–8, 1985, p. 17 (CIDAI, UCA).

[49] Quoted in *El Mundo*, July 24, 1985.

FIGURE 4.2 Sindicato Agua Leadership: Benítez, middle row, far left; Adela Amaya, middle row, far right; Grande Preza, top row, third from right; Ruperto Torres, top row, far right
(courtesy Adela Amaya)

the broad congruence with the AIFLD/CGT objectives, Sindicato Agua's actions had their own logic and dynamic.

THE COOPERATIVE DREAM

Benítez had an important objective that did not figure prominently on the agenda of any of the union's backers. During the third month of the strike, along with other Sindicato Agua members, he formally constituted a cooperative fishing enterprise. On May 8, in a declaration to the president of the Legislative Assembly, Benítez and CGT leader Preza Grande asked the body to study the legal requisites for the expropriation of the company – given that it was using a national resource – and its conversion into a worker-owned cooperative. The down payment for the plant and the fishing fleet would be the "salarios holgados" (wages owed by the company during the strike). As a first step toward that end, Benítez and Preza Grande wrote, by virtue of the fact that we are hard-working men, all of the Pezca workers have agreed to constitute a cooperative in Puerto el Triunfo with which we will contribute with our own grain of sand together with you, shoulder to shoulder in order to achieve that deeply desired common good of all Salvadoran brothers, through our collective efforts as workers.[50]

Although the cooperative was but a paper organization, it laid claim to a serious goal, namely to expropriate one of the largest enterprises in the country and turn it over to its workers. Following a breakdown in the negotiations with Pezca, Benítez delivered a second letter to the Assembly, reiterating the call for expropriation. Over the next five years, Sindicato Agua continued to lobby and struggle for the cooperative goal.

Some members of the Duarte government and the National Assembly supported the expropriation of Pezca S.A. and the creation of a cooperative. Such a goal was broadly congruent with the Christian Democratic agenda. However, the expropriation of Pezca would have satisfied more strictly partisan goals, given the rightist politics of its owners. Moreover, Benítez believed that the project was viable and that the Christian Democratic government would effectively support it. Producer cooperatives had been a cornerstone of Christian Democratic philosophy and practice since the 1960s when the movement established a major presence in Latin America. CLAT, with whom the CGT was affiliated, promoted a vision of *autogestion* (worker self-management) as the key element of a democratic socialist strategy. Emilio Máspero, the longtime head of CLAT, viewed cooperatives as fundamental institutions that contributed to the movement for a nonauthoritarian version of socialism. Of course, the anticommunist orientation of the federation made it virtually impossible for Máspero to establish any alliances that would have made viable his cooperativist goal.

A left-wing Christian Democratic analyst commented on the Duarte administration's position vis-à-vis the Pezca strike and the cooperative:

For the Christian Democrats the solution is to transform the company into a cooperative as long as the beneficiaries remain under their political control. When you realize that shrimp is currently the fourth source of foreign exchange one realizes the importance of the second intention of the Party: divide the economic right wing, by stimulating those productive branches that rely on intensive labor while simultaneously coopting the organizational bases of those industries.[51]

---

[50] Mauricio Ascencio Benítez to the president of the Asamblea Legislativa, letter, July 8, 1985 (AAL).

[51] *Víspera,* June 1985, 3 (bulletin of the Movimiento Popular Social Cristiano).

The analyst perceived a broader Christian Democratic strategy that would neutralize the agro-financial elite (tied to the rightist ARENA Party) and create a cooperative industrial base, under their political control. The financing for such a bold, transformative move would have to come at least indirectly from the Reagan administration and international lending agencies. Both sources were committed to a neoliberal project that did not encompass a cooperative model of development.

Cold War blinders and imperatives make it hard to penetrate to the core of Duarte's thought. However, it seems likely that the analyst was largely correct. There is no doubt that Duarte took great pride in the numerous cooperatives established through the agrarian reform of 1980.[52] Moreover, the Christian Democratic Party (PDC) was in an historically deadly battle with the Right and the idea of displacing the agro-financial elite from economic dominance was a necessary element of the party's strategy for future advancement.

On a local level, the cooperative ideal gained acceptance among Sindicato Agua's rank and file in part perhaps because the fishermen's experience of direct appropriation reinforced their sense of control over production. They also implicitly assumed that such a cooperative would solve the employment problem of the *marineros eventuales*.

Ricardo Jovel, the leftist general secretary of SIP, recalls discussing the cooperative idea with Benítez (whom he claims to have often counseled over the years). Jovel expected that the plant workers would democratically own and run the packinghouse operation. Jovel thus repeatedly encouraged Benítez, "I will support you." He told other SIP militants, "If Mauricio pulls this off, we do as well."[53] Sindicato Agua received several visits from the Ministry of Labor, which consistently offered support for the cooperative.[54]

---

[52] There were limits to Duarte's promotion of cooperatives as evidenced by his March 1985 veto of a bill highly favorable to that form of organization. See *Proceso*, Mar. 15, 1985.

[53] Ricardo Jovel, interview with the author, San Salvador, May 2014.

[54] Jovel recalls, however, a conversation with the Minister of Labor who exclaimed, "Benitez is crazy! Duarte can't do that ... he can't expropriate capital." Ruperto Torres, interview with the author, Puerto El Triunfo, 2013; Adela Amaya, interview with the author, Puerto El Triunfo, 2013. The US labor attaché talked with Ministry of Labor officials who claimed there was no legal basis for expropriation but stated that Pezca lawyers claimed that if the company became bankrupt then a co-op could take over. US Embassy to Secretary of State, "No Sign of Let-Up in Four-Month Strike against El Salvador's Largest Shrimp Exporter," May 28, 1985, San Salvador, 6659, r282355z,

Ovidio Granadeño recalls that the Minister of Labor and Luis Hidalgo, a Christian Democratic deputy from Usulatán, visited the port and met with SIP militants, trying to persuade them to support the cooperative.[55] Granadeño and other SIP activists rejected the offer primarily because of the bad blood between the unions; they were tired of being called "reds" or "subversives" when such an appellation could be a death warrant. SIP militants assumed that government backing would ensure Sindicato Agua control over the cooperative. Such a move would be congruent with their efforts to wrest control of the plant from SIP. The SIP militants also assumed that they would lose all benefits because "they would be owners and not employees."[56] Signifying an even deeper level of mistrust, they were convinced that "la movida" would not end with a cooperative. They also recognized that the cooperative plan did not explicitly challenge the hierarchy that placed inordinate power and income in the hands of the *patrones de barco.*

Ideological and political considerations also entered into Sindicato Tierra's decision to reject Jovel's position on the cooperative. Regardless of political allegiance, SIP leaders took seriously their membership in FENASTRAS, an organization that was broadly allied with the Left. In the words of Cirilo Hueso in 1985, the labor confederation no longer had a formal affiliation with the Frente Democrático Revolucionario (FDR – an exiled group allied with the FMLN) but rather "a convergence of objectives."[57] FENASTRAS's ideological affinity with the FDR played out in the port. Hueso, who had more prestige and influence among the SIP leadership than Jovel, strongly counseled against supporting the cooperative. According to Granadeño, "Cirilo told us that the cooperatives formed part of a counterinsurgent strategy and thus we had to oppose them."[58] Such a statement would be in keeping with FMLN intransigent opposition to the land reform. The Left had opposed the agrarian reform from its promulgation in 1980, despite its broad congruence with agrarian reforms promoted by leftist governments in Guatemala (1952) and Nicaragua (1981). The opposition stemmed in part because of the military nature of the expropriations and organization of

no. Co562655, case F-2013–1010925 (obtained under the Freedom of Information Act from US Department of State, Washington, DC).

[55] Ovidio Granadeño, interview with the author, Puerto El Triunfo, May 2014.   [56] Ibid.

[57] Quoted in Shirley Christian, "Newly Active Unions a Challenge for El Salvador," *New York Times,* June 16, 1985.

[58] Ovidio Granadeño, interview with the author, Feb. 2016.

the cooperatives. More significantly, the Left opposed the reform because it aimed to weaken its own peasant base. That said, it is difficult to ascertain what tipped the balance among SIP militants against the port cooperative. The negative and nearby example of the cooperative on Juan Wright's expropriated hacienda, *La Carrera*, surely influenced them; it was under-financed and highly militarized.[59] Indeed, the FMLN staged an attack on *La Carrera* that destroyed much of the cotton crop. The war also weighed on cooperatives throughout the country. Duarte's plans to finance them ran up against defense budget realities despite massive US aid.

IMPLACABLE FOES: BENÍTEZ AND MENA LAGOS

Beyond the opposition of SIP, Benítez also faced an intransigent manage-ment whose hostility became increasingly personalized as the strike progressed. Immediately following the outbreak of the strike, Mena Lagos, the company president stated:

During his entire tenure, Sr. Benítez had maintained a threatening attitude towards the company, trying to impose his points of view arrogantly, up to the point of trying to force the company to fire its principal representatives in Puerto El Triunfo. Ultimately, he is trying to undermine company authority and adminis-trative autonomy.[60]

The last point had an important historical referent: many of SIP's suc-cesses in the 1970s came precisely through the union's ability to curtail company authority at the point of production. The repression of the early 1980s had done a great deal to restore managerial authority.

Beyond the seemingly transcendent principle of managerial authority, the personalization of the strike responded to Benítez's reputation as possessing a "strong character," not given to reasoned compromise and to his *caudillo*-like qualities: virility and defiance. The Embassy con-sidered him to be "erratic and difficult."[61] An Embassy source claimed

---

[59] The La Carrera cooperative had a heavy military presence on it. In February 1986, the FMLN attacked the cotton-processing plant on the hacienda. They killed or wounded 40 troops and caused 3.8 million colones worth of damage to the cotton crop. Irene Sánchez Ramos, "El Salvador, 1986: El carácter global de la contrainsurgencia," in *El Salvador: proceso político y guerra*, Cuaderno de Divulgación, no. 4 (San Salvador: Centro de Investigación y Acción, 1987), 64.

[60] "Posición de Pezca S.A. frente a la huelga ilegal promovida por el Sr. Mauricio Ascención Benítez," Jan. 21, 1985 (AAL).

[61] US Embassy to Secretary of State, "End May Be Near for 186 Day Strike," July 1985, 08542 (obtained under the Freedom of Information Act from US Department of State);

that the Pezca management "hated Benitez" and wanted to see him "finished as a labor leader."[62]

Mena Lagos considered Benítez as mentally unstable – a view he conveyed to the US Embassy. He also considered the union leader as "corrupt" and a "Mafioso."[63] Most directly, the Pezca president feared that the Sindicato Agua leader would derail his project to rationalize shrimp production. Indeed, he considered that the strike was fundamentally a response to Mena Lagos's incentive program to combat illegal sales. From the company president's perspective, Sindicato Agua's push for expropriation and for the cooperative were simply an extension of Benítez's gangsterism. The illegal sales were, in a sense, a proto-cooperative, appropriating a significant share of Pezca's wealth. Short of expropriation, Mena Lagos recognized that Sindicato Agua's fundamental goal was to eliminate SIP, thereby gaining a stronger position to contest power relations in Pezca. Much to the consternation of the US Embassy, Mena Lagos favored relations with the "Marxist" SIP because they behaved like "professionals," a rational, bread-and-butter union, weighing company solvency as they argued for better pay and working conditions. From the Embassy's perspective, Mena Lagos was playing a "dangerous game," given SIP's "Marxism."

According to Mena Lagos, Sindicato Agua's intransigence aimed to bankrupt Pezca to facilitate the expropriation. In response, the company president pledged his resources to outlast Sindicato Agua, despite AIFLD's support. Pezca mobilized its business-class support to pressure the Duarte administration to intervene, as they were legally required to do, given the judicial declaration of the strike's illegality.[64] According to the US Labor Attaché, "Pezca's docks are occupied by the strikers and Mena Lagos alleges the Duarte administration will not clear the docks because it is partial to the strikers."[65] Mena Lagos's recollection of his

Ovidio Grandeño, interview with the author, Puerto el Triunfo, 2015; Ana Alvarenga, interview with the author, Puerto El Triunfo, 2016; Ruperto Torres, interview with the author, Puerto El Triunfo, 2013.

[62] US Embassy to Secretary of State, "196 Pezca Strike," Aug. 7, 1985, San Salvador, 10119, r072316z, no. C05624766, case F-2013–10925 (obtained under the Freedom of Information Act from US Department of State).

[63] Alfredo Mena Lagos, interview with the author, San Salvador, 2016.

[64] Campo Pagado, "Pezca S.A. ante las autoridades de Defensa y Seguridad Publica, de Trabajo y Economía, y ante la conciencia nacional expone," *La Prensa Gráfica,* June 25, 1985.

[65] US Embassy to Secretary of State, "No Sign of Let-Up in Four-Month Strike against El Salvador's Largest Shrimp Exporter," May 28, 1985, San Salvador, 6659, r282355z, no.

conversation with President Duarte is tinged with his political resentment against the Christian Democrats. He recalls that he did not address him as "Sr. Presidente" but rather as "Ingeniero" (Engineer). "Duarte exclaimed to me: 'This strike is because you don't pay good salaries.' I shoved a folder across the table and told him to read it. 'See, my captains earn more than your ministers!'"

Not surprisingly, the meeting was inconclusive. As the strike wore on through July making it the longest and most costly in the country's history, the Labor Ministry pushed harder for concessions from both sides.[66] The issue of the *salarios holgados* was sent to a special arbitration commission that decreed that the company would pay 30 percent of the strike days or roughly half of the amount that the union demanded. On August 1, union and management agreed to the compromise and the strike ended. Although all fired workers were rehired, the cases of the three management employees were referred to a special commission; they ultimately remained on the job.

The US Embassy labor attaché devoted time and consideration to the "longest strike in El Salvador's history." His report underscored that, as a result, the country lost US$4.5 million in export earnings, in addition to more than a quarter of a million dollars in tax revenue. The report continued,

Both Pezca and SGTIPAC [Sindicato Agua] have claimed victory. It does not appear, however, that the union gained anything by the strike. Pezca believes that it has SGTIPAC under its thumb because SGTIPAC does not have the strength to call its workers back on strike. Therefore, PEZCA does not plan to grant any significant salary concessions when the collective contract talks begin.[67]

Yet, Pezca did grant major concessions to SGTIPAC. The discrepancy between Pezca's optimism recounted in the Embassy report and the results of the negotiation a month later derives from the ascension to

C0562655, case F-2013–1010925 (obtained under the Freedom of Information Act from US Department of State).

[66] The company continued to play the two unions against each other and to emphasize the illegality of the strike (as declared by a Labor court). It attempted to maintain a positive public image as eager to negotiate, but they would not budge on any issue relating to its "authority," including a refusal to rehire 16 of the 82 fishermen whom they had fired. Given the illegality of the strike, it steadfastly refused to offer to pay "salarios holgados" (payment for strike days). May 8, 1985 (AAL).

[67] US Embassy to Secretary of State, "196 Pezca Strike," Aug. 7, 1985, San Salvador, 10119, r072316z, no. C05624766, case F-2013–10925 (obtained under the Freedom of Information Act from US Department of State).

the presidency of Rafael Escalón (to be discussed in Chapter 5). As the negotiations began, Mena Lagos resigned as president of the company. He had tired of dealing with Benítez, on the one hand, and a board of directors, on the other hand, who refused to support his modernization plans and whom the Pezca president viewed as less than loyal to the company.

Regardless of the proximate causes, the union won a guaranteed minimum salary for a *marinero* of US$30 a day (a 400 percent increase) at a time when the industrial minimum wage was US$3.00 a day (inflation had increased some 20 percent in 1985). A contentious final proviso required the payment of 80 percent of salaries when the fishing boats could not set sail on time.

Despite their substantial victory, Sindicato Agua did not achieve its objective to win representation of the plant.[68] SIP militants argued that the strike "had as its objective the destruction of our union in Pezca, S.A. but that goal was not fulfilled due to the conviction and clarity of our members."[69] At least part of that clarity was gendered. The strong majority of female union members harbored negative feelings toward the fishermen's union, at least partially rooted in their scorn for female SIP activists and in general due to their treatment of women.[70] That treatment included a marked disdain for family stability and open displays of womanizing. Moreover, as noted in the preceding text, SIP had earned the loyalty of its rank and file through its successful battles during the 1970s and its continued capacity for negotiation during the mid-1980s.

Yet, such was its commitment to work with management that rank and filers began to view SIP leadership with a degree of suspicion. In 1987, a rank-and-file insurgency led by Ana Alvarenga threw out the secretary general of the Pezca Local and several other leaders whom they accused of having "sold out" to the company. Regardless of the leftist ideological sympathies of the leadership that still made them targets of occasional death squad violence, SIP behaved like a moderate, bread-and-butter union.[71] Sindicato Agua's dramatic victory in the contract negotiations

---

[68] Dirección General de Trabajo, Oct. 30, 1985.

[69] FENASTRAS, *Memoria anual de labores, 1984–1985*, FENASTRAS, Nov. 7–8, 1985, p. 16 (CIDAI, UCA).

[70] Perhaps 20 percent of female Pezca workers were married or living with fishermen. Fewer than half of those women joined the rival union despite spousal pressure to do so.

[71] A death squad gunned down the secretary of conflicts of the Atarraya local in March 1985. The killing was related to a conflict with a company foreman. See FENASTRAS,

revealed their competency as a union and in so doing maintained their threat both to the company and to SIP. That Benítez became a member of the CGT national leadership added to his luster.

Retrospectively, we can see that the strike of 1985 created the space to reverse locally the global trend toward the casualization of labor. SIP's failure to support the cooperative plan that would have resisted casualization was a *desencuentro* I and II that derived, in part, from their failure to understand the full range of Sindicato Agua's ideology and practice that we will examine in the following section. Cold War blinders affected the leadership of both unions thus impeding their view of a common ground. Ironically, Benítez, who quite radically promoted the expropriation of the shrimp company, long a dream of port socialists, sabotaged the plan in part by consistently referring to SIP as the "subversive union."[72]

WORKING-CLASS POPULISM: CHRISTIAN DEMOCRATIC STYLE

Benítez's rhetoric and militancy appealed to the *marineros eventuales*, the most abject segment of an increasingly impoverished port population. The official national unemployment rate in 1985 was 16.9 percent with the inflation rate at 15 percent. Those rates both soared throughout the following year. Moreover, at least 1,500 war refugees arrived in the port during the 1980s exacerbating employment pressures. *Marineros eventuales* had great difficulty finding supplemental work and the rising cost of foodstuffs translated into hungry children. Whatever else may have motivated Mauricio Benítez, he related to their plight. Some of his fellow union members believe that Benítez's passion, obstinance, militancy, and commitment to the *eventuales* derived, at least in part, from his experience as a despised drunkard. "People would kick him on the street."[73] That is, he sought at once to redeem himself in society's eyes, but he also had a chip on his shoulder, a smoldering resentment that he managed to harness in the labor struggle. Something of his compelling worldview may be

---

Memoria anual de labores, 1984–1985, FENASTRAS, Nov. 7–8, 1985, p. 18 (CIDAI, UCA).

[72] Ovidio Granadeño, interview with the author, Puerto El Triunfo, July 2013.

[73] Ruperto Torres, interview with the author, Puerto el Triunfo, Feb. 2016.

gleaned from an unpublished manifesto, penned by the Sindicato Agua leaders in 1987.

Although the local leaders wrote the document, their contact with the CGT and CLAT acquainted them with progressive Christian Democratic discourse. With the qualified exception of CLAT, Latin American Christian Democrats rarely broke out of a Cold War box that impeded them from developing some of their more progressive core tenants. Throughout the hemisphere during the 1970s, leftist elements influenced by Liberation Theology had broken off from the main parties. Yet, during the 1980s, many Latin American Christian Democrats, especially trade unionists affiliated with CLAT, still promoted the "social market" and "comunitarismo" and democratic socialism in opposition to oligarchic and/or foreign-dominated capitalism. CLAT's efforts to chart a proworker, socialist course between US imperialism and "Stalinism" undoubtedly inspired Benítez.

The oligarchic Right in El Salvador, organized in the ARENA Party, viewed the Christian Democrats as an equal threat to that posed by the guerrilla Left.[74] For the hard Right, the guerrillas were ultimately the responsibility of the US and Salvadoran military. Since the 1932 massacre of some 10,000 mostly indigenous peasants, the landed elite had relied on military regimes to maintain their economic power. So, in a sense, the civil war, for them, was a continuation of their political strategy by other means. For the oligarchs, the Christian Democrats were "watermelons," green on the outside and red on the inside who severely challenged their class interests and, therefore in the words of a contemporary social scientist, ARENA opposed all measures of the Duarte government with "a profound ideological intransigence."[75] They complained to Reagan administration officials that there was no reason to defeat the FMLN if the Christian Democrats were going to be allowed to carry out their program.

In the position paper, "Posición SGTIPAC frente a la realidad que vive actualmente el país como pueblo salvadoreño" (The position of SGTIPAC

[74] See Ignacio Ellacuría, "Las organizaciones populares ante la nueva situación," in *El Salvador entre el terror y la esperanza: Los sucesos de 1979 y su impacto en el drama salvadoreño de los años siguientes*, ed. Rodolfo R. Campos (San Salvador: UCA Editores, 1982).

[75] US Embassy to Secretary of State, "196 Pezca Strike," Aug. 1985, San Salvador, 10119, r072316z, no. C05624766, case F-2013–10925 (obtained under the Freedom of Information Act from US Department of State).

faced with the reality the Salvadoran people face) replete with a myriad of orthographic errors typical of grade-school educated Salvadorans, the local leadership laid out their view of society and politics.[76] The writers venomously attacked the oligarchy, blaming the *terratenientes* for El Salvador's ills. They viewed the rise to power of the elite as a consequence largely of the illiteracy of the bulk of the rural population that allowed the small group to appropriate state lands, converting themselves into "latifundistas who exploited the land and the working class with extremely low salaries. Relatively speaking, socially, they did the same with industry, where there is much social injustice."[77] Politically, the document argued that the oligarchy depended on its alliance with the military both to maintain the unequal distribution of land and to repress workers who struggled for their rights. Similarly, the union writers signaled the land reform of 1980 as a major step toward redistributive justice. At this juncture in the document, the writers stake out new ground, veering toward what seems like fantasy:

those who made major investments to buy arms to bring into the country and using the organized sectors in clandestine organizations promoted violent revolution trying to cause a coup d'état in order to take power.[78]

The Sindicato Agua writers posited an alliance between the FMLN and the oligarchy that would allow the elite to recover its land. They "manipulated the revolutionary leaders so that they would boycott the haciendas taken over by the agrarian reform, burning coffee and cotton plantations, and harvests. They also burned factories, manipulating the labor movement, all in order to obstruct the revolutionary movement."[79] In fact, in 1986, FMLN guerrillas had destroyed more than US$600,000 worth of cotton in an assault on the neighboring "la

---

[76] The orthography strongly suggests that José Luis Grande Preza was not involved in drafting the handwritten document. Located in SGTIPAC archive.

　　Jorge Cáceres Prendes, "Estado, sociedad y política de un contexto de insurgencia popular: El Salvador 1980–1987," *Anuario de Estudios Centroamericano* 14, nos. 1–2 (1988): 38.

[77] "Posición SGTIPAC frente a la realidad que vive actualmente el país como pueblo salvadoreño," 1987 (SGTIPAC Archives).

[78] "[L]os que isieron grandes inverciones para comprar armas para introducirlas en el país, y usando sectores organisados en organisaciones clandestinas impulsaron la rebolucion com mas auge biolento; buscando con esto el golpe de estado que les permitiera yebar a poder." Ibid., 2.

[79] Ibid., 3.

Carrera" hacienda, expropriated from Pezca owner Juan Wright and organized in a cooperative.[80]

Here the Sindicato Agua militants portray themselves as the true revolutionaries. They present a *sui generis* form of anti-communism; its emphasis is on class, rather than patriotic betrayal. The Sindicato Agua statement also outlines an original form of populist discourse that helps to explain strong support among the *eventuales* and other sectors of the port population.

Working class–inflected populism bursts through the text on every line, situating a popular bloc composed of campesinos and workers against the oligarchy, allied with sectors of the military. At the same time, however, the union militants transform the discourse of the "two devils," "the two extremes," or "between two fires." The continent-wide discourse held that the extreme Left and the extreme Right were equally guilty for the widespread violence and massive human rights abuses of the 1970s and 1980s. In this local version, the extreme Left and extreme Right worked in concert to thwart the fundamental reforms – financial and agrarian – that the Christian Democratic–backed junta had enacted and that the country needed so desperately.

Although the union writers offer no empirical evidence to support their claim of an oligarchic-FMLN alliance, their insistence warrants attention precisely because it speaks to a discursive space that scholars and activists have not acknowledged. It is a position that does seem absurd: the revolutionary Left and the oligarchy were locked in deadly combat. To the Sindicato Agua militants, however, there was abundant evidence of the alliance starting with the implacable and vitriolic opposition of both the Left and the Right to the Christian Democratic government. Of course, the hostility of the right-wing press to the 1985 strike and its apparent sympathy for SIP added to the local credibility of the argument. Similarly, Mena Lagos's palpable support for SIP despite (or, in Sindicato Agua's eyes, because of) his identification with the "derecha recalcitrante" (recalcitrant Right) offered further evidence of the alliance. The "patronalismo" (the pro-company actions) of the SIP leadership further put into question the sincerity of the Left. Even more damning, in 1986 Roberto D'Aubuisson claimed that the leftist Unión Nacional de Trabajadores Salvadoreños (UNTS) was more democratic than the Unión Nacional de Obreros y Campesinos (UNOC),

---

[80] Sánchez Ramos, "El Salvador, 1986: El carácter global de la contrainsurgencia," 64.

the pro-Duarte labor confederation to which Sindicato Agua belonged. Finally, the aforementioned guerrilla attack on a cooperative built on Wright's former hacienda, but a few miles away, drove the point home.[81] Every act of revolutionary sabotage against the land reform, transportation, or industrial production, in the eyes of Sindicato Agua, bespoke clear links between the FMLN and the Right. The establishment of a key premise made this position plausible. The structural reforms were necessary to bring social justice to the country and the Left had long promoted the very same reforms. Therefore, its hostile opposition could only indicate betrayal through an opportunistic alliance with the oligarchy.

The Left viewed the government of Duarte as its primary antagonist. The FMLN promoted resistance to the structural reforms out of suspicion over their counterinsurgent goals and their militaristic implementation. The Left's rejection of cooperatives flowed from its strategic opposition. However, there was a serious cost to that position and its accompanying *desencuentros*. Hundreds of thousands of campesinos either joined the cooperatives or expected to benefit from the land reform. Though mismanaged, at times militarized, and usually underfunded, the cooperatives still stood as an attractive option for the landless. The Sindicato Agua document naturally scorns the leftist opposition but, at the same time, silences the counterinsurgent aspect of the land reform along with the role of the United States in the country's affairs. After removing the highly consequential US political and military intervention from the discourse, the union's manifesto becomes a coherent call for labor rights and redistributive justice. Those goals appealed to the port rank and file of both unions. Yet, everyday gender relations, *la movida*, and Cold War–inspired political invective impeded an understanding let alone an alliance between the leaders of Tierra and Agua. This, indeed, was a fundamental *desencuentro* with devastating local consequences. Two unions shared fundamental goals of a dignified life for their members, yet they could not join forces to save their livelihood.

The eventual arrival of tropical deindustrialization to Puerto El Triunfo was a complex and contradictory process involving Cold War policies, harsh gender relations, *la movida*, and different forms of corruption. As we shall see in Chapter 5, a massive bank fraud perpetrated by

---

[81] Ernesto Cruz, "Crónica del mes, marzo–abril," *Estudios Centroamericanos* 450 (Apr. 1986): 342.

owners of Pezca S.A. directly contributed to the collapse of the shrimp industry and mass unemployment in the port. And yet the bitterness and anger are reserved for the fishermen and their union; the fraud merits but rare mention in the recollections of the packinghouse workers. This harbinger of neoliberalism – the crudest form of financialization of formerly productive activities – remains submerged beneath the chasm that at once caused and symbolized the onset of neoliberal social relations, in particular the rupture of bonds of solidarity. Following the highly consequential repression of 1980–81 that rupture occurred largely independently of the violent repression that operated throughout the country over the next few years.[82]

Today, the threat of violence again permeates the port. Not death squads but gang youths symbolize that fear. Until very recently, an internecine struggle among subaltern youths replaced the workers' struggle. Calle 18 and their MS-13 rivals for years have engaged in frequent gun battles over turf, recreating in a horribly distorted and fashion the divisions that wrought Puerto El Triunfo in the 1980s. The Right, the bankers, and the owners wreaked their havoc, but largely behind closed, wood-paneled doors or through invisible, ghost accounts and untraceable wire transfers. Today, the military occasionally patrols the streets to protect the port residents from gang violence. Ovidio views those soldiers with deep ambivalence. The army had broken into his rancho in 1979, ready to kill him and his family. In 1981, they surrounded his house day and night. The new presence of the military reenacts a tragedy; it is certainly no farce.

---

[82] David Harvey's concept of "accumulation by dispossession" is also useful to understand this global phenomenon. See David Harvey, *A Brief History of Neoliberalism* (New York: Oxford University Press, 2005).

5

The Far Right and Fraud

For three years The Reagan Administration has pretended that it did not
know that death squads and military butchery are intrinsic features of the
government and military of El Salvador. For three years, the administration
has known the names and involvement of wealthy Salvadoran exiles living
in Miami, Florida, who organize, fund, and direct right wing death squads.

Robert White, US Ambassador to El Salvador, 1980–81

The uneven geographical development of neoliberalism, its frequently
partial and lop-sided application from one state and social formation to
another, testifies to the tentativeness of neoliberal solutions and the complex
ways in which political forces, historical traditions, and existing institutional arrangements all shaped why and how the process of neoliberaliza-
tion actually occurred.

David Harvey, *A Brief History of Neoliberalism*

Even before his graduation from Menlo College in California in 1974,
Alfredo Mena Lagos became active in his family businesses. In 1973, he
was on the board of directors of Pesquera del Pacífico, one of the fishing
companies tied to Pezca, of which his father was president. The following
year he returned to El Salvador and continued to work in the company.
He also developed friendships with right-wing political figures including
the famous General Jose Alberto Medrano, the founder of Organización
Democrática Nacional (ORDEN), an organization that, by the late 1970s,
became a 100,000-member-strong paramilitary organization based in the
countryside.

As the Sandinista Revolution gathered momentum, Mena Lagos, along
with fellow rightists, increasingly feared the triumph of the revolutionary

Left in his country. He also recognized the corruption and inefficiency of the military regime. Joining forces with some friends including future president Armando Calderón Sol, he co-founded the Movimiento Nacionalista Salvadoreño (MNS). This political group planned to stage a *coup d'état* to install a government that would deal with the Left implacably and efficiently. Around the same time, Roberto D'Aubuisson, the second in command of the intelligence agency, Asociación Nacional de Seguridad de El Salvador (ANSESAL), approached the president, General Romero with a plan for what amounted to a coup to push the military into an even harder-line stance against labor and the Left. When General Romero rebuffed him, D'Aubuisson approached Mena Lagos. As the latter recounts:

We were very annoyed with the military due to their inability to contain the subversión, whom we saw becoming bolder by the day. Thus, when D'Aubuisson came to my house to explain his disagreements with his superiors and his support for our political movement, I had no confidence in him.[1]

Mena Lagos asked Major D'Aubuisson for proof of his loyalty.[2] Following the October 15 coup, D'Aubuisson brought the proof: a cache of secret documents that he and his partner Fernando "el Negro" Sagrero had taken from the ANSESAL archive. Those documents were largely reports on "subversives" and opponents of the Right. Mena Lagos and D'Aubuisson were both convinced of the leftist sympathies of the new government and recognized the need for decisive action. The MNS operated on at least two fronts: the political and the military. The most famous target of D'Aubuisson's death squads was Monseñor Oscar Romero, gunned down March 24, 1980.[3] For the far Right, the archbishop, "the voice of the voiceless," and an implacable foe of violent repression, was a dangerous communist. The MNS (subsequently transformed into the Frente Amplio Nacional – FAN) and some military officers conspired to overthrow the Junta Revolucionaria de Gobierno (JRG). In May 1980, Colonel Adolfo Majano, a member of the second Junta Revolucionaria

---

[1] Geovani Galeas, "Roberto D'Aubuisson, un hombre derrotado," *El Salvador Times*, Oct. 13, 2016.

[2] Ibid.

[3] See Matt Eisenbrandt, *Assassination of a Saint: The Plot to Murder Óscar Romero and the Quest to Bring His Killers to Justice* (Berkeley: University of California Press, 2017), 158. Although US government reports alleged Mena Lagos's links with death squads, there is no evidence of his connection to the Romero assassination. Ibid.

(military-Christian Democrats) ordered a military raid on Finca San Luis (owned by the Guirola family) where D'Aubuisson and some 25 active and retired military were attending a meeting cum fiesta. The raid uncovered documents that linked, but without conclusive proof, D'Aubuisson and Alvaro Saravia to the assassination of Romero. Mena Lagos's name also appeared along with others apparently connected to the conspiracy.[4] They also uncovered evidence of a plot to overthrow the JRG. Although the arrests might have led to the weakening of the extreme Right, even the moderate military leaders were appalled at Majano's move against active officers.[5] In addition to key elements of the armed forces, the far Right organized effectively against the arrests and within a week the charges were dropped. D'Aubuisson, Mena Lagos and other members of the FAN relocated to Guatemala. Within two years, Mena Lagos returned to El Salvador.

Although Mena Lagos had no regrets about his participation in the FAN, he transitioned away from a full-time political commitment. In 1982, the board of directors of Pezca S.A. appointed him to the presidency. He thus became one of the youngest presidents of a major company in the country's history.

Through no fault of Mena Lagos, during his tenure, the company suffered what David Harvey has called "accumulation by dispossession." Harvey argues that the main achievement of neoliberalism has been to redistribute wealth toward elites and "dispossession" has been the "main mechanism" to achieve this goal. He cites four of its key features: privatization and commodification; financialization; management and manipulation of crises; and state redistributions. With respect to financialization, Harvey writes: "Deregulation allowed the financial system to become one of the main centres of redistributive activity through speculation, predation, fraud, and thievery."[6] For Harvey, "[T]he most devastating of all [practices has been] the use of the credit system as a radical means of accumulation by

---

[4] At some point, Robert White suggested the connection between the diary of Alvaro Saravia, who was definitely connected to the plot, and D'Aubuisson because the diary appeared on the stationary of Mariscos Tazumal, a company founded by D'Aubuisson and Fernando "El Negro" Sagrera. And copies show an image of the ruins of Tazumal, the archaeological site. As a US official pointed out later, however, the company was founded in 1982 and that assertion seems to be correct. There is little doubt that, despite the mistake, D'Aubuisson was linked to the diary and the plot. Of course, he probably liked the patriotic symbolism of Tazumal.

[5] José Napoleón Duarte, *Duarte: My Story* (New York: Putnam, 1986), 126; Eisenbrandt, *Assassination of a Saint*, 6.

[6] David Harvey, *A Brief History of Neoliberalism* (New York: Oxford University Press, 2005), 161.

dispossession."[7] This chapter will explore this striking but virtually illegible form of accumulation in Puerto El Triunfo, a key component of the triumph of neoliberalism in the port and beyond.[8] At the same time, we will continue our discussion of the shrimp company owners outlined in the introduction of this book.

Despite the far Right opposition, in early March 1980, the second JRG carried out land and financial reforms that directly affected the shrimp and plantation owners, many of whom were part of the oligarchy and related to one another. Juan Wright Alcaine, the principle stockholder in Pezca, was also the owner of la Carrera, a 7,000-acre cotton plantation, the largest in the country, near Puerto El Triunfo. The Wright family, originally from San Francisco, California, was intermarried with the de Sola family, one of the original "14 families." Roberto Daglio, a similarly prominent member of the old oligarchy, was the owner of Atarraya S.A. as well as important coffee plantations. Rafael Guirola's oligarchic family owned Mariscos de El Salvador and San Rafael (in La Unión). Roberto Mathies Regalado, another major stockholder in Pezca, a graduate of Georgetown, similarly belonged to an oligarchic coffee family. The land and banking reforms of March 1980 directly affected all five families; La Carrera, the cotton plantation, became a peasant-owned cooperative.

All the families supported far Right politics. In 1971, a nascent guerrilla group, the ERP, had executed Ernesto Regalado Dueñas in a botched kidnapping. Not surprisingly, his nephew, Roberto Mathies Regalado, 46, eagerly supported the FAN and its paramilitary operations. The owner of a Volkswagen dealership, he donated a Passat to D'Aubuisson's group; the car carried Monseñor Romero's assassin to the church where he was conducting mass.[9] Following the reforms, the Wright and Daglio families relocated to Miami, citing the threat of kidnappings. Miami also provided a safe haven for De Sola, Mathies Regalado, and other elite families. They formed part of the nucleus of what would become the Alianza Republicana Nacionalista (ARENA) Party.

In January 1981, a cable from the US Embassy in El Salvador to the Secretary of State cited an interview with an exiled lawyer who reported the existence of the Miami Six – a group of millionaires who actively supported death squads, threatening and cajoling other Salvadoran

---

[7] Ibid., 159.
[8] See introduction to Carlota McAllister and Diane M. Nelson, eds., *War by Other Means: Aftermath in Post-Genocide Guatemala* (Durham, NC: Duke University Press, 2013).
[9] Eisenbrandt, *Assassination of a Saint*, 86.

millionaires to support the rightist cause. Specifically, they promised to execute anyone who collaborated at all with the Junta Revolucionaria and intimidated those who kept open their businesses. They aimed to destabilize the JRG and, if necessary, to eliminate "hundreds of thousands of Salvadorans suspected of liberal or leftist sympathies."[10] The cable stated that the "[Miami Six] organize, fund, and direct death squads through their agent, Roberto D'Aubuisson."[11] According to the Embassy source, over the previous year, the six exiles often summoned Salvadoran businessmen to Miami, sat them at a long table, and then threatened them with death or kidnapping if they continued to collaborate with the government.[12] Roberto Daglio was one of the Miami Six. The owner of Atarraya had business and personal ties to Juan Wright. The report also identified investors in Atarraya, Juan and Ricardo Salaverría, as among the six.

According to the testimony of former Ambassador Robert White in 1984 in front of a House Foreign Affairs subcommittee, "[O]ver the last three years, the Reagan Administration has suppressed the facts" about the Miami Six.[13] White bore particular animus toward the Reagan administration as Secretary of State Alexander Haig had him not only dismissed as ambassador but also drummed out of the foreign service for his refusal to whitewash the Salvadoran government's failure to investigate the rape and assassination of three American nuns and a religious worker in December 1980. The Reagan administration's excuse for failing to investigate the Miami Six was that the Embassy had lost contact with the key informants who had furnished the information about the death squad financiers.[14]

Under considerable congressional pressure, the CIA and the State Department apparently began a joint investigation of death squads in January 1983. In November, at the prompting of the State Department, the FBI began to investigate the Miami connection. The Embassy furnished the FBI with an expanded list of 29 individuals, residing in Miami, who supplied funding to death squads. Four of the 29 reputed death squad financiers had important connections to the shrimp industry: Roberto Daglio, Alfredo Mena Lagos, Roberto Mathies Regalado, and

[10] US Embassy to Secretary of State, "Millionaires Murder Inc.?," cable, Jan. 6, 1981, "El Salvador: The Making of U.S. Policy, 1977–1984" collection, ES01131, p. 3 (DNSA, George Washington University, Washington, DC).
[11] Ibid., 2.
[12] Joel Brinkley, "Ex-Envoy Accuses 6 Salvadoran Exiles," *New York Times*, Feb. 3, 1984.
[13] Ibid.   [14] *New York Times*, Feb. 7, 1984.

Juan T. Wright.[15] Newspaper reports, however, did not discuss the expanded list and only referred to the Miami Six. Those individuals all rejected the charges. Daglio, for example, suggested that the claims were merely veiled political attacks against President Reagan. That White had misidentified one of the six did not help his credibility.[16]

The FBI investigation was not thorough.[17] Agents interviewed 33 individuals, including 13 State Department employees and 2 US Army officers. The FBI only interviewed 3 of the 29 Salvadorans cited for funding death squads. Their document – most of the reports on interviews with Salvadorans were redacted – concluded: "None of the various people interviewed could furnish evidence or first-hand knowledge of persons in the U.S. furnishing any type of support or direction to the Salvadoran death squads."[18] Given this conclusion, not surprisingly, there were no indictments.

Several factors probably affected the investigation. First, given the FBI's past apathy with regard to the activities of the extreme Right, the Reagan administration most likely did not signal great interest. Second, the FBI was devoting significant resources toward investigating and harassing American solidarity activists who opposed US policy in Central America, primarily those in the Committee in Solidarity with the People of El Salvador (CISPES). Ambassador White stressed that the administration sat on documents that strongly implicated D'Aubuisson in the assassination of Archbishop Romero, due to his position as president of the Constituent Assembly from 1982 to 1983. Third, it would have been extremely difficult to separate the legitimate financing of the ARENA Party (founded in 1981) from those of death squads, connected, however loosely, to the party. Finally, the wave of death squad assassinations had diminished significantly by late 1983 when the FBI began its

---

[15] Federal Bureau of Investigation, "Furnishing Funds and Weapons to Salvadoran Death," cable, Dec. 9, 1983, EL01373, "El Salvador: War, Peace, and Human Rights, 1980–1994" collection, p. 2 (DNSA). In the response of the Miami Six to White's charges, Julio Salaverría claimed that the former ambassador had to be referring to someone else, and that his brother Juan Ricardo had died in a car accident in 1982. Three Salaverria's (including one whose name must be wrong) appear in the list of 29. See AP story, "Salvadoran Rebuts Charge of Death-Squad Link," *New York Times*, Feb. 7, 1984.

[16] Eisenbrandt, *Assassination of a Saint*, 89.

[17] Federal Bureau of Investigation, "Unknown Subjects; Furnishing Funds and Weapons to Salvadoran Death Squads in El Salvador," cable, May 15, 1984, EL01374, "El Salvador: War, Peace, and Human Rights, 1980–1994" collection, p. 24 (DNSA).

[18] Ibid., 4.

investigations. Thus, the few Salvadoran witnesses whom the FBI interviewed might have spoken truthfully in the present tense about their lack of knowledge of death squads.

A STENCH OF CORRUPTION

The FBI cable that listed the 29 individuals also stated that on November 23, 1983, "A visa had been granted to Roberto D'Aubuisson to visit the United States. D'Aubuisson planned to visit Rafael Escalón over the Thanksgiving holidays and weekends. This information was furnished due to the allegations that D'Aubuisson was closely connected to the right-wing death squads in El Salvador."[19] That D'Aubuisson had such an important governmental position surely made US authorities wary of attacking him publicly and probably induced the curious use of "allegations." The document also signaled the friendship between Rafael Escalón and the death squad chieftain cum founder of ARENA and president of the Constituent Assembly.

The scion of a once-prominent oligarchic family, Escalón had owned and managed coffee plantations, but he was not wealthy by elite standards. During the early 1980s, he became general manager of Atarraya S.A. His marriage to the daughter of Juan Wright solidified his social, if not economic, standing. By 1984, at age 42, he was moving back and forth between Miami, San Salvador, and Puerto El Triunfo. The FBI report on their interview with Escalón is quite revealing, despite the redaction of key phrases. He fervently defended someone – most likely Bobby Daglio – from the charge of financing death squads. Previously Escalón had worked for Daglio's coffee operations. He had known him for 25 years and "remained extremely close." In support of his friend, Escalón also cast doubt about the existence of death squads because "the hate between classes that is now prevalent has generated the killings in a random fashion without any organization directing the murders ... [redacted] believes that the communists both in El Salvador and throughout the world have originated the idea of death squads."[20]

Escalón further remarked that he traveled between "El Salvador and the United States approximately every two weeks specifically on business ... he had to return to El Salvador to try to counteract the

---

[19] According to an informant, D'Aubuisson, in fact, stayed with Escalón on his visits to Miami. Ibid., 3.

[20] The inclusion of Escalon's name as the interview subject was clearly an oversight by the redactors, given that his name is redacted in the text. Ibid., 66.

individuals who are stealing [redacted] and causing the company heavy losses."[21] Shifting gears, from the difficult state of affairs in the port, Escalón mentioned his active support for D'Aubuisson's presidential campaign, assuring the FBI that his support only took place in El Salvador. The interview occurred shortly before the ARENA leader's second-round electoral loss.

In addition to Escalón, D'Aubuisson had strong ties to Bobby Daglio. Those ties became stronger in 1982. The Latin American branch of the World Anti-Communist Federation, based in Guadalajara, Mexico, helped to finance D'Aubuisson's purchase of eight shrimp fishing boats and the founding of Mariscos Tazumal S.A.[22] Apparently, Daglio also helped to finance the purchase. Atarraya, owned by Daglio and managed by Escalón, processed the shrimp. Both companies had offices in the same building in San Salvador. D'Aubuisson's friend "El Negro" Sagrera, similarly linked to the far Right, also worked in Mariscos Tazumal throughout the 1980s.

Escalón managed Mariscos Tazumal until Lieutenant Carlos "Sandi" Zacapa took over in 1984.[23] They worked closely together. Sandi Zacapa was executive officer of the Cavalry Regiment of the armed forces. From 1982 until 1986, Zacapa and his uncle, Colonel Joaquin Zacapa, while continuing to foment death squad activity, operated a kidnapping ring on the side. Disguised as FMLN guerrillas, they kidnapped and extorted wealthy Salvadorans, often fellow members of ARENA.[24] In 1988, Mariscos Tazumal briefly made the news: its letterhead appeared in a compromising fax that sought to oppose extradition of Saravia from Miami where he was being held. Presumably, D'Aubuisson and others feared a trial in El Salvador that might reveal facets of the Romero assassination that they wished to remain buried. US Ambassador William Walker commented to his superiors in the State Department: "[the fax] clearly links the Saravia defense with an entire realm of coup plotters,

---

[21] Ibid., 67.

[22] *Diario Oficial*, Mar. 15, 1983. Alvaro Marín, Daglio's legal representative was granted a fishing license for *Mariscos Tazumal*, on Mar. 9, 1983. He requested the license on November 26, 1982.

[23] *Diario Oficial*, May 17, 1984, 40. Zacapa is listed as the *apoderado general* of Mariscos Tazumal.

[24] The threat was that the military appeared reticent to move against members of la Tandona (the graduating class of 1966). US Embassy to Secretary of State, "Kidnapping Case Threatens Duarte Government," cable, Apr. 2, 1986, EL00907, "El Salvador: War, Peace, and Human Rights, 1980–1994" collection, p. 4 (DNSA).

death squad chiefs, kidnappers, baby robbers, mad bombers, car thieves and assorted other criminals."[25]

The shrimp industry's far Right connections extended to the employment of Alvaro Saravia as head of security at Atarraya. Saravia had worked closely with D'Aubuisson and had participated in the plot to assassinate Monseñor Romero.[26] During his brief stint at Atarraya, he was able to become financially solvent as Daglio allowed him to stay at his home (modeled on a castle) in San Salvador. Unfortunately, Saravia had a drinking problem that eventually led to him losing his job and his family.

Despite their powerful presence in Salvadoran politics, the far Right militants had little impact on port society. The military, however, did have major influence, in particular, in Atarraya, where SIP operated within the parameters set by the silent partners of the rightist owners.[27] And, as mentioned previously, high-level military officers were deeply implicated in "*la movida.*"

D'Aubuisson, Sagrera, and Saravia arrived after the wave of death squad threats and assassinations was over. Moreover, they spent relatively little time in the port and, of course, people were wary of them. Ricardo Jovel, SIP leader, recalls a curious encounter.

I was working on a problem in Pezca, when someone came up to me and told me that Major D'Aubuisson wanted to meet with me. I took my time as I had a lot of work to do with our members. When I finished, I went over to the company pool. He was in the water with a drink in his hand. El Negro Sagrera was standing outside of the pool, with a submachine gun in his hand. "So you're Ricardo Jovel ... why didn't you want to come here and meet with me?"

"Well I had a lot work I had to finish."

"I've heard a lot about you. Good things people say. I just wanted to get to know you. Do you want a drink?"

"No sir," I responded, "I don't drink."

"So do you like women?"

"Well sure I do."

"Let me see what I can do."

"Well thanks but right now I still have work to do."[28]

[25] US Embassy to Secretary of State, "The Saravia Extradition and the D'Aubuisson Mafia," cable, Oct. 3, 1988, EL00969, "El Salvador: War, Peace, and Human Rights, 1980–1994" collection (DNSA).

[26] Carlos Dada, "Así matamos a monseñor Romero," *El Faro*, Mar. 22, 2010.

[27] See Joel Millman, "El Salvador's Army: A Force unto Itself," *New York Times Magazine*, Dec. 10, 1989. He also recounts the long-standing practice of shrimp companies making payments to military officers for "protection."

[28] Ricardo Jovel, interview with the author, San Salvador, 2014.

This exchange reveals little except perhaps for D'Aubuisson's mundane exercise of power. He didn't have an active role in Mariscos Tazumal or in Pezca. And yet, he wanted Jovel to at least realize that he was under surveillance. Perhaps D'Aubuisson was also reminding Jovel of his power drawing a distinction between his role in the early 1980s when he could easily have had Jovel executed for working with Federación Nacional Sindical de Trabajadores Salvadoreños (FENASTRAS) and affirming his current role as a prominent politician cum businessman. Or, he hinted at both roles. Rather than a gesture of bribery, the offer to procure a woman spoke more to the common language of machismo and the status of women as perks to be conferred.

It is not entirely clear whether Mariscos Tazumal financed the paramilitary and/or political activities of ARENA or simply supplemented the income of D'Aubuisson, Sagrera, and Zacapa. Some allege that they might have engaged in the cocaine trade. Indeed, the relation of rightist politics and port social and economic activity is not very legible. Mena Lagos, president of Pezca from 1982 to 1985, as we have seen had been deeply involved in politics and had worked closely with D'Aubuisson. Notwithstanding his rightist political identification, he did not engage in especially authoritarian labor relations in Puerto El Triunfo. As revealed in Chapter 4, Mena Lagos preferred working with the leftist-led SIP much more than with the Christian Democratic–affiliated SGTIPAC. Despite their political differences, SIP rank-and-file leaders remember him somewhat fondly as an honest and reasonable boss.[29]

Rafael "Lito" Escalón fit this pattern of semi-benign management as well. Despite his far Right ties, he was not a particularly autocratic general manager.[30] As noted in the FBI report, however, he was, like Mena Lagos, very concerned about "*la movida*." Apparently in response to the practice of illegal shrimp sales, Escalón promoted a new system whereby Atarraya rented the fishing boats directly to the captains who received an advance from the company for all expenses. The captains then sold the product to the company at market prices, thereby recouping their rent and paying back the expenses. Under such a system, there was less incentive to sell on the high seas as the captains' self-interest militated against *la movida*. As a secondary benefit for the company, the new system would seriously debilitate the union because the captain would

---

[29] Similarly, despite Bobby Daglio's ownership and the brief role of Saravia, there was nothing especially repressive about Atarraya's management.

[30] However, Rolando Franco, SIP leader in the 1980s, recalls a well-connected port resident informing him that Lito Escalón had placed a hit on him.

become an employer and the five-member crew would be impeded from functioning as a union. In the case of Atarraya, Sindicato Tierra seems to have accepted the arrangement without much opposition in part because it seemed to guarantee more production even if it meant losing union members among the *marineros*.

THE BIGGEST FRAUD IN HISTORY

In March 1985, Rafael Escalón made a momentous decision that affected not only his own life but also moreover that of the shrimp industry. During the early stages of the Sindicato Agua strike, Escalón, still the general manager of Atarraya, forged a deal with his father-in-law Juan Wright, the principal stockholder of Pezca S.A. to defraud the Banco Agrícola Comercial (BAC) of more than US$20 million. They worked with Rafael Tomás Carbonell, president of the nationalized bank, to facilitate the loans. Politically, Carbonell and Escalón were far apart, as the former was tied to the Duarte government, yet they clearly saw a splendid business opportunity.[31]

What were the conditions of possibility for Escalón's daring move? It is hard to imagine that when Escalón formed business partnerships with Sandi Zacapa he was unaware of his criminal activities, and it is equally hard to imagine that such an association had no effect on his moral fiber. The idea of taking over the largest shrimp company in Central America appealed to him but the task surely seemed daunting. As noted previously, Escalón was extremely frustrated with the illegal sales of shrimp on the high seas and could not be sure he could contain them at Pezca. Moreover, he probably shared Mena Lagos's extremely negative view of the Sindicato Agua's leader Mauricio Benítez (and his mental stability) and was unsure how he could deal with him, given his Christian Democratic allies in high places. By taking over Pezca and defrauding the bank, Escalón could potentially partake in some very rich cake and eat it too. He could run a major company, reach some kind of *modus vivendi* with the fishermen, while possibly siphoning millions into private accounts.

Politics also shaped the fraud. As noted earlier in the chapter, both Wright and Escalón were deeply enmeshed in the rightist ARENA Party and were closely aligned with the agro-financial sector of the oligarchy. They bitterly opposed the structural reforms promoted by Duarte and the

---

[31] He was the brother-in-law of Antonio Morales Ehrlich, prominent Christian Democratic politician and mayor of San Salvador (1974–76 and 1985–88).

military in 1980 that included the nationalization of the banking industry and the land reform that affected all of the shrimp company owners. Indeed, a very small group of businessmen defaulted or fell in arrears on loans – more than US$150 million, representing 243 percent of the total capital and bank reserves.[32] There is anecdotal evidence to suggest that some of these "debtors" refused to pay back loans as form of political pay back, debilitating a pillar of Duarte's program.[33]

Although the specific financial dealings between Carbonell and Escalón are unclear, the BAC director unilaterally approved 57 million colones (more than US$10 million) of loans to 13 dummy (or "straw") corporations between March and November 1985. Later, BAC made loans to five Pezca subsidiaries (fishing companies) under similar conditions. In October 1985, the bank made an additional loan of 5 million colones to Pezca, by then under Escalón's control. By the end of the year, the BAC had loaned 87 million colones (roughly US$16 million) to enterprises in which Escalón had a significant role. Ultimately, Escalón and his cohorts swindled the bank for approximately 140 million colones.[34] Carbonell approved the loans unilaterally on the same day (or the following day) that they were requested, thereby infringing prescribed national banking rules. Regardless of any other charges, Carbonell's infraction was never in doubt and he would be charged with "fraud against the public economy." He left the country as soon as the BAC fired him in May 1987.

The fraud was meticulously planned. Escalón often used accountants and other lower-level employees to sign loan applications as owners. At times, he told them that he could not sign, due to "security measures," an excuse that resonated in wartime.[35] In one case he promised an employee 10 percent of the profits that, of course, would never be realized. In another

[32] "El sistema financiero de El Salvador: Análisis y perspectivas," *Cuadernos de Investigación* (San Salvador: Centro de Investigaciones Tecnológicas y Científicas [CENITEC], May 1989).

[33] Licenciada Ivette Bará recalls that bank officials were threatened with violence by the extreme Right when they tried to push for loan repayment. Ivette Bará, communication with the author, 2017.

[34] Information on the case has been gleaned from several thousands of pages of reports of a judicial investigation, found in the archives of the Second Criminal Court. Also see, *Los Angeles Times*, July 26, 1991. At the official 1985 rate, the loans were worth US$56 million and at the official rate of 1986 they would have been worth US$28 million dollars. Over the next year, those corporations, under the nominal directorship of low-level employees, secured loans from the BAC for some 140 million colones.

[35] Testimony of Victor Pineda, Apr. 1989, Pieza 53, p. 3 (Juzgado Segundo de lo Penal, Corte Suprema de Justicia, San Salvador).

case, he persuaded an insurance agent who had long managed the Atarraya account to sign the loan request for a dummy corporation. Escalón approached the agent, hinting that he would need a policy for new boat licenses. The agent signed as director of the company because he assumed that favor would get him the fishing boat account and that his signature "did not implicate him in anything." Later, Escalón informed the gullible agent that he had purchased an insurance company and could not offer the account to the agent.[36]

To legitimate the new companies, Escalón presented photocopies of checks for 100,000 colones that purported to represent their social capital. He and his confrères alternatively never placed the money in the corporations or at other times immediately withdrew the funds and deposited them in Escalón's accounts. After receiving the millions in loans, he then exchanged most of the colones on the black market. In one instance, he turned a 5 million colones loan into US$800,000 that reportedly ended up in his bank account in Miami.

At least once, Escalón relied on Juan Wright Alcaine for a loan signatory. Otherwise, Wright removed himself from any association with the deal. In August 1985, Wright called up Margarita Najarro de Rivera, who had worked for his family since 1955. When Wright departed for Miami in March 1980, Najarro de Rivera was left in charge of his businesses as his legal representative.[37] From Miami, he informed her that Rafael Escalón would show up at her office. Four days later Escalón did appear in her office and presented her with various documents to sign. She signed them, each requesting 5 million colones loans from the BAC. When Najarro realized that she appeared as legal representative of various straw corporations, about which she had no knowledge, she asked Escalón to explain. He replied, "I thought Don Juan had told you about this."[38] She dutifully signed.

Regardless of the origins of the loan, Escalón's financial operations were not entirely illegitimate. He and others used 33 million colones toward the purchase of Pezca S.A. stock. By October 1985, Escalón had become president of the board of directors of the company, replacing Mena Lagos.

[36] Testimony of Jose Roberto Imberton, 1989, Pieza 53, 7263 (Juzgado Segundo de lo Penal).

[37] Unidad Ejecutiva de la Comisión de Investigaciones de Hechos Delictivos, "Unidad de investigaciones de la Unidad Ejecutiva de la Comisión de Investigaciones de Hechos Delictivos," report, May 3, 1989, Pieza 54, 10631 (Juzgado Segundo de lo Penal).

[38] Ibid.

Escalón's route to the presidency of Pezca S.A. hinged on the BAC loans and on the backing of Wright. He also relied, in part, on the support of Sandi Zacapa and D'Aubuisson, who shifted the operations of *Mariscos Tazumal* over to Pezca, which began to process its shrimp catch. That move apparently annoyed Bobby Daglio (reputed by the CIA to be hotheaded), who fired Escalón from his position as general manager of Atarraya. That said, even as energetic a man as Escalón might have had trouble running two large companies. Zacapa, D'Aubuisson, and Sagrera allowed Mariscos Tazumal to financially support the creation of Productos Pesqueros del Mar in March 1985. Although Productos Pesqueros resembled the other dummy corporations in in its founding date and the quantity of initial loans, Escalón and his partners wanted this company to succeed as a business enterprise.

Indeed, early during Escalon's takeover of Pezca, it seemed to many locals that he intended for Productos Pesqueros to supplant the venerable shrimp company. Eventually, Productos Pesqueros became one of the larger fishing companies – with six to nine vessels in el Puerto – that supplied Pezca. When it shut down its operations in Puerto El Triunfo in 1988, it had 60 employees. In the port of La Unión, however, Productos had as many as eight other fishing boats.[39]

Sandi Zacapa played an active role in Productos Pesqueros as he did with Mariscos Tazumal. Zacapa and Escalón clearly expected to make these fishing enterprises profitable in the short run while using them as collateral to obtain even more financing from the BAC. Presumably, they assumed that they could pocket the excess of the loan beyond the operating expenses of Productos Pesqueros and Tazumal. Both men built new houses in the exclusive Colonia Escalón (named for a distant relative) in 1985. More significantly, they purchased controlling shares in the Aseguradora Centroamericana S.A., the largest insurance company in the country. That company would, of course, insure Pezca's operations.

In 1986, however, Zacapa's kidnapping past began to catch up with him.[40] In August, a military judge ordered Zacapa along with his five partners in crime, including three other military officers, to stand trial. Although only charged with arms trafficking, their kidnapping ring had

---

[39] Throughout 1985 and 1986, Productos received loans totaling more than 5 million colones to purchase boats, but investigators could find no receipts.

[40] The Banco Hipotecario was trying to embargo Zacapa's goods but could neither locate an address or a legal representative. Raúl Beltrán, "Military Court to Try Officers in Military Court," *United Press International (UPI)*, Aug. 23, 1986; *Diario Oficial*, Sept. 3, 1987, 296.

been exposed: they had extorted five businessmen for nearly US$4 million. Their Far Right connections could not help them, given the animus of the elite toward those who would kidnap members of their class. Zacapa and his uncle Colonel Joaquin Zacapa opted to flee the country; Sandi made it to Brazil.[41]

The dealings of Escalón and Zacapa are worth considering. They both worked in a netherworld, between the legitimate and the illegal and immoral (evil, in the case of Zacapa). Their partnership suggests the very porous borders between astute and illegal business practices, on the one hand, and the potential links between rightist politics and financial capital, on the other. Recall the military had arrested Zacapa at the coup-plotting meeting with D'Aubuisson and Mena Lagos in May 1980. Although Escalón had no direct dealings with that group, much less with the kidnapping ring, he did maintain close ties with key members of the paramilitary Right. They were self-styled revolutionaries in their defense of a free El Salvador, and they dispensed with any notions of bourgeois justice and morality. Nothing in this ethos militated against personal enrichment. Similarly, at least since 1980, although they espoused no productivist agenda, they did enshrine private property. Yet, there was at least one clear exception to this model: Alfredo Mena Lagos. Although identified with the Far Right and prepared to launch a coup against the first and the second JRG in 1979–80, Mena Lagos assiduously adhered to managerial norms and was clearly repelled by the activities and attitudes of Escalón and others on the Pezca Board of Directors.

When Escalón assumed control of Pezca in October 1985, he did just the opposite of what Mena Lagos intended.[42] He granted Sindicato Agua an extremely favorable contract, guaranteeing a high daily wage, regardless of the catch, a guarantee that directly undermined Mena Lagos's initiative to combat "*la movida.*" On the contrary, the guaranteed wage was an invitation to engage in "*la movida*" because the fishermen would not be penalized for bringing in smaller catches. Described as an "ideal contract" for labor, another stipulation held that if a boat could not depart on time due to maintenance issues, the company would pay 80 percent of the daily wage. Various former workers claim that some

---

[41] Some suggested that Zacapa set up a shrimp business in Rio. May 2, 1989, Pieza 54 (Juzgado Segundo de lo Penal).

[42] US Embassy to Secretary of State, "196 Pezca Strike," Aug. 7, 1985, San Salvador 10119, r072316z, no. C05624766, case F-2013–10925, p. 2 (obtained under the Freedom of Information Act from US Department of State).

fishermen sabotaged boats to recoup this benefit.[43] These are terms to which Mena Lagos would never have agreed, and they beg the question as to why Escalón did so. Mena Lagos's assessment, acknowledged by the Embassy, was most likely correct that SGTIPAC did not have the strength to carry out another strike in support of their demands. Their strike funds were depleted after nearly eight months, and it is hard to imagine that many fishermen wanted to engage in another work stoppage. Most likely, Escalón calculated that ultimately, he would be successful in converting Pezca to a subcontracting system in which case the contract would no longer be operative. The generous contract would buy labor peace for some time as he consolidated control over the company and converted portions of the BAC loans into personal capital.

In May 1987, however, Escalón began to feel some heat. Under pressure from the right-wing media that hoped to undermine the Duarte government, the Fiscalía General de la Nación (the equivalent of the leading federal prosecutor) began a formal investigation into the BAC and its loans to the shrimp industry. Throughout the latter part of 1985 and 1986 the fraud scheme had been working well. While the key stockholders and Carbonell enriched themselves, Pezca and its affiliates seemed to be functioning without serious problems. Carbonell, however, could not do all the work himself. In 1986, he assigned a lifelong acquaintance and longtime colleague, BAC Vice President Marlena Posada de Gomez, to process the refinancing of all the 1985 loans.[44] In effect these new loans would allow Pezca and its allies to pay off interest and meet their payroll obligations. Subsequently, she claimed that, in July 1986, she began to spot the anomalies in the loans: more than US$15 million with no collateral (with the notable exception of the Pezca installations and boats). She went outside the BAC to report what she considered to be grave and consequential offenses, informing the Minister of Defense Carlos Eugenio Vides Casanova and Fidel Chavez Mena, Minister of Planning and Director of the Junta Monetaria de Reserva, as well as a key leader of the Christian Democratic Party. She also reported anomalies to the head of the Banco Central de Reserva, which ordered an audit of the BAC and its loans to Pezca and affiliates.[45]

[43] Ruperto Torres (former SGTIPAC leader), interview with the author, Puerto El Triunfo, Feb. 2016.

[44] In fact, she had worked on many of the initial loans.

[45] Later Posada was also accused of the fraud given her position in charge of corporate credits of the BAC throughout 1985. Testimony of Marlena Posada de Gómez, Pieza 53/3, 7298 (Juzgado Segundo de lo Penal).

As a direct result of Posada de Gomez's reports, in May 1987, the bank fired Carbonell and named her as interim president. She immediately "placed a judicial embargo" against Pezca and its affiliates.[46] Then the scandal broke. The right-wing papers (the only important ones) emphasized the role of Carbonell and his Christian Democratic Party (PDC) connections.[47] The papers did not mention either Pezca S.A. or Escalón or Wright, despite alluding to the BAC's intervention in the companies that acquired the loans. In June, the Fiscal General de la República began a formal investigation into the fraud that would last over the next two years.

During the course of the entire investigation, Escalón continued to serve as president of Pezca, Productos Pesqueros, and other allied fishing companies. He continued to deal with the BAC. He explained that he was unable to repay the loans due to the illegal sales and to the strikes. Moreover, he continued to argue for new financing to get the fishing industry back on its feet. He promised that, if he obtained the loans and if the BAC (and Pezca) could settle the strike (that began July 26, 1987 – see Chapter 7), he would install a subcontracting system that would foment a newly prosperous shrimp industry. Indeed, Escalón managed to create a subcontractural labor system in Productos Pesqueros, operating out of the port of La Unión.

From very early in the investigation, Escalón, Wright, and Roberto Mathies Regalado mounted a defense that hinged on a selective reading of history replete with facts, distortions, and silences. The legal defense statement of Mathies Regalado summarized their basic arguments revolving around the man-made and natural "catastrophes" the owners had to face. First, it laid out a conjunctural analysis of the early 1980s. The major stockholders of Pezca had been hit hard by the structural reforms and by the increase in illegal sales:

> The morale of the stockholders had deteriorated a great deal ... By 1982, robbery on the high seas had become so widely practiced that there were boats that after days on the high seas returned with so little shrimp that it didn't even cover the normal costs of a trip.[48]

The 1985 strike, falsely depicted as lasting more than a year (its duration was seven and a half months) drove "some stockholders to sell their

---

[46] After a month, she was named vice president of BAC, a position she held until her resignation in October 1987. Testimony of Marlena Posada de Gómez, Pieza 53/3, 7299 (Juzgado Segundo de lo Penal).

[47] *Diario de Hoy*, July 2, 1987.

[48] Defense of Roberto Mathies Regalado in front of Juez Segundo del penal, upon issuing of warrant for his arrest, June 12, 1991, Pieza 56/2, 7405 (Juzgado Segundo de lo Penal).

stock." The latter point was undoubtedly true, as Mena Lagos and his family did divest themselves of Pezca and related company stock. Yet, the sloppy chronology obfuscates the reality that the loans originated in the early stages of the strike well before there were any indications that stockholders would sell. Mathies Regalado also emphasized the fact that in September 1985, Trakel Maritime Company, based in Miami, performed an appraisal of Pezca S.A. and valued the plant and its 29 boats at US$13 million. He suggests that was more than ample collateral for the company's loan. He neglected to mention that, at the time, Pezca was deep in the red and the strike made their indebtedness worse.[49]

Although the loans to Pezca were significant, the bulk of the prosecutor's case against Mathies Regalado, Escalón, Wright, and Carbonell had to do with those made to the 13 fictitious corporations with no collateral. Mathies Regalado resorted to dissimulation when he claimed that Pezca was paying off its loans in a timely fashion until the last months of 1986, when various catastrophes hit the company. On the contrary, according to an internal report of the Fiscal General, Escalón and his associates had paid back only two million of the 87 million colones (four-year) loans that had been acquired at 15 percent annual interest.[50]

For Mathies Regalado, those catastrophes included a decline in the capture of *camarón blanco*, the highest priced shrimp. That decline derived from the negative effect of El Niño, pollution from surrounding haciendas, years of overfishing, and the problem of illegal sales. Mathies Regalado omitted the role of the company in blocking the enactment of temporary shrimping bans. To these factors, they added a vague chronological reference, "[A]nd, if that weren't enough, political movements manipulated workers who then caused new labor problems, hurting their own livelihoods."[51] Once again, the lack of chronological specificity is telling because it allowed the defense to suggest that the "labor troubles" were the primary cause of company owners' inability to repay the loans.

---

[49] Pezca was 1.7 million colones in the red at the end of 1984. The strike would have significantly increased its insolvency.

[50] There is some confusion around this point. Pezca obtained 29 million colones in loans from BAC in 1986 and apparently used 9 million colones of that loan to pay back the 1985 loans. Even so, they were 6 million colones in arrears. The original Fiscal report claimed that Pezca had paid back nothing in 1986. "Memorandum de la investigación," Pieza 46/1, 6914 (Juzgado Segundo de lo Penal).

[51] Defense of Roberto Mathies Regalado in front of Juez Segundo de lo Penal, upon issuing of warrant for his arrest, June 12, 1991, Pieza 56/2, 7405 (Juzgado Segundo de lo Penal).

The Duarte government, in this selective reading, caused the industry's distress. Despite their best efforts to repay the loans, the Sindicato Agua strike of 1987 compounded the existing problems making it impossible for them to keep up with the loan payments.[52] In reality, the strike could not have impeded Escalón and others from repaying the loan at the moment of the embargo because the labor action came two months later. In the long run, however, the strike became a key part of the tale of the beleaguered and somewhat heroic *empresarios* who faced all odds to save the Salvadoran economy from the wretched and corrupt mismanagement of the Christian Democrats. In a similar vein, their defense challenged the BAC and the courts. After explaining that the BAC had been utterly negligent in safeguarding the plant and the fishing boats as was their duty, Mathies Regalado exclaimed:

And now they accuse us of committing non-existing crimes. Crimes were committed by those who incited illegal strikes and the destruction of jobs.
Crimes were committed by those who systematically refused to combat robbery of shrimp; crimes were committed by those who promote that robbery.[53]

For Mathies Regalado and Escalón, the Duarte administration had practiced a "policy of business extermination."[54] The Christian Democrats had promoted the strikes to ruin the company. Presumably, the Pezca owner imputed the tactic to Duarte's resentment against the Right. But the statement might also refer to Sindicato Agua's demand for cooperative ownership that would emerge out of the ruins of Pezca.

Although Mathies Regalado's public posture cast all the blame on Duarte and labor, privately he offered a different version. According to a US Embassy official in 1990,

this long time contact ... [is] embarrassed by his role in Pezca. He blames managing director Escalón for the corruption and mismanagement that ruined the company and admits that he should have watched it closer. He also blames Juan Wright for not keeping a tighter rein on his former son-on-law. He claims that he can do little without Juan Wright who refuses to negotiate with the workers ... As a major debtor of a non-performing loan, he will be blacklisted for new credit under the newly privatized banks.[55]

---

[52] The letter suggests that they were paying back the loans punctually until the strikes. Pieza 55, 6438 (Juzgado Segundo de lo Penal).

[53] Defense of Roberto Mathies Regalado in front of Juez Segundo de lo Penal, upon issuing a warrant for his arrest, June 12, 1991, Pieza 56/2, 7412 (Juzgado Segundo de lo Penal).

[54] Rafael Escalón to Ramón González Giner, Mar. 12, 1992, Pieza 56/2 (Juzgado Segundo de lo Penal).

[55] US Embassy to Secretary of State, "No Resolution in Sight," June 13, 1990, R132130Z, p. 3 (obtained under the Freedom of Information Act from US Department of State).

Regalado managed to shift the blame onto Wright and Escalón and limit his own role to a problem of being distracted and not exercising sufficient oversight of the operations. The formerly united front of right-wing oligarchic stockholders thus crumbled when faced with the reality of the strike, the criminal investigation, and the BAC intervention.

Once the BAC intervened and the judicial investigation began, Escalón and his partners searched for alternatives to regain control of the industry and to avoid criminal prosecution. As a first move, they hired Salvador Perez who had worked for 20 years at the BAC.[56] The bank had fired him along with Carbonell, as he served on its executive board during the loan process. Escalón wanted Perez to figure out a strategy to mollify the BAC, revivify the industry through new loans, and pay back some of the extant loans to avoid criminal prosecution. Escalón's repeated attempts to negotiate with the BAC over the next three years would also contribute to his defense narrative, but the informal conversations accomplished far more for him. First, Escalón managed to establish a bridge of interests with the very institution that had initiated an investigation against him.[57] Now that the BAC was putatively running the company, its real owners necessarily had the same goals to ensure labor peace and earn substantial profits. Second, when Sindicato Agua launched a strike on July 26, 1987, both Escalón and the BAC faced the same antagonist. That complicity probably allowed Escalón to enshrine his narrative about the politicization of the strike and its main consequence for the Pezca owners: their inability to pay back the BAC loans.[58] This historical frame served them in their legal battle, especially when the rightist ARENA Party gained power, winning the congressional elections in 1988 and the presidency in 1989. Their public defense also helped to shape a historical narrative about the Christian Democrats and labor and more locally about the perfidy of Sindicato Agua and their struggle to form a cooperative that would replace Pezca.

---

[56] Pieza 53, 7294 (Juzgado de lo Penal).

[57] The issue is, however, more complex. Marlena Posada who served as vice president the BAC even as she was being investigated by the Fiscalia apparently promoted the cooperative idea with Sindicato Agua, a goal that was of course anathema to Escalón and his confreres. Her resignation in October 1987 might have been due to that pro-labor position or to the investigation or both. Pieza 53, 7295 (Juzgado Segundo de lo Penal), refers to the conversations with Roberto Morales, the new BAC president.

[58] The clear insinuation of the document is that the Duarte government specifically promoted the Sindicato Agua strike to ruin the company. Pieza 55, 6379 (Juzgado Segundo de lo Penal).

According to a *Los Angeles Times* article about the fraud case, "Much of the initial information came from Escalón and Wright, who apparently felt they were being set up to take most of the blame, sources said. They hoped to head off any punishment by exchanging information and promising to pay back the loans."[59] In Salvadoran law, a perpetrator of fraud can avoid criminal prosecution, if he or she pays back the amount that had been obtained. Eventually, Escalón and Mathies Regalado did, in fact, pay off some of the loans. In the latter's case, in 1993, he turned over a number of fishing boats worth 3.7 million colones (that somehow had avoided embargo) and some land to the BAC. Yet, there is no evidence at all to buttress the notion that they supplied the initial information to the investigators. It is clear, however, that Escalón continually sought to maintain a dialogue with the BAC and obtain more funding that would allow him to reestablish a fishing fleet if not a processing plant based in La Unión.

The US-trained Special Investigative Unit (SIU) carried out a methodical investigation, as indicated by the more than 3,000 pages of testimony, the most voluminous case in the country's history.[60] The SIU turned over its findings to the judicial authorities in mid-1989. US reporters allege that the case then lay dormant for a year due to local political pressure given the connections of many of the accused to the ruling ARENA Party and to the Cristiani government. Once apprised of the case, the US Congress applied pressure to the Salvadoran government, by refusing to grant US$20 million in aid unless the judiciary showed signs of proceeding expeditiously with the case. Following the indictments, the congressional appropriations committee again held up US$20 million in aid because none of the money was being repaid to the BAC while the United States was trying to help the banks privatize "on a sound basis."[61]

US congressional pressure probably did contribute to Judge Daniel González's issue of a large number of indictments. On July 12, 1991, Gonzalez issued warrants for 21 individuals, many of whom were prominent members of the Salvadoran elite – notably Wright and Mathies Regalado. A diplomat stated, "This has knocked the ruling class of this

[59] Kenneth Freed, "Salvadoran Government Shows Signs of Losing Interest in Bank-Looting Scandal," *Los Angeles Times*, July 26, 1991.
[60] *La Prensa Gráfica*, June 19, 1991.
[61] US Congress, Senate, "Foreign Operations, Export Financing, and Related Programs Appropriation Bill, 1993," 102–419 Cong. Rec. S29 (Sept. 23, 1992).

country on its rear end."[62] The president of the Central Reserve Bank called it "the biggest fraud in [Salvadoran] history."[63]

Considering the amount of time in which the case lay "dormant," it is somewhat surprising that the judge ended up making such sloppy indictments. He charged the 21 people with "administración fraudulenta."[64] There had been a vigorous debate within the judiciary over this charge, and its weakness was quite evident. Defense attorneys were quick to point out that only bank administrators could be charged with such an offense. Therefore, Escalón, Wright, and Mathies Regalado could not be convicted on such charges. Furthermore, the BAC president in 1991 had argued strenuously but to no avail to limit the indictments to the two principals, Escalón and Carbonell, given that the third important figure, Wright, never signed any documents and therefore would be hard to convict. Yet, the judge responded to the evidence that many higher-ups in the BAC and others had participated directly in the fraud and therefore should be punished. Some alleged that Judge González wished to make a political splash. It is also possible that the initial charges were intentionally flawed. In any event, the indicted had plenty of time to flee the country and to prepare their defense.

By 1993, the court cleared Rafael Escalón of the charges; no one served jail time. And Pezca – the enterprise that he so enthusiastically set out to revivify – was dead. A highly placed official in the judiciary explained: "These people have powerful friends."[65] An understatement for a new era.

* * * *

As we shall see, the bank fraud would eventually destroy Pezca S.A. and with it the dreams of their workers for a dignified life. Yet the fraud was invisible to the people of Puerto El Triunfo. Even after the Fiscalía launched its investigation, the unions resisted Pezca (and the BAC) policies with no clear understanding of the direct consequences of the fraud or the course of the investigation. When, in 1991, the US

---

[62] Quoted in Lee Hockstader, "Indictments Startle Salvadorans: Prominent Families Cited in Bank Case," *Washington Post*, July 8, 1991.

[63] Ibid. Also see, Douglass Mine, "Bank Fraud Scandal Rocks Salvador's High Society," *Associated Press*, July 9, 1991.

[64] However, during that period the BAC prosecutor, the Fiscal, and judges argued about the specific charges that needed to be filed.

[65] Mine, "Bank Fraud Scandal Rocks Salvador's High Society."

government – at the tail end of its multi-billion-dollar effort to stamp out the leftist insurgency – pushed the Salvadoran government for "transparency" it would be too late for the workers. For a brief moment, Puerto El Triunfo became a microcosm of the global transition to neoliberalism, marked at once by a powerful discursive call for transparency in all transactions and a reality in which the most decisive actions that affected ordinary lives took place in society's shadows.

6

Solidarity and Discord in the Labor Movement, 1984–1989

Due to its division and relative submission to other powers, [the labor movement] does not impact in the way it should either the immediate defense of its own interests or the construction of a social and political order that would favor the popular majorities. Nevertheless, it represents a real power and even greater potential.

Ignacio Ellacuría, 1987

If we were to shed tears for everyone of us who is murdered, for every disappearance, for every worker tortured who is disappeared, for every unionist in prison, the waters of Lake Ilopango would overflow their shores.

Pedro Cruz, Salvadoran Hospital Workers' Union, December 1988

Shortly before 3:00 AM on June 2, 1985, several men carried a person in a stretcher past a picket line and into the emergency room of a San Salvador hospital. Once inside, they pulled out guns and pointed them at doctors, nurses, and employees of the hospital. The gunmen were plainclothes members of the Policía Nacional on a mission to evict the strikers who had occupied the premises for nearly a month. Chaos ensued as soldiers barged through the barricades. Imagining a guerrilla assault, the police opened fire. In the ensuing firefight, four policemen were killed. The soldiers grabbed doctors, nurses, and paramedics and forced them face down on the floor. The soldiers tied them up and then combed through the hospital searching for "arms." In the process, they removed babies, so they could search their cribs. They found no arms; doctors claimed that a patient suffered cardiac arrest during the shooting and they couldn't help her because their hands were literally tied. At 5:00 AM, Colonel Enzo Rubio, Chief of Department III of the police force, triumphantly turned over the hospital to its director, Dr. Jorge Bustamante. They carted away four union leaders. Troops raided 25 other hospitals and clinics as part of the anti-strike effort.[1]

Without the tragicomedy, this scene could have easily taken place in 1979 under military rule, when union activists' lives were on the line daily. Nevertheless, the action took place under the democratically elected government of José Napoleón Duarte. Still under the Christian Democrats, anti-union repression, though often severe, was nothing like that of 1979–83 when an estimated 5,000 urban and rural labor activists were gunned down or disappeared. To wit: a few days later, thousands marched through the streets of San Salvador to protest the repression at the hospital. There were no arrests or killings; the four imprisoned hospital union leaders were released days later when the strike was settled on terms favorable to the union.

The erratic, rather than systematic, use of repressive tactics characterized the Duarte administration from its inception. As noted in Chapter 4, the Christian Democratic Party (PDC) was elected with the support of the Unión Popular Democrático (UPD). Despite those ties, in August 1984, the UPD (the peasant/labor federation) publicly demanded that the president carry out the "social pact" (discussed in Chapter 4) to which Duarte had subscribed. The Reagan administration, however, did not want to see the progressive agenda of the "pact" implemented. There were very few in Washington who supported an extension of the land reform.[2] Moreover, they viewed the strident demand for peace talks to be subversive of US political and military strategy.

The AIFLD began to undermine what it considered to be the left-leaning leaders (despite their Christian Democratic identification) within the UPD.[3] As AIFLD'S subsequent leadership recognized, this was not the

---

[1] *Proceso*, June 10, 1985.

[2] In particular, outside of AIFLD there was very little support for the implementation of Phase II of the land reform that involved expropriating lands between 250 and 1,250 acres. That measure would have affected mostly coffee plantations still the fulcrum of oligarchic power; it was never implemented.

[3] Robert Alexander, *A History of Organized Labor in Panama and Central America* (Westport, CT: Praeger Publishers, 2008), 201–2; William Bollinger, "El Salvador," in *Latin American Labor Organizations*, ed. Gerald Michael Greenfield and Sheldon L. Maram (New York: Greenwood Press, 1987), 322.

organization's finest hour.[4] Regardless of the veracity of the myriad of charges against them, there seems little doubt that the international arm of the AFL-CIO practiced an extremely odd form of labor solidarity during the period 1984–86: rewarding friends and punishing dissidents from what amounted to the US political-military line. They also formed parallel unions in an attempt to debilitate putatively leftist ones. Most significantly, AIFLD successfully divided and weakened the UPD and helped to create a new labor confederation, the Central de Trabajadores Democráticos (CTD) that would more closely follow the policies and directives of the Duarte administration and Washington, mainly an implacable hostility to the Left.[5]

The policy of AIFLD toward the UPD directly contradicted its goal of fomenting democratic union activity. Indeed, it could have touted the labor/peasant organization as a success story, in part, an outcome of the land reform, so reviled by the Left and Right. Although the UPD had a weak presence among factory workers, it did have a significant base of support among cooperativized peasants, the beneficiaries of the Christian Democratic–inspired land reform, who represented some 15 percent of the rural population (roughly 300,000 people). It also had significant support among construction and transport workers.

The Duarte government was complicit with AIFLD efforts to halt the UPD's perceived leftward tilt. At the same time, however, the government opened up space for the entire labor movement, including the Left. Whereas in 1983, 2,600 workers participated in 15 strikes (10 in construction), in 1984 some 26,000 workers participated in 41 strikes. Teachers, public works' laborers, land reform technicians, and telephone

---

[4] For the debate on AIFLD's role in El Salvador, see J. Michael Luhan, "AIFLD's Salvadoran Labor Wars: A Painful Record of Political Arm-Twisting," *Dissent* 33, no. 3 (July 1986): 340–50. For the reply see David Jessup, "El Salvador Unions – the Real Story," *Dissent* 33, no. 4 (Sept. 1986): 514–17 and J. Michael Luhan's reply, 517–18. Also see Chris Norton, "Build and Destroy," *NACLA Report on the Americas* 19, no. 6 (1985): 26–36, for a sharp critique of AIFLD. Also see, Harry Bernstein, "US Unions Split on Central American Aid," *Los Angeles Times*, May 14, 1986. For a broader critique of AIFLD, see Kim Scipes, *AFL-CIO's Secret War against Developing Country Workers* (Lanham, MD: Lexington Books, 2010); Frank Smyth, "AFL-CIO Is Spanish for Union Busting," *Washington Monthly*, Sept. 1, 1987. It should be underscored that later labor attachés and AIFLD directors (such as Frances Scanlon and Norman Schipull) attempted to some degree to avoid such crass intervention as took place with the UPD.

[5] Norman Casper, "El IADSL y la corrupción del movimiento sindical de El Salvador," *Estudios Centroamericanos* 41, no. 449 (Mar. 1986): 214–15; Luhan, "AIFLD's Salvadoran Labor Wars," 340–50. For the reply see David Jessup, "El Salvador Unions – the Real Story," 514–17 and Luhan's reply, 517–18.

workers launched strikes that all ended with at least partial victories and without notable repression.

The growth and militancy of public-sector employees conditioned Duarte's erratic policy toward labor. Public employees composed more than 60 percent of the strikers in 1984.[6] The shift in locus from the private to the public sector would have powerful effects on the labor movements. The private sector became increasingly hard to organize because of narrowing profit margins caused by globalization and casualization; moreover, anti-union repression was easier to practice. On the contrary, public-sector employees were very much in the public view and thus blatant repression was harder – yet, as we saw in the vignette at the beginning of the chapter, far from impossible – to enact. Public-sector unionism had its costs. First, as neoliberalism took hold, constant pressures to downsize public employment conditioned union struggles so that they emphasized the protection of employment that was dependent on taxpayers. With relative ease, the government could counteract their rallying cries for solidarity by stressing the strikes' "anti-popular" character: the strikers were paid by the citizens to serve them. Second, that pursuit along with the workers' distance from the means of production also seems to have had an impact on the employees' political and social imaginary. Socialism became more of an abstraction, as labor unions became removed from any alternative strategy of accumulation or labor relations. That said, the opening of space for union activity represented a significant change for previously terrorized and silenced labor militants. In the official words of a Federación Nacional Sindical de Trabajadores Salvadoreños (FENASTRAS) bulletin: "[1984 has been a year] of resistance and major struggles ... After nearly three years of absence from the streets of our capital, the workers reconquered the right to express ourselves freely."[7]

Both the Duarte and Reagan governments faced a similar dilemma. To different degrees, they wanted at least the appearance of democracy

---

[6] There is a discrepancy between the 36 strikes listed by the ILO and the 47 strikes listed by Rafael Guido Béjar, in "El movimiento sindical después de la Segunda Guerra Mundial," *Estudios Centroamericanos* 45, no. 504 (Aug. 1990): 883. Government employees per se were not legally allowed to organize unions although they could form associations. Employees of autonomous institutions such as telecommunications, light and power, and water and sewage could form unions, though legally they were not allowed to strike. Rural workers legally continued to be barred from unionization.

[7] It seems likely that Guido Béjar's figure, based largely on those strikes recorded in *Proceso* included illegal strikes (e.g., by state employees) and short-lived ones that might not have been recorded by official statistics. *El Mundo*, Jan. 11, 1985.

including the right to organization and expression without repression. And yet those democratic forms gave rise to a resurgence of the urban labor left that threatened their interests both politically and economically. Thus, the Confederación General de Trabajo (CGT) fit the needs of Duarte and Washington (especially AIFLD) to foment a labor federation that would be prepared to do battle with perceived leftist labor leaders while attempting to represent peasant and worker interests and preserve the appearance of democratic forms.

That commitment to democratic forms was strongly endorsed by the Reagan administration, which needed a passable record on human rights to present to Congress to receive the necessary funding for its counterinsurgency strategy. The respect for human and labor rights, however, conflicted with two other imperatives to which the Duarte administration needed to adhere. First, the government could not respect all labor rights because, along with the US Embassy, it operated under the assumption that leftist labor activists, in effect, carried out orders from the FMLN. For Duarte, they were enemy agents. Second, the Reagan administration and the International Monetary Fund promoted an early version of a neoliberal agenda that emphasized sharp reductions in government programs and expenditures and strong support for private enterprise. Duarte had no choice but to back this austerity program that would come to fruition in the *Paquetazo* of January 1986 against which all sectors of the labor movement mobilized. Such government measures and repression tended to promote solidarity among unions, but powerful forces, including AIFLD and the Embassy, on the one hand, and the FMLN, on the other, often thwarted unity.

Labor relations from 1985 to 1990 in Puerto El Triunfo, as we shall see in Chapter 7, followed the national pattern of repression, solidarity, and discord but with significantly different timing. The distinct rhythm of union activity in the port reflected the valence of the local forces. In particular, the special quality of gender relations and the mass adherence of *marineros eventuales* to the pro-Duarte union tended to accentuate the divisions in the labor movement more than in the capital. Thus, the wave of neoliberalism that swept over the Americas blew in with gale force across the Bay of Jiquilisco at a moment of labor discord with devastating consequences for port society.

Nationally, the very rhetoric that linked the guerrillas and unions pushed Duarte and the military into repressive action. Days before the Left staged the largest May Day demonstration in five years, with 10,000–15,000 participants, the military released the testimony of two FMLN deserters who claimed that the guerrillas exerted direct control over FENASTRAS and other leftist-led labor groups. The US Embassy and AIFLD also promoted the view that FENASTRAS was merely a front group for the guerrillas. An Embassy report stated:

In the spring of 1985, the FMLN coordinated strikes at the Social Security Institute [ISSS] and the Sewage and Water Works [ANDA] public sector strikes along with teacher work stoppages. During these strikes, strike leaders made no attempt to disavow support from the FMLN's clandestine Radio Venceremos or to separate themselves from death threats against ISSS and ANDA directors.[8]

Using the same discourse that linked the union to the FMLN, ANDA fired more than 240 labor activists, while death squads eliminated two militants and disappeared another. The director of ANDA claimed that most of the union activists were "infiltrators sent in by armed groups."[9] Throughout the year, organized workers struck, and management responded by stationing troops on the premises. Military officials captured and tortured individual union activists. By October, despite large marches and solidarity work stoppages, the ANDA workers were defeated.

The government applied repression very selectively. In Puerto El Triunfo, as we saw, the pro–Christian Democratic SGTIPAC was able to carry out a seven-and-a-half-months-long strike without experiencing any governmental repression. Yet, elsewhere during a six-week period in October and November, authorities struck hard against those identified with the Left: they captured 47 union activists, 11 militants were killed, and 4 disappeared. Notwithstanding, most strikes in 1985 resulted in at least modest victories. Public-sector unions and associations led 54 of the 78 strikes. As with those of the private sector, most strikes involved a struggle for survival: unions fought for raises to compensate for the three-year wage freeze that ended in 1984 and a 30 percent annual inflation rate.

In November 1985, more than 15,000 public employees, including several ministries and the telephone company went on strike against anti-union repression and a demand for a 300 colones (US$60) monthly raise. In response, the government militarized several institutions, including the telephone company, allowing for military tribunals to sentence union activists, among other forms of repression. This time Duarte had a harder time finding the justification for massive repression, given the

[8] US Embassy, "Labor Trends in El Salvador," 1987, US Department of Labor, Bureau of International Labor Affairs, Washington, DC, p. 8.
[9] *Memoria de FENASTRAS*, 1985 (CIDAI, UCA), 21.

pro–Christian Democratic leadership of most of the unions involved in the strike movement. On November 22, he made a speech that blamed the FMLN for creating the conditions that led to the strike through sabotage and "infiltration."[10] The president claimed he would protect union rights but that many activists had fallen into "a fatal trap" set by the Left to destabilize the government.[11] At the same time, Duarte made concrete efforts to end the strikes. He granted monthly raises of 100 colones (US $20) and a US$120 *aguinaldo* (Christmas bonus). Nevertheless, selective repression against leftist-led unions, in particular the telephone and the ANDA unions, continued and was even apparent to international observers. A West German labor delegation registered the following protest: "the efforts by Duarte to disarticulate independent unions and to intimidate workers are both systematic and serious."[12]

Duarte's charges of collusion between the guerrillas and the unions raise the questions: what was the relationship of the FMLN to the left wing of the labor movement? Were they "independent"? Up to a point, the evaluations of Duarte and the US Embassy were accurate. Some key union leaders did have clandestine ties to the FMLN. The heads of FENASTRAS, in particular, often belonged to the Fuerzas Armadas de Resistencia Nacional (FARN, one of the five guerrilla organizations conforming the FMLN). Yet, as Ignacio Ellacuria argued, the labor movement had its own rhythms, demands, and tactics regardless of the affiliations of leaders.

One thing is for the FMLN to make use of certain organizations or that they sometimes support the Frente's positions and something entirely distinct is to say that these organizations are empty shells that hide guerrillas.[13]

In his memoir, Mario Cabrera, a former leader of the Unidad Nacional de Trabajadores Salvadoreños (UNTS), essentially agreed with the Duarte/Embassy assessment. Commenting on the situation when he rejoined the movement in 1987, he wrote, "The general command of the FMLN again committed the error that they committed in the seventies; they reactivated the mass organizations only because they needed cadres and the organizations would provide them."[14] However,

---

[10] US Embassy, "El Salvador, 1984–87," 1987, Foreign Labor Trends, p. 30 (US Department of Labor, Washington, DC).

[11] *Proceso*, Dec. 15, 1985.   [12] *Proceso*, Feb. 3, 1986.

[13] Ignacio Ellacuría, *Veinte años de historia de El Salvador (1969–1989), tomo II, escritos políticos* (San Salvador: UCA Editores, 1991), 786.

[14] Mario Cabrera, *Piruetas* (San Salvador: Palibrio, 2012), 380.

on the following page, he modifies this position: "some FMLN leaders understood the concept of autonomy for the mass organizations."[15]

Cabrera's ambivalence reflected the shifting relations between the distinct guerrilla organizations and other sectors of the labor movement. The FMLN leadership typically desired to exert ultimate control over the popular movement and to use it when necessary to achieve precise objectives. Yet FMLN militants in the labor movement spent most of their time struggling for a minimal standard of living and to resist the repressive tactics of the government and management. Whether due to a strategic initiative or out of necessity, leftist labor activists were often open to alliance with pro–Christian Democratic unions. Similarly, despite Duarte's unremitting hostility against the Left, most of the Central Latinoamericana de Trabajadores (CLAT)-affiliated unions (nominally under Christian Democratic influence) opted to work with FENASTRAS. That experience of solidarity was remarkable given the state of civil war that pitted their allies against each other in military combat.

In February 1986, the center-left labor alliance protested against Duarte's economic austerity measures (*el paquetazo*), which included an end to food and energy subsidies, and wage, price, and governmental hiring freezes. Tens of thousands joined the demonstration that also announced the creation of the UNTS. Centrists initiated the new labor federation to which leftist labor groups adhered. Carried out in an entirely peaceful atmosphere, the demonstration in which 150 labor and peasant organizations participated posed the greatest political challenge to Duarte since his election.

The government's response was immediate. In early March, a group of pro-Duarte union and peasant leaders announced the foundation of the Unión Nacional de Obreros y Campesinos (UNOC). Led by José Luis Preza Grande, Mauricio Benitez's advisor and closely tied to AIFLD, UNOC staged a dramatic inauguration in the capital. On March 15, the new labor federation organized a massive demonstration, mobilizing significantly more people than had attended the UNTS rally. The forces of UNOC were largely made up of campesinos who had benefited from the land reform of 1980. The SGTIPAC formed the largest union within the CGT, in turn one of UNOC's constituent federations. The demonstration made it clear that Duarte had not lost much political support in the countryside. UNOC did share some key objectives with

UNTS, especially demands for the deepening of the land reform, serious peace negotiations, and modifications of the *paquetazo*. Despite important areas of agreement, the two organizations did not cooperate until later in the decade.[16]

Internal dissension soon wracked and weakened UNTS, provoked by political pressures from the government and to some degree from AIFLD. UNTS attempted to organize various work stoppages in support of demands for salary increases and peace negotiations. In response, centrist public employee unions withdrew from the labor organization. Later in the year, the UPD, by then a primarily campesino organization with a base among land reform beneficiaries, also withdrew from UNTS.[17]

Working in tandem with the Duarte administration, AIFLD attempted to create parallel unions with the express aim to weaken the Left, and they did so in factories and governmental institutions. An internal AIFLD report issued in 1993 stated:

In the area of trade unions, AIFLD has worked toward a principal objective of strengthening non-leftist independent unions, and to do so, has focused on two sub-objectives. First, in order to strengthen independent unions, it had to be sure that the unions were, in fact, independent, and that meant free of control by the left. Therefore, a certain portion of AIFLD's energies were dedicated to wresting control of the union movement from leftists and in keeping non-leftist unions strong.[18]

When necessary, AIFLD set up parallel unions and provided them with funding that kept the new unions "afloat." Also, AIFLD supported "independent" union efforts to achieve decent contracts because that would strengthen the "democratic" labor movement. Notwithstanding, this two-pronged strategy had its drawbacks. AIFLD's refusal to support the struggle of leftist unions, at times, made it appear anti-union. And to employers, the majority of whom were influenced by rightist ideology, their support of unions, such as Sindicato Agua, made the Cold War–inspired labor organization appear pro-Communist. Overall, though, AIFLD was quite pleased with its efforts to thwart leftist hegemony over the labor movement.[19]

[16] *Proceso*, May 7, 1986, 16.
[17] UNTS ascribed their withdrawal to AIFLD influence. There is, however, no evidence that the American labor organization played a direct role in the UPD's withdrawal.
[18] Stephen Stewart and Danilo Jimenez, "Final Report: Midterm Evaluation: AIFLD-AID Cooperative Agreement in El Salvador," June 1993, El Salvador, submitted to USAID, Washington, DC, 23–24.
[19] On one successful AIFLD intervention in a Japanese-owned textile mill, see *Proceso*, June 18, 1986; US Embassy, "El Salvador, 1984–87," 1987, Foreign Labor Trends, p. 31 (US Department of Labor). There were constitutional protections for union leaders.

There is, however, no documentary evidence to implicate AIFLD in governmental or rightist repression such as occurred on July 7, 1986, when heavily armed men in civilian clothes grabbed textile union and FENASTRAS leader, Febe Velasquez, from a minibus. Mass protests ensued until several days later Duarte personally brought Velázquez (Ricardo Jovel's *compañera*) to union headquarters.[20] A virtual repeat performance took place a month later. The leader of Sindicato de Empresa Trabajadores de ANDA (SETA) (the water company union) was kidnapped and brought to the air force facilities, where he was kept for a day without food and water. Once again, solidarity strike actions and international pressure compelled the government to liberate the union leader. President Duarte freed him in a public act. In the government's defense, he exclaimed that "there is guerrilla infiltration everywhere ... and that is the reason behind the capture of the union activist."[21]

Analysts at the Universidad Centroamericana considered Duarte's response to the kidnappings and to a new wave of solidarity strikes to be "clumsy and improvised."[22] His erratic behavior is worth pondering. Duarte needed labor support to maintain his political legitimacy. As mentioned in the preceding text, Duarte, the US Embassy, and AIFLD obsessively believed that every action by leftist labor was, in part, an act of war in that it obeyed the dictates of their military foe, the FMLN. This contradiction between anti-leftism and the democratic tolerance of labor led to such theater-of-the-absurd behavior as the death squad–like kidnapping of union leaders and their personal liberation by Duarte.

Public- and private-sector strikes erupted in the metropolitan area from August until October 1986. Beyond salary raises, the most typical demand was for the rehiring of fired workers. As the putative resolution of previous strikes unraveled, union activists simply refused to accept defeat and continued to support their unemployed *compañeros*. As the UCA analyst (most likely Ellacuría) remarked:

In the first place, the growing solidarity demonstrated by the working classes is notable. There is no other way to interpret this but as the consolidation of greater class consciousness, able to overcome to some extent the divisions that existed in previous years.[23]

---

[20] *Proceso*, July 18, 1986; Camelia Cartagena, *El silencio de los culpables: El Salvador, luchas sindicales, dos décadas de oro 1970–1989* (San Salvador: Servicios Gráficos El Salvador, 2015), 281.

[21] *Proceso*, Aug. 27, 1986.

[22] Ibid., 11; *Estudios Centroamericanos* 454–55 (Aug.–Sept. 1986).

[23] *Proceso*, Oct. 8, 1986.

The analyst goes on to highlight the maturity of the movement. Not cowed by the militarization of the work sites, the unions consistently offered to negotiate. For the first time, the unions used hunger strikes to dramatize their opposition to repression. Despite ample evidence to the contrary, for the US Embassy and for the Duarte administration, this strike movement had as its sole purpose to buttress the FMLN and weaken the government at the negotiation table. Indeed, the Embassy's own statistics showed that half of all negotiated contracts involved leftist unions. In short, they engaged in the characteristic behavior of an ordinary trade union.

Despite its successes, UNTS played into Duarte's hands, driven in part by FMLN strategy. Once key centrist elements departed UNTS, the Left began to operate in ways that seemed to give credence to the Duarte/ Embassy allegations against them. During the first six months of 1987, in response to relentless anti-labor repression, the UNTS organized several protest marches that turned violent. A multi-class group aligned with the Ejercito Revolucionario del Pueblo (ERP) (one of the five guerrilla groups of the FMLN); the Movimiento Pan, Tierra, Trabajo, y Libertad (MPTL) joined the UNTS demonstrations. They burned buses and gasoline stations and "saturated the walls of the city with combative *pintas*." Their militants also provided security for the marches with "firearms and iron bars."[24] In other demonstrations, this largely student group, connected to the ERP, also burned vehicles and telephone booths. Although the UNTS leadership pushed the MPTL to tone down its actions, the radical group continued to operate as a "fuerza de choque" (shock force) and as a defensive unit at demonstrations and marches.[25]

The US Embassy had no doubt that the UNTS played a key role in the FMLN strategy to overthrow the government, claiming: "This period (1987–88) was marked by FMLN reliance on economic sabotage and strike activity to worsen economic conditions on the theory that this would turn workers against the democratic system."[26] During this same period, the UNTS (following the FMLN line) called for Duarte's replacement by a government of "broad participation." Early in 1987, the

[24] Cabrera offers an insider's view from the vantage point of the leadership of UNTS, though he joined in 1987. Thus, his view that the organization was born "bajo la influencia y como apendice del FMLN" is not accurate. By the time he joined the leadership, the organization was under the guerrilla front's indirect control. Cabrera, *Piruetas*, 383.

[25] Ibid., 416.

[26] US Embassy, "El Salvador, 1988–89," 1990, Foreign Labor Trends, p. 10 (US Department of Labor).

government levied what was popularly called a "war tax" that mainly affected private enterprise. In response, ANEP, the rightist organization of businesspeople, staged a nationwide strike (really a lockout) that was more than 90 percent effective. The Supreme Court then struck down the tax. The FMLN saw this battle as a sign of the impending collapse of Duarte and the US-backed counterinsurgent strategy. For Humberto Centeno, UNTS leader and Communist Party militant, the call for a new government represented "un salto cualitativo" (a qualitative leap) in that the labor organization made a specifically political demand.[27]

For Ellacuría and other independent observers, the UNTS leadership was myopic. For many, if not most, Salvadorans the achievement of democratic government represented a victory against the oligarchy. The radical political position of UNTS also impeded a functional alliance with the centrist labor groups that were committed to electoral democracy.

Tracy Fitzsimmons and Mark Anner, in a study of post–Peace Accord labor movement, ascribe the weakness of the Left and center unions to their political attachments during the 1980s. "For years during the Salvadoran Civil War, leftist labor groups served as the strategic rear guard for the guerrillas awhile the center labor unions functioned as the mainstay of the U.S. counterinsurgency program." They then underscore the way in which the FMLN seemingly guided UNTS into a preparatory phase for what would be the November 1989 insurrection.[28]

Notwithstanding leftist labor sectarianism and violence, throughout 1987, workers launched 100 strikes, the highest number since 1979. Public employees staged 48 strikes from January to July and only 6 during the rest of the year.

Governmental repression was primarily responsible for the decline in labor activity during the second half of the year. In May 1987, for example, soldiers captured two leaders of the coffee workers' union and held them incommunicado for three weeks. In response, workers at 18 coffee processing plants went on strike.[29] More ominously, in July, police opened fire on protesting social security workers, injuring at least

---

[27] *Proceso*, May 11, 1988.

[28] Mark Anner and Tracy Fitzsimmons, "Civil Society in a Postwar Period: Labor in the Salvadoran Democratic Transition," *Latin American Research Review* 34, no. 3 (1999): 110–11. They quote a leftist labor leader, "We created activists for sabotage and mobilizations, not for sustained organizational activity." Ibid., 111.

[29] Cartagena, *El silencio de los culpables*, 292; "El movimiento laboral atenazado," *Estudios Centroamericanos* 42, nos. 463–64 (May–June 1987): 347.

15 people. The following day, UNTS carried out a protest strike, involving 18 unions, representing 60,000 workers.[30]

Many labor conflicts dragged on from year to year as beaten-down union militants arose once again to demand the reinstatement of their union and their fired *compañeros*. Such seemingly endless conflicts occurred primarily in the autonomous institutions of the state, such as ANTEL (telecommunications), ISSS (clinics and hospitals), and ANDA (water and sewage). The hydro-electrical workers, to cite an important example, had been at the forefront of the labor upsurge during the late 1970s. In 1980, the second Junta Revolucionaria de Gobierno (JRG) had imprisoned its leadership and dissolved the union STECEL by force. Since 1986, the union had tried to reconstitute by legally calling itself an association. For two years, the state-owned company refused to recognize the association, citing a constitutional provision that inhibited the organization of public service workers. On June 15, 1987, the hydro-electrical workers went on strike demanding recognition and the rehiring of 53 *compañeros*, fired for union activity. The strike's effects were dramatic because workers failed to repair the damage wrought by guerrilla sabotage.[31]

General Jaime Abdul Gutiérrez, a member of the JRG when it dissolved STECEL, was the director of the Executive Hydroelectric Commission of the Río Lempa (CEL). He claimed that the union was illegal and acting under FMLN orders. A US labor investigative team reported:

On June 25, seven strike leaders in Ahuachapán were captured by army troops who turned them over to the National Police where they were handcuffed. Refusing to sign statements linking ATCEL to the FMLN, they were beaten. Local military commanders threatened ATCEL strikers with arrest or disappearance.[32]

The demand to sign a document linking labor and the guerrillas is a striking admission of the bankruptcy of the reigning ideological framework. Simply put, most political and military authorities could only understand labor activism as a function of the war. However, Colonel Mauricio Ernesto Vargas, the army operations chief, dissented. He claimed that the government was incorrect to argue an identity between

---

[30] "Police Shoot Strikers, Unrest Grows," *Central America Report*, July 17, 1987.

[31] *Proceso*, Jan. 18, 1989.

[32] In 1980, Abdul Gutiérrez was a member of the JRG that oversaw the imprisonment of STECEL (hydroelectric workers' union) leaders and the closure of their union. National Labor Committee in Support of Democracy and Human Rights in El Salvador (NLC), *Labor Rights Denied in El Salvador: An On-Site Investigation by a Delegation of Labor-Legislative-Religious Leaders*. Labor Campaign: El Salvador, New York (Dec. 1988), 12.

the unions and the FMLN. Referring to the strikers, he stated, "They have unfulfilled needs and can be used to generate violence, but to say that these groups are communist is not true."[33] The strike continued for more than a month ending after a commission in the National Assembly promised to study and resolve the issues.

It is hard to measure with any accuracy the effect of the strikes and the sabotage on the Salvadoran economy or on the popularity of Duarte. Similarly, there are no clear gauges to measure capital flight or other forms of rightist resistance.[34] Two things are evident: firstly, socioeconomic conditions for ordinary Salvadorans had not improved during Duarte's first four years in office. Between 45 and 50 percent of the population was unemployed or underemployed. Inflation remained more than 30 percent and real wages had not recuperated since their precipitous decline in the early 1980s. Secondly, Duarte quite consciously did not attempt to deepen the land and financial reforms of 1980. His failure to support the original intent of the reforms contributed directly to their relative failures. Both the FMLN and the oligarchic Right were pleased with Duarte's retreat. For the oligarchy, the dampening of reforms protected their interests and, for the FMLN, the limits on land reform weakened the strategy of counterinsurgency.

In large part as a repudiation of Duarte, the rightist ARENA Party soundly defeated the Christian Democrats (PDC) in the March 1988 legislative and municipal elections. Its significant quota of political power did nothing to lesson anti-labor repression.[35] That repression, the continuation of the Civil War, and rank-and-file insistence on inter-union solidarity slowly pushed the labor movement toward unity.

Following the implosion of Duarte's labor and popular support, in March 1989, the right-wing ARENA Party won the presidential elections. A modernizing faction of the party led by Alfredo Cristiani took over the reins of government. The PDC's electoral defeat was due in part to the growing apathy and anger of its popular bases over Duarte's failure to respond positively to the demands of the labor and peasant movements.

Despite the promise of Cristiani to respect freedom of association and his meetings with all factions of the labor movement, during his first two

---

[33] Quoted in "The Army and Politics," *Central America Report*, Aug. 21, 1987.

[34] Some estimates state that US$5 billion in private capital left El Salvador from 1978 to 1981. See Walter LaFeber, *Inevitable Revolutions: The United States in Central America*, 2nd ed. (New York: Norton, 1993).

[35] ARENA made a very limited play for labor support with an eye to the March 1989 elections.

months in office, police and the military committed abuses against 116 *sindicalistas* always with the pretext that a given union or federation was but a "fachada" (front group) for the FMLN, bent on carrying out subversion. At the same time, the economic plan of Cristiani was gearing up for massive reductions of public expenditures mainly through layoffs and privatization of public institutions.[36]

Faced with ARENA's anti-labor repression, neoliberal agenda, and open hostility to land reform, labor activists of all ideological tendencies moved toward unity. UNOC, aligned with the PDC and CLAT, began to question what they had previously believed: the intertwined identity of UNTS and the FMLN. One UNOC leader stated simply, "We represent different tactics of struggle but there is mutual respect. Anyone who says that the UNTS is an arm of the FMLN is completely mistaken."[37] In response to this rapprochement between unions, the ARENA government began to apply the epithet "FMLN front group" to UNOC.[38]

UNOC, UNTS, and other labor groups met and drew up joint resolutions denouncing the ARENA government for its "anti-popular" character.[39] In the words of another UNOC activist, the new administration's major achievement was to unite the labor movement:

In the first year of the Cristiani government, unionists, cooperativists, and workers have been assassinated and disappeared with impunity. The Armed Forces have stepped up their arbitrary and illegal arrests of working people as well as illegal searches and constant harassment of workplaces and the houses of labor leaders."[40]

During the first year of the ARENA government, authorities captured 633 unionist activists many of whom were tortured; 30 were disappeared. The armed forces staged 26 raids on union offices. Yet, in retrospect, such acts of repression were but rehearsals for one act of terror. On October

---

[36] *Proceso* 394, July 26, 1989, 9–10.

[37] It is worth noting that Grande Preza, the CGT leader and Benítez advisor, pulled his federation out of UNOC over its growing ties to UNTS. The CGT leader, however, suffered a loss of prestige due to his inability to win or negotiate the SGTIPAC strike. NLC, *Labor Rights Denied in El Salvador*, 15. See, US Embassy, "El Salvador, 1989–1990," 1990, Foreign Labor Trends, p. 12 (US Department of Labor).

[38] Grande Preza, ever loyal to AIFLD, bolted from UNOC to form a new group. See interview with author, Jose Luis Grande Preza, San Salvador, 2014.

[39] *Proceso* 397, Aug. 23, 1989, 9.

[40] NLC, *El Salvador 1990: ARENA Repression Unites the Salvadoran Labor Movement*, Labor Campaign: El Salvador, New York (Sept. 1990), 3.

31, 1989, at noon, as workers, union activists, and others lunched in the cafeteria, a powerful bomb blew up FENASTRAS headquarters, killing 10, including Febe Velásquez. This act of rightist terrorism was the culmination of a bipartisan campaign that for years had equated labor activists to subversives.

Citing the bombing of FENASTRAS as a pretext, the FMLN launched an offensive on November 11 that reached the exclusive barrio of *Escalón*. The offensive, however, failed to spur a mass insurrection. The FMLN, the government, and the Embassy all came to recognize that a negotiated peace was the only viable option. During the offensive, a military battalion entered the Universidad Centroamericana and brutally executed six Jesuit scholars, their housekeeper, and her daughter. Ignacio Ellacuría, at once a brilliant analyst of the popular movements and the leading proponent of the peace process, was the primary target of the death squad. In the days preceding his execution, the vice president of the republic had accused Ellacuria of having "poisoned the minds of the nation's youth" and a high-level army officer had labeled the university a "haven for terrorist leaders."[41]

The decade ended with a largely united but scarred and debilitated labor movement and a rightist government fully pledged to achieving peace and to the implementation of neoliberal policies. The ARENA government also had fresh blood on its hands: 10 FENASTRAS militants and the Jesuit intellectuals, 16 people with vast stores of courage and knowledge who would have helped pave a more just, peaceful, and equitable transition away from war.

Puerto El Triunfo, as we shall see, ended the decade on a similarly dark, if far less bloody note.

---

[41] Quoted in Teresa Whitfield, *Paying the Price: Ignacio Ellacuría and the Murdered Jesuits of El Salvador* (Philadelphia, PA: Temple University Press, 1995), 307, 329.

7

The Longest Strike in History

Todo o nada, eso era su verso [All or nothing that was their refrain]
Ana Alvarenga

You give us 75% or we'll torch the whole place and all the boats.
The gasoline is ready.
Ruperto Torres (recalling the final negotiation)

Crises are moments of truth. They bring to light conflicts that in daily
life are buried beneath the rules and routines of social protocol, behind
the gestures that people make automatically, without thinking of their
meanings and purposes. In such moments, the contradictions that lay behind
the rhetoric of social harmony, consensus, hegemony, or control are exposed.
Emilia Viotti da Costa

Seeing the writing on the wall and in the ledgers, in March 1987, Joel
Morán Olmos resigned as general manager of Pezca after some five years
in that post. By the time the Banco Agrícola Comercial (BAC) intervened in
May 1987, the signs of a severe crisis of liquidity were ubiquitous. Subsidized meals for live-in white-collar employees ceased and only seafood was
available.[1] The company stopped providing shrimp to its unionized workers
as a monthly benefit. More seriously, by April, only 10 of the company's
32 boats were functioning; the others were docked due to a lack of

[1] Ivette Bará was *subgerente de personal* in Pezca S.A. during the first six months of 1987.
Ivette Bará, communication with the author, 2017.

maintenance funds. The company began to fire and lay off fishermen and fell behind in salary payments to all its workers. From January to June 1987, monthly production in the entire shrimp industry dropped from 136 to 26 metric tons as the number of docked fishing boats increased from 37 to 78.

Benítez and the Sindicato Agua (SGTIPAC) leadership analyzed Pezca's crisis, within its radical populist framework in a public declaration:

The fraudulent administration of Pezca [is] the cause of their supposed bankruptcy; we workers are not willing to pay for the dishes broken by the rich kids of private enterprise affiliated with the recalcitrant Right, guilty of the pain that today we suffer, caused by the War that social injustice caused, fomented for years by these gentlemen.[2]

Beyond the scorn directed at the rich-kid rightist owners, the text connects the company's mismanagement and fraudulent activity to its antisocial rightist ideology. For Sindicato Agua, their rightist ideological identification and practice – along with that of the rest of the oligarchy – were the primordial causes of the civil war and its consequences. Sindicato Agua called on the government to investigate the fraud but, at the same time, with the phrase "they attempt to make us believe" insinuated that in fact Pezca's liquidity crisis and its impending bankruptcy were, at least to a degree, manufactured.

Their argument ran along these lines. Sindicato Agua had struggled hard to achieve a decent shake for its members. Now, due to the fraud and mismanagement, the company faced some financial difficulty. Pezca, however, was trying to resolve its problems not only by reneging on its contractual obligations but moreover by breaking the union through the creation of a system of subcontracting. In a different statement, the leadership wrote,

[T]hey are trying to make the public believe that they are bankrupt so that they can change the administration of the company ... that will let them evade the payment of benefits and salaries stipulated by the collective contract ... the mechanism that they seek to implement will involve the rental of the boats, converting the captains into contractors.[3]

[2] "La Administración fraudulenta de Pezca S.A., causa de la quiebra que pretende dar a creer ante el pueblo salvadoreño porque los trabajadores ya no estamos dispuestos a pagar los platos que quiebran los niños de la empresa privada afiliados a la Derecha recalcitrante, y culpable del dolor que hoy en día sufrimos ... con esta Guerra que originó la injusticia social que tantos años fomentaron estos señores." "Comunicado de prensa de SGTIPAC afiliado a CGT, Mauricio Ascencio Benítez," communiqué, June 12, 1987 (SGTIPAC Archive, in possession of the author).
[3] "Carta de SGTIPAC al Ministerio de Trabajo y la Corte Suprema," letter, Feb. 29, 1988, pp. 8–9 (SGTIPAC Archive).

For Sindicato Agua, the subcontracting system was designed, in part, to break the union, and every move the company made furthered those goals. In effect, the captains would become employers of four workers. The fishing companies could no longer be considered management, much less Pezca S.A. Under such conditions, it would be virtually impossible to maintain the integrity of the union.

The material desperation of the *eventuales* was the key source for Sindicato Agua's militancy. Eastern Salvador faced the highest unemployment rates in the country and inflation drove people to the edge of hunger (nationally both indices were more than 30 percent). Puerto El Triunfo had become a center for war refugees and hosted between 1,500 and 3,000 during the decade. Most of the male refugees sought work in the port's only industry and joined the ranks of aspiring *eventuales* on land and sea, thus harshly exacerbating the labor situation. Benítez, an *eventual*, continued to have an almost millenarian following among the temporary fishermen with whom his radical populist rhetoric resonated. A successful subcontracting system would undermine that support, disrupt the union's organizational coherence, and pit the two sectors of marineros against each other.

Pezca's public discourse suggested that the subcontracting plan had nothing to do with union busting. Rather, the company spokesmen confronted the gaping lacuna in Sindicato Agua's discourse; "*la movida*" was the direct target of the new system. The problem had only worsened. Whatever Escalón's motives for granting the guaranteed daily wage in 1985, it had done nothing to dampen the illegal sales. As early as 1986, a US Embassy report had observed, "the corruption is bringing Pezca to the brink of failure and has caused the company to lay off half of its plant workers."[4] Although most of the shrimp ended up in neighboring countries or Salvadoran restaurants, illegal sales surely account for much of the discrepancy between the 6.42 million pounds of exported shrimp reported by the Salvadoran government and the US Department of Commerce's report of 8.17 million pounds of imported Salvadoran shrimp. A government study in 1990 stated: "The robbery of the products reached an unimaginable magnitude ... and it was aggravated by those assigned to stop it."[5]

---

[4] US Embassy to Secretary of State, "Crisis in the Shrimp Industry," Mar. 22, 1985, San Salvador, 6659, r221606z, no. 6659, case (obtained under the Freedom of Information Act from US Department of State, Washington, DC).

[5] This figure does include some robberies of shrimp boats, a growing phenomenon in the late 1980s and early 1990s. According to a report published in *Diario de Hoy*, Aug. 30, 1992, losses due to "robbery" (both kinds) amounted to more than US$15 million a year.

The Pezca management requested that Sindicato de la Industria Pesquera (SIP) leaders participate with them in an informal commission to explore ways to control *la movida*. They also enlisted the support of the Marina Nacional (despite strong allegations of their involvement in the practice) in the investigation. Presumably, the SIP leadership grasped the implications of their participation in the commission, which would mean an intensification of their antagonism with Sindicato Agua. Moreover, subcontracting was the obvious solution to the illegal sales. That practice would risk the erosion of SIP's own membership in the fishing fleet as it had done at Atarraya (the other remaining shrimp company in the port). In short, the SIP leadership was ready to behave like the company union Sindicato Agua accused them of being to protect their members, many of whom depended on production quotas; all plant workers, of course, depended on the survival of the company. Escalón repeatedly promised to the BAC that he would eliminate the illegal sales problem through the implementation of the new subcontracting system. There is only anecdotal evidence from Atarraya to bolster the claim. The captain, as renter and employer, would develop specific material interests that would set him apart from the crew and thus militate against *la movida* that had always depended on the unanimity of the captain and the crew.

The company's public position was also silent about its own role in its collapse, namely that the failure to use and pay back the bulk of the more than US$20 million in loans blocked the necessary credit to get the fleet repaired and productive again. Moreover, Pezca could not pay the fishermen the considerable sum of money that was owed to them. The company's contractual obligation to pay them 80 percent of their salaries when they could not work because the boats were undergoing maintenance increased that sum. The BAC fraud had left no alternative for Pezca: the lack of credit, illegal sales, and shortage of the high-priced *camarón blanco* (due to overfishing and pollution) compelled the company to push through the subcontracting system. Thus, they threw permanent marineros onto the street and would have to withstand the fury of Benítez and Sindicato Agua who, by June, were already threatening a strike.

Despite their albeit vague knowledge of Pezca's own "robbery," the SIP leadership offered their support to the company and directly confronted the fishermen: "We are aware that the companies are going through a precarious economic situation due to a lack of financing in addition to the contraband of shrimp on the high seas."[6] They also

---

[6] "Carta Abierta, SIP," paid advertisement, *Diario de Hoy,* July 29, 1987.

claimed that Marlena Posada, acting president of the BAC, was attempting to work with Benítez to create the cooperative at Pezca. At the same time, she was holding up payment of salaries to the plant workers and fisherman.[7]

Faced with what they perceived to be the collapse of the industry, the SIP leadership opted to side with the company and its BAC intervenors, rather than with the fishermen whom they viewed with increasing antagonism. In a June 12 negotiating session with Raúl Marroquín, the intervenor, SIP complained about the failure to pay salaries and the withholding of five weeks of union dues. Marroquín responded that the extreme illiquidity was due to the generalized contraband, the company's indebtedness, and the ubiquity of fishing licenses.[8] He claimed that they were trying to increase exports, and salaries would be the first priority – those of the plant workers in particular. Despite their resentment against the company, in private and in public, they accepted Pezca's arguments.[9] Indeed, in a series of letters sent at the end of July, SIP fully embraced the new model of production that represented "economic advantages for labor, which we are already enjoying, since about 30 fishing boats are operating under this new plan."[10]

Although sympathetic to revolutionary goals, SIP leaders consistently rejected Sindicato Agua's proposed expropriation of the industry and cooperative ownership and management. Moreover, the SIP leadership was willing to accept the new management subcontracting plan for its fishermen members connected to Atarraya. Ultimately, the leftist leadership viewed company stability as their priority.

It is striking how the different kinds of silence intensified the *desencuentro* II between the two union leaderships. In Chapter 4, we discussed how the silence about *la movida* made communication difficult between plant workers and fishermen. The liquidity crisis and the Sindicato Agua's strike preparations compelled the SIP leaders to violate what had been an implicit subaltern understanding: you don't rat out your *compañeros de clase*.

---

[7] Ibid.

[8] It is unclear why the government was granting additional licenses beyond the traditional limit of 72 in Puerto El Triunfo. It was possibly a move to boost production but probably derived from corruption.

[9] "Acta de Reunión between Pezca and SIP," June 12, 1987, San Salvador (SIP General Archives, Puerto El Triunfo, Usulután, El Salvador).

[10] It seems that SIP was referring to Atarraya. "SIP to Cmdt. Jimenez Aguilera," letter, July 26, 1987 (SIP Virtual Archive, in possession of the author).

SIP's public denunciation of *la movida* and its participation in the commission set up to investigate the practice provoked the Sindicato Agua leadership to respond with heretofore unknown verbal and even physical aggression. Ricardo Jovel, despite his prior working relationship and even friendship with the Sindicato Agua leader, stated: "We charge Fidel Angel Chávez and Mauricio Benítez with the responsibility ... for the personal integrity and safety of all plant workers ... we have nothing to do with the SGTIPAC's conflict." Jovel then claimed that Sindicato Agua militants had beaten a member and issued death threats to the SIP leadership.[11]

Jovel and his *compañeros* also remained silent about the fraud and the managerial practices that had brought the company to the brink of bankruptcy. Moreover, the SIP leadership accepted what they called the "new economic model of production" without publicly recognizing its implications not only for its assault on Sindicato Agua but also for all forms of unionization on the sea.

Throughout July, the levels of tensions between the unions intensified along with the breakdown in negotiations between Sindicato Agua and Pezca, which had passed under nominal control of the BAC. For Sindicato Agua, the behavior of SIP confirmed its own populist analysis of the political conjuncture: the Left leadership worked with the oligarchic Right to subvert the rights of workers. SIP's campaign against the threatened strike only confirmed that analysis.

Indeed, the SIP leaders had become so concerned about the strike that they asked the military to intervene to protect the plant installations and themselves from the strikers. Several times they called on the authorities to intervene to stop the strike. On July 20, 1987, they sent a letter to Eugenio Vides Casanova, Minister of Defense, and head of the National Guard from 1979 to 1983, the period of its worst human rights abuses. The union leaders knew that his hands were soaked in blood: "Thus, we ask for your collaboration so that if in a given moment, they launch a strike you will ensure order so that our work will not be disturbed."[12] They made their pleas for intervention to this man considered by many to be a war criminal, with no apparent recognition of the irony that their union had experienced lethal repression earlier in the decade. Not surprisingly, the Sindicato Agua strikers viewed SIP members as scabs.

[11] Ricardo Jovel and SIP, "Carta Abierta," *Diario de Hoy*, July 29, 1987.
[12] SIP and Subseccional Pezca to General Carlos Eugenio Vides Casanova, letter, July 20, 1987 (SIP General Archives).

FIGURE 7.1 Fishermen unloading shrimp
(courtesy Mario Sáenz)

On July 26, Sindicato Agua went on strike against Pezca and its five allied fishing companies against the contract violations that accompanied the gradual shutting down of the company's operations, in particular the failure to pay severance pay to 27 fishermen whom the company had fired. Most significantly, the companies owed a considerable sum to all the fishermen because of its contractual obligation to pay 80 percent of the daily wage when maintenance issues prevented the fishermen from working.

The contract also included the payment of back pay. Benítez's slogan "LO CONQUISTADO NO SE ENTREGA" (We will not hand over what we have won) summarized the union's position that it would not give up the hard-won benefits it had won, despite the apparent inability of the company to pay. In the buildup to the strike, Benítez and the other Sindicato Agua leaders did not publicly discuss their cooperative goal. Yet, it is hard to imagine that they expected a favorable resolution of their strike because only a massive infusion of bank or government funds would have allowed the company to meet the union demands. Presumably, they assumed that cooperative ownership would be the fruit of their struggle, a position that had deep support especially among the *eventuales* who saw it as the only way to overcome their own precarious situation. If SIP's allegations were accurate, at least one key figure in the BAC, connected to the Christian Democrats, was pushing for such an outcome.[13]

Because Benítez had scrupulously followed the complicated procedure laid out in the Labor Code, he obtained a court ruling in the union's favor, perhaps aided by his friendly relations with the Duarte administration. Benítez's ties had solidified thanks to his election to the post of secretary of conflicts of the pro–Christian Democratic Confederación General de Trabajo (CGT). This was the first legal strike in the country since 1984. The legality of the strike became extremely important both for propaganda purposes and because the Ministry of Labor was obliged to promote negotiations. Moreover, the companies legally had to pay strike days. As the strike dragged on month after month, the bill owed to the workers continued to climb. Benítez and his *compañeros* used that debt as a powerful bargaining chip. Either the company negotiated the demands, handing over the back pay owed and wages for the strike days, or the government should compel the company and the BAC to turn over the companies to the union in compensation.

Shortly after the court ruling in favor of Sindicato Agua, the union pickets unexpectedly faced the navy "on the pretext that the strikers were attempting to occupy the facility [the plant]."[14] The strikers had seized a delivery truck owned by the US Marines as part of their effort to shut down all operations.[15] Although they immediately released the driver and his passengers, the union charged that the navy "provoked and beat" its picketers.[16] Later, the union's version of the incident reduced it to a "minor fracas" caused by the company tricking the military. In this version offered to a US Embassy official, the company had called in the military on false pretenses. In any event, the union agreed to let plant

---

[13] Marlena Posada would not last out the year at the BAC and her position in favor of a cooperative solution did not represent that of the rest of the bank leadership.

[14] Embassy officials traveled to the port to investigate a denunciation of anti-labor violence made by America's Watch. Curiously, Benítez and the others offered a story that deemphasized any military wrong doing, quite different than their original version. US Embassy to Secretary of State, "Shrimp Workers' Strike in Puerto El Triunfo," July 26, 1988, 026051z (obtained under the Freedom of Information Act from US Department of State); *La Prensa Gráfica*, Aug. 26, 1987.

[15] Presumably the marines were on a mission to obtain provisions.

[16] Campo Pagado, "La CGT condena inoperancia del Ministerio de Trabajo," *Diario de Hoy*, Nov. 13, 1987.

workers continue to work and to allow container trucks enter and depart from the premises. They allowed the plant workers to continue to process shrimp from five other companies, including Productos Pesqueros whose workers and fishermen belonged to SIP.

When Sindicato Agua launched the strike, they seemed to have a relatively strong position, despite the implacable opposition of SIP. Marlena Posada, as noted, offered hope that the BAC would work with them to create a cooperative. Moreover, AIFLD was firmly behind them. Although AIFLD legally could not directly deliver strike funds, through an educational program they funneled US$1,600 a month to the union.[17] Sindicato Agua also obtained limited support from other international labor organizations such as Central Latinoamericana de Trabajadores (CLAT).

Yet despite the CGT's good relations with the Ministry of Labor and the Duarte administration, the union activists were disappointed with their political allies. In October, the CGT and Sindicato Agua denounced the Comandante of the Navy (who they claimed had stock in Pezca) for attempting to break the strike, by allowing boats to bring diesel fuel into Puerto El Triunfo with the aim of resuming fishing in the companies on strike.[18] In October, the company through the Ministry of Labor made a proposal to Sindicato Agua that involved the payment of 70 percent of the money owed to the workers and 70 percent of the severance pay for all of the workers in the fishing companies. The companies would then be free to start up again and implement the subcontracting system.[19] Not surprisingly, the CGT and Sindicato Agua rejected the proposal because they "did not go on strike for severance pay" but for the company to respect their contract and to thwart the subcontracting plan. They demanded that the Ministry of Labor intervene in the negotiations to lessen the social injustice that had increased thanks to the "evil mentality of the rightist sectors." The unions also asked the Duarte administration to order the military to keep out of the conflict.[20]

Framing their struggle in broadly populist terms, the Sindicato Agua leadership even denounced foreign ownership of the company. In fact, no

---

[17] The money was paid as a stipend to Sindicato Agua leaders to participate in educational programs. They used it for food for the strikers. Interview with Ruperto Torres, Puerto El Triunfo, Feb. 2017. Francis Scanlon (former US labor attaché), phone conversation with the author, 2014; Norman Schipull (former director of AIFLD in El Salvador), electronic communication with the author, Sept. 17, 2014.

[18] *Diario Latino*, Oct. 20, 1987.

[19] Pagado, "La CGT condena inoperancia del Ministerio de Trabajo."   [20] Ibid.

foreigners owned stock in Pezca though an American company did own part of Atarraya. It is possible that some union militants considered the oligarchs "foreign" due to their different skin color, clothing style, and accents, but it is more likely that this allegation was merely a propaganda ploy. The declaration also had a particular anti-militaristic twist. Although clearly positioned against the FMLN, Sindicato Agua's rhetoric and forms of struggle were not at all compatible with the broad contours of Duarte's (or his US allies') discourse. Despite the political framing of the struggle, Benítez always stressed the apolitical nature of the struggle.

Sindicato Agua's rejection of the company offer was not surprising; it would have been an abdication of both the short-term objectives and the goal of establishing a cooperative. In his speeches, Benítez employed the slogan he had used in the 1985 strike: "todo o nada," with its powerful resonance among his base; it was his rallying cry to reject any company offer for less than the full back pay it owed the workers.[21]

SIP leaders suspected that the strike had the cooperative as its ultimate goal once the union pushed the company into bankruptcy. They assumed that a deal with the Duarte administration would lead to Sindicato Agua's control over the cooperative. Most fundamentally, SIP members believed that the fishermen's union guided by anti-communism and greed had contributed to the destruction of their livelihood. In a letter to the Minister of Labor, in October 1987, they lashed out at Benítez:

[H]e is responsible for the destruction of our livelihood; the destruction of a town whose life depends on the companies; of the personal and irrational reactions that will ensue when the companies are destroyed.[22]
This last line was prescient.

Both the antagonism between the two unions and the inertia of the Ministry of Labor prompted the Sindicato Agua leadership to expand the strike. On December 9, 1987, they declared a strike in the five remaining fishing companies tied to Pezca. SIP had the support of the workers and fishermen in Productos Pesqueros del Mar that in turn had administrative control over the other companies. All the companies, operating out of the

---

[21] Interviews with Ana Paniagua, Virginia Reyes, Elsie Castellón, Carmen Parada, Maura de Zelaya, and Ovidio Granadeño, Puerto El Triunfo 2012–14. The back pay derived from the clause in the 1985 contract that obligated to pay 80 percent of salaries when the fishing boats could not set sail due to the company's responsibility.
[22] SIP to Miguel Ángel Gallegos, letter, Oct. 2, 1987 (SIP Virtual Archive).

Pezca installations, had been subcontracting with *patrones del barco*. Sindicato Agua upped the ante by shutting down what they considered to be strike-breaking operations. More significantly, they believed that Productos Pesqueros had been created as a ploy whereby Rafael Escalón could decapitalize Pezca and start up the new company and, in so doing, eliminate all retirement benefits to the Pezca workers. Benítez argued that the union had been trying to negotiate contracts with these fishing companies for months and had followed the same Labor Code steps toward the legalization of a strike. Nevertheless, the departmental court declared it illegal. After the legal setback, Sindicato Agua exerted its coercive force. According to the testimony of Productos Pesqueros workers as related to the Juez Civil of Usulután:

On December 30, 1987 a group of union members affiliated with SGTIPAC, led by Sr. Mauricio Ascencio Benítez ... proceeded to violently enter the installations where we work for these companies; they also beat a guard and threatened him with a gun ... Since they took over the premises they will not allow us to enter nor to work and we have been threatened if we seek to work.[23]

Claiming that Sindicato Agua did not represent them, the SIP workers demanded legal action to allow them to work on the docks and on the boats. Notwithstanding the dramatic entrance into the plant, the Sindicato Agua strikers harmed no SIP workers. The plant workers then staged their own action by occupying the plant and its immediate surroundings. They locked up the cold storage unit where they kept the shrimp they had processed, as a means of pressuring the companies to pay them for the previous six weeks of work. However, the strike did end production work in the plant. Leading the resistance to Sindicato Agua and the defense of their livelihood was the new SIP leader, Ana Alvarenga.

ANA ALVARENGA AND SINDICATO TIERRA

Ana Alvarenga's brutalized childhood and young adulthood had steeled and prepared her for union leadership. When she became Secretary

---

[23] "Que el día 30 de Diciembre 1987 a las 5:30 horas un grupo de sindicalistas afiliados a SGTIPAC dirigidos por el sr. Mauricio Ascencio Benítez ... procedieron a irrumpir violentamente las instalaciones donde nosotros normalmente laborábamos para estas empresas; ademas golpearon y amenazaron con arma de fuego al vigilante ... Que a partir de los violentos incidentes y la toma del lugar donde operábamos el SGTIPAC no nos deja entrar, ni laborar y hemos sido amenazados si intentamos trabajar." Employees of Productos Pesqueros to the Usulután civil judge, letter, Jan. 8, 1988 (SIP General Archives).

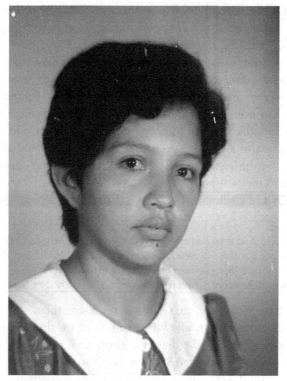

FIGURE 7.2 Ana Alvarenga early 1980s
(courtesy Ana Alvarenga)

General of the SIP Local she had become a brave, forceful, and intelligent woman, dedicated to her children and the membership. When she was six, her father, an artisanal fisherman, was lost at sea. She was one of nine children and her mother faced a near-impossible task to feed them all. Her mother and some of her brothers found work in Pezca to help make ends meet. When she was in third grade, Ana was charged with taking care of her siblings and cooking for the family. She also had to deliver food to her siblings who worked in the plants. The pressure on her was enormous. One of her brothers beat her if she did not have the tortillas ready or if she delivered their lunch late. Although she was an excellent student, she could not finish high school due to her familial responsibilities. The beatings continued. They physically hurt and psychologically scarred her. She could not overcome a sense of dread in her everyday existence. When she was 17, she got a job at Pezca so she could leave behind her domestic burden. Soon she met a *patrón de barco* and, after a short courtship, they married. At first, the marriage felt like liberation. Not for long. For 14 years he beat her.

During the 1970s, she worked in Planta II. Eventually she was promoted to Planta I where she worked sorting shrimp, a far easier job than peeling *chacalín*. Although she participated in SIP activities, during the 1979 strike when she was eight months pregnant with her first child, Alejandro relieved her of picket duty and sent her home. As SIP reorganized following the repression from 1980 to 1983, Ana continued to participate in meetings. She began to notice the corruption of some of the leaders of the Pezca Local and she denounced what she witnessed – namely unauthorized meetings between some of the union leaders and management. To Ana's eyes, those leaders often caved to management and also seemed more prosperous as time went on. The Pezca Local leadership in the 1980s was a male sphere. Yet, some of the male leaders were not corrupt and they admired Ana's courage. They nominated her for a leadership position and the union assembly voted her into office in May 1987 just before the Sindicato Agua strike broke out.

Ana's position on the Sindicato Agua strike was similar to the rest of the leadership. She saw no benefit at all for packinghouse workers. She also had to confront Sindicato Agua's efforts to win over SIP members. She recognized that SIP had lost members due to its corruption and its cozy relations with management. She thus took firm stands against corruption and made public all management overtures to her. Her anti-corruption discourse, combined with her day-to-day activities on behalf of the membership, persuaded some of the defectors to return from Sindicato Agua, and SIP stopped losing membership. She recalls: "One guy who had tried to seduce me before and had then left SIP, came up to me after I joined the leadership and told me that he recognized that I was honest and a fighter, so he was going to return to our union. He brought back others as well."[24] In a conscious response to prevailing gender norms, whenever she could, Ana would bring her along her children to meetings in San Salvador. Yet, she was simultaneously becoming aware of her identity as a female labor militant. In September 1988, she attended a feminist-inspired conference in San Salvador specifically devoted to women's issues including domestic abuse.[25]

During the first months of the strike, the plant workers continued to process shrimp from Productos Pesqueros and some allied companies.

---

[24] Ana Alvarenga, interview with the author, Montreal, 2016.   [25] Ibid.

As recounted in the preceding text, in December 1987, Sindicato Agua pushed the fishermen to strike in most of the remaining companies and forced Productos Pesqueros to close operations.

In early 1988, following the expansion of the Sindicato Agua strike, the Pezca Local membership elected Ana to its highest post, secretary-general. For the first time, a woman held that position in a SIP local union. As her first action, she promoted the full-scale occupation of the Pezca plant with the express purpose of protecting and maintaining the machinery and grounds. The occupation became a means to pressure the companies to pay the workers for the previous six weeks. Subsequently, and for the duration of the strike, the *toma*'s primary aims were to keep the machines and tools in good shape and protect them from vandalism or theft, awaiting the day they could go back to work.

SIP deployed a classic form of Salvadoran labor militancy for such unusual goals. The occupation, in part, had neoliberal objectives. For the union was pushing for an acceptance of Pezca's subcontracting plan and the occupation was an effort to preserve the possibility of a job. No one considered trying to figure out how the workers might produce and process shrimp – reaching some kind of arrangement with independent shrimpers, for example. Yet, the solidarity that SIP mobilized was legitimate in their eyes and those of the leftist federation, Federación Nacional Sindical de Trabajadores Salvadoreños (FENASTRAS). They were defending years of hard-fought improvements in their labor and living conditions. They survived largely thanks to donations from the labor federation and from churches.

Regardless of its goal, the collective nature of the occupation evinces in Altagracia Granadeña (Ovidio's sister) and others a sense of nostalgia.

We had to defend our jobs. We spent a lot of time occupying the plant. Other organizations brought us rice, beans, and corn. We cooked with a wood stove. We formed groups and we took turns. We kept our small kids with us.[26]

Plant workers, organized by shifts, camped out in the area just outside of the buildings, where all took share in the work equally.

The former plant workers recognize their unusual deployment of labor solidarity; some of their justification for their defensive *toma* derived from their assessment of Mauricio Benítez. He continued to gnaw away at the

---

[26] "Teníamos que defender nuestro trabajo. Pasamos bastante tiempo adentro. Nos traían las demás organizaciones – arroz, frijoles, y maiz. Cocinábamos con una cocina de leña. Formamos grupos y nos tornábamos. Allí estábamos juntos con los hijos pequeños." Altagracia Granadeño, interview with the author, Puerto El Triunfo, 2014.

SIP membership. Sindicato Agua activists would cajole plant workers: "If we get more members, we'll win the strike."[27] This was the period of Sindicato Agua's greatest success in recruiting SIP members. Before Ana's election, the suspicions of corruption were at their highest point. Ana helped stem the tide of defections and probably no more than 10 percent switched unions. She and other SIP militants belittled Benítez and his base of *eventuales* as people who "had only gone on out on two or three trips" and were not genuine fishermen.

There were times when SIP activists did reach out to Benítez. We have already seen how Ricardo Jovel had developed a reasonable relationship with the Sindicato Agua leader and that he supported the idea of a cooperative. Yet, part of the problem was that Jovel did not enjoy unanimous support either from the rank and file or from the other leaders. Despite his leftist orientation, many thought he was too cozy with management and some suggested that his reception of gifts of modest amounts of shrimp and fish entailed a degree of corruption. Such allegations were sufficient for FENASTRAS to remove him from his position in the federation. Some recall that his withdrawal from SIP as a reflection of his need for clandestine activity. Jovel claims that he had developed serious migraine headaches (who wouldn't have under such circumstances?). Regardless, his departure in 1987 removed one interlocutor in SIP for Benítez. Nevertheless, as the strike wore on, SIP began to take a more belligerent position with respect to the company and, subsequently, the BAC when the former declared bankruptcy. They also began to share their food with the strikers. Moreover, they offered some level of support for the cooperative. Rolando Franco recalls the situation in these terms:

Some of us began to realize that the cooperative was our only solution. We also realized that Benítez had been right. SIP had been becoming "patronalista" and "corrupt." So, we started talking with him, trying to figure out ways we could work together. But it was too hard. We realized that in the end he needed to become *the* spokesmen for the workers, he needed to be the head honcho.[28]

Here, it seems that the possibility for a united labor movement and the success of the cooperative hinged on the personality of Benítez. Was it really his personality, described by Mena Lagos and by the Embassy as "unstable" and "erratic?" Perhaps. Was it the deep mistrust fostered by Cold War alliances that derailed the cooperative efforts? Did the level of

[27] Ana Alvarenga, interview with the author, Puerto El Triunfo, 2015.
[28] Rolando Franco, interview with the author, Los Angeles, 2016. Emphasis added.

female hostility to the *machista* lifestyle of fishermen and their aggressive attitude toward SIP impede unity?

When Sindicato Agua launched the strike in Productos Pesqueros and the other fishing companies, they also took possession of seven boats. Those boats soon became an important issue in the dispute. Confronted with Sindicato Agua's "impounding" of the boats, Escalón opted to move his remaining fleet to the port of La Unión. The union, however, exerting some of its remaining influence with the Duarte administration, persuaded the Ministry of Agriculture to block the unloading of shrimp in La Unión. The companies then anchored the boats in the bay where, over the next few months, storms and vandalism destroyed most of them. This loss fed seamlessly into Escalón's narrative about the politicized strikes impeding the repayment of the loans. Moreover, his lawyers continued to contest the ruling until the ministry relented in August 1988 and four of Escalón's shrimp boats began to operate out of the port of La Unión.[29]

The Duarte administration claimed to sympathize with the strikers and, in January 1988, the president wrote to Pezca "recommending an immediate settlement of the dispute."[30] Although management did sit down several times at the bargaining table, it did not substantially change its initial offer, in part because it was no longer playing an independent hand. In May 1988, Pezca formally filed for bankruptcy and the BAC became the owner of the plant and the boats. The presence of the fishermen on the docks and in the boats, however, blocked the BAC's access to their new possessions.[31]

At this moment of impasse, the labor attaché from the US Embassy, Bruce Thomas, entered the discussions in an attempt to resolve the conflict.[32] The BAC was, above all else, interested in getting the loan money back and did not see payment of Pezca's debts to the laborers through the creation of a cooperative as a viable route. AIFLD surely informed Thomas about the situation; the AFL-CIO's international branch actively supported

---

[29] Rafael Escalón to the BAC, letter, Nov. 4, 1988, Pieza 56/1 (Juzgado Segundo de lo Penal, Corte Suprema de Justicia, San Salvador).

[30] US Embassy to Secretary of State, "Shrimp Workers' Strike in Puerto El Triunfo," July 26, 1988, 026051z (obtained under the Freedom of Information Act from US Department of State).

[31] In May 1988, in the offices of the Ministry of Labor, the company paid some 225,000 colones owed to the plant workers for work carried out processing shrimp brought in by fishermen working with Productos Pesqueros. That was the last transaction before it formally declared bankruptcy.

[32] Ruperto Torres, interview with the author, Puerto El Triunfo, 2016; Migdonio Pérez, interview with the author, Puerto El Triunfo, 2013.

the CGT and its allied labor confederation, the Union Nacional de Obreros y Campesinos (UNOC). After some consultation with the BAC, Thomas met with the Sindicato Agua leadership. The Embassy official informed the union activists that the bank claimed that the bankrupt Pezca owed it some US$8 million in addition to the amount the company owed to the workers. Thomas then urged Benítez and the others to negotiate with the BAC. According to Ruperto Torres, he said "We can do this – bargain with them [the BAC] – my government is very concerned."[33] Thomas suggested that the Embassy could help Sindicato Agua come up with the money to cover what the BAC was owed by Pezca, though he wanted the union leaders to negotiate the price down. Despite the potential offer that Thomas extended, the BAC stalled, avoiding committing to or even commenting about the idea. Then Thomas left his position as labor attaché to join the Foreign Service and the March 1989 Cristiani election removed union friends from high places.

The bank therefore blocked every move that Sindicato Agua made toward converting Pezca's debt to them into ownership of the facilities. Indeed, it had continued conversations with Escalón up until the bankruptcy under the hope that the very person responsible for the sinking of the company would restore the shrimp industry. Regardless of ideological differences, class prejudice and identity prevailed. In the words of Angel Escobar,

[The corporate and bank officials] ... acted on a mean-spirited impulse [*un capricho mesquino*]. There were incorrect ties between the rich and the politicians. Like it has always been in our country. Those on top could give a crap about the people who always end up screwed.[34]

The election of Alfredo Cristiani in March 1989 spelled the end of any real hope for the cooperative because the right-wing government would have no interest in backing such an initiative. Rather, its primary goal was to privatize the banks, and the financial dispossession of the BAC certainly did not fit in with the plan.

THE LONG FINALE

At 5:30 PM on June 29, 1989, 500 soldiers from the army's Sixth Battalion, shooting in the air, stormed the docks. They occupied the area

---

[33] "Esto podemos hacer – regatéolo ... mi gobierno está muy preocupado." Ruperto Torres, interview with the author, Puerto El Triunfo, 2013.

[34] Ángel Escobar, interview with the author, Los Angeles, Feb. 2017.

until the next day. At 3:00 AM, they boarded the six fishing boats involved in the "illegal" strike and evicted the strikers who were living on board. UNOC denounced the action: "the soldiers, pointing their guns, evicted the workers from the Pezca installations and took six boats in order to move them supposedly to La Unión." The troops injured some fishermen who tried to resist the eviction.[35] The union claimed that one of the boats had 15,000 colones (US$3,000) on board destined for food for the strikers as well as many of their tools and implements. The troops departed at 6:30 AM on June 30.

The military action cracked what had been unflinching unity among the Sindicato Agua members. The evicted fishermen who had been involved in the December 1987 expansion of the strike now had to find another place to live (they had been living on the boats), and their cause became even more desperate and more separate from those of the "legal" strikers. To add insult to injury, Atarraya and other fishing companies in the western port of Acajutla had created a blacklist, blocking any chance of employment for Sindicato Agua members. The union protested to the International Labor Organization where they received a favorable ruling but with no consequential governmental action.[36]

Despite the relative political weakness of their position, in October, Benítez was able to call a union meeting on the docks with an estimated participation of 500 permanent and *eventuales* members. In the prelude to a union election, he outlined the latest BAC proposal that offered the union members 50 percent of their wages since April 1987 plus 50 percent of their severance pay. The BAC would then end all the contracts and install the subcontracting system, effectively eviscerating the union and its contract, that in Benítez's words, "we had won with so much effort and sacrifice." Migdonio Pérez, another union leader, urged his fellow workers, "[D]on't let the psychological warfare employed by the BAC weaken us."[37] Another union member stood up and offered the possibility of compromise on the condition that if the BAC refused, then the union would demand that its members be granted cooperative ownership

[35] Campo Pagado, *Diario de Hoy,* July 1989; US Embassy to Secretary of State, "No Resolution in Sight as Three-Year Strike Drags On," June 13, 1990, 132130z (obtained under the Freedom of Information Act from US Department of State).

[36] ILO, Case 1506, *Definitive Report, Complaint against Government of El Salvador by SGTIPAC,* 1990.

[37] SGTIPAC minutes, act 109, Oct. 14, 1989 (SGTIPAC Archives).

of Pezca. No one publicly suggested accepting the BAC's offer. In the ensuing elections, Benítez beat out Fidel Angel Chavez, 378–122.[38]

Two weeks after the meeting on the docks, right-wing terrorists blew up the FENASTRAS headquarters in San Salvador, killing 10 people including Febe Velásquez, secretary general and *compañera* of Ricard Jovel. The event saddened and frightened members of both unions in Puerto El Triunfo; whatever their feelings about Jovel, the loss of Febe in such horrific fashion was painful. Right after the bombing, rumors of an FMLN offensive began to circulate. Benítez decided that it was time for him to take up some long-standing invitations from the US labor movement.

Although he claimed he feared for his life, the FMLN bore Benítez no particular animus; it was not clear who would be targeting the union leader. Other Sindicato Agua militants contended that the military knew exactly where everyone lived; they all faced the same risk. Some considered his departure an act of cowardice and betrayal. Once the November offensive waned and the capital and the port returned to their semblance of peaceful normality, Fidel Angel Chavez and the other Sindicato Agua leaders decided to reopen negotiations. They reached a "partial settlement" with the BAC and the company that would allow fishing operations to start again. However, Benítez returned immediately following the negotiations and denounced the settlement as an act of "cowardice." For the other leaders, his departure had been a "betrayal" of the struggle and an internecine conflict broke out. Ruperto Torres recalls, "In the CGT office in San Salvador, we came to blows. It was serious."[39]

Benítez was able to reassert his control, drawing on his reserves of support among the *eventuales*. The union voted to rescind the agreement with the BAC. He commented to an Embassy official that the acceptance and rejection came from a "leadership dispute."[40] He again pushed for a cooperative, claiming that the company assets, with the degradation of its fleet, had dropped to some US$4 million, whereas the company owed them US$5 million in back salaries (including strike pay) and benefits. In public, the union slammed the bank and the company:

[38] It is unclear whether during the election, Chavez suggested compromise, but he clearly did so with the backing of other union leaders in December 1989. Ruperto Torres, interview with the author, Puerto El Triunfo, Jan. 2016.

[39] Ibid.

[40] US Embassy to Secretary of State, "No Resolution in Sight as Three-Year Strike Drags On."

FIGURE 7.3 Ruperto Torres on fishing boat, 1980s
(courtesy Ruperto Torres)

[W]e are faced with a fraudulent bankruptcy originated by ill-intentioned policies that decapitalized the companies and defrauded the Banco Agrícola Comercial. The money obtained by some of the businessmen ended up in foreign bank accounts.[41]

The union demanded that the bank and government cease charging the workers for the bosses' corruption. The union then insisted that the Ministry of Agriculture activate fishing licenses so that the 32 boats under their control could start to work. Yet, once again, neither the government nor the BAC was interested in allowing the cooperative to get off the ground.

[41] "[S]e asiste a una quiebra fraudulenta originada por políticas malintencionadas que ejecturaron acciones de descapitalización de las empresas y estafa al Banco Agrícola Comercial, ya que el dinero obtenido por algunos empresarios lo han depositado en bancos extranjeros." Campo Pagado, SGITPAC, and CGT, "Exigimos solución al conflicto de Pezca S.A.," July 16, 1990.

FIGURE 7.4 Ruperto Torres on fishing boat
(courtesy Ruperto Torres)

In June 1990, the US Embassy sent several of its officials to the port
to see if they could help find a solution to the stalemate. The US government and AIFLD had been interested in the strike since its inception
but now had the added incentive to aid the bank privatization process.
Privatization was the key goal of the Cristiani administration whose
ideological agenda meshed perfectly with that of the George H. W. Bush
administration. The Embassy officials offered a somber portrait:

In Puerto Triunfo today, there is no evidence of the once thriving fishing business.
The concrete block building that once housed the plant – and still houses operable
machinery – ... is now empty. On a recent visit [we] hiked down a long, muddy
path and over a dormant swine to reach the sunny wharf where ex-fishermen
lounged and played cards. The rusty fishing boats are tied to the docks but haven't
left the port for three years.[42]

---

[42] Ibid., 2.

As part of the same investigation, Embassy officials interviewed the BAC president who not only reiterated his opposition to a cooperative but moreover underscored his legal strategy to dislodge the strikers from the plant and wharf. Following their eviction, he planned directly to operate the company "until investors were found." A new court ruling had lifted the obligation to pay back salaries to the strikers and thereby emboldened the BAC's opposition to the union demands.

President Cristiani, however, supported a compromise. He made it clear to both the strikers (with whom he met) and members of his administration that he wanted to find a quick solution and the Embassy officials lauded his commitment to do so despite the newly privatized bank's opposition. His motivations are not entirely legible. Most likely, he wished to highlight the moderate credentials of his faction of ARENA against the hard Right that had founded the party and continued to inform its national and international image. Moreover, a constructive stance toward the strike was congruent with Bush administration objectives.

The Embassy report concluded on a note of despair: "Thirty-four perfectly serviceable fishing boats sit alongside a wharf in Puerto Triunfo begging for a solution."[43] The officials did something else that day. They managed to converse privately with some of the other Sindicato Agua leaders about Benítez's role in the union. They made it clear that the Embassy would help reach the best agreement possible for the strikers, but they would do nothing as long as Benítez remained in the leadership. In the words of Migdonio Perez, "[T]hey were fencing him in until the Embassy stated that if Benítez stayed in the leadership, they would not help."[44]

The leadership group, already embittered by his actions since November 1989, approached Benítez and informed him, "Either you leave, or we'll make you leave."[45] Recognizing that he had no room left to maneuver, the labor *caudillo* did not stand for reelection. In September, around the time of his final decision to withdraw from the election, Benítez issued a statement to the union membership. He signaled the source of the workers' plight: "the situation caused by the fascistic mentality of the businessmen stockholders of our country who constantly

---

[43] Ibid., 3.   [44] Migdonio Pérez, interview with the author, Puerto El Triunfo, 2013.
[45] "[O] te apartás, o te apartamos." Ruperto Torres, interview with the author, Puerto El Triunfo, 2013.

react repressively against our actions." Referring directly to the Pezca strike, he charged interference by "the whorish justice system that protects those who have a lot of money."[46]

The statement combined populist militancy with a certain vagueness and abstractness that perhaps reflected his own sense of ambivalence. Given that the bulk of the union membership was idled by the strike, it is somewhat odd that he referred back to the fraud and to "*la movida*": "In order to keep up the smokescreen that allows them to cover up the social injustice and the bank financing, they keep on defaming the compañeros about illegal shrimp sales."[47] This was one of the few times that Benítez referred to "*la movida*." Although the strike had made the practice largely irrelevant, the fraud at the root of the crisis was still quite salient. He seemed to choose the moment when his own honor and reputation were under assault to defend the honor of his fellow workers. He then insinuated that some workers had sold out to the bosses, though the vagueness of his prose makes it unclear if he was referring to his fellow Sindicato Agua leaders who had demanded his removal. Finally, he signed off his last declaration, with a phrase that might have been uttered by any leftist militant over the previous two decades: "Only united can we achieve the power necessary to fight back against the oligarchy who oppresses us.[48]

Although it is possible that the militant declaration was meant to rally his troops one last time, it more likely reflects a moment of anguish. The labor leader simply had no alternative to offer except his anger and resentment against oligarchic power. Within a year, at the age of 42, he started a new life with his mother in Australia.

Even with Benítez gone and with US backing, the negotiation was not easy. Although the union realized it could not win the cooperative, it fought for a deal that would grant the members 75 percent of the strike pay and 75 percent of severance pay and benefits owed the membership. The BAC was opposed to these terms and stuck to its original figure of 50 percent. This time, however, due to a favorable ruling (the "justicia ramera" in Benítez's words), the BAC was under no legal obligation to pay back wages. An official of the Ministry of Labor sided with the bank. Ruperto Torres recalls the official almost spitting at them "You're not worth 50%!"

[46] "Carta Abierta Para los Afiliados al SGTIPAC," Sept. 17, 1990 (SGTIPAC Visual Archive).
[47] Ibid.   [48] Ibid.

Despite its lingering Cold War–infused distaste for SIP, the Embassy concurred with the Minister of Labor that SIP needed to be included in the final negotiations. After years of discord, the two unions came together and jointly pushed back against the BAC position. Ruperto Torres recalls the final negotiating session when one of them shouted at the bankers: "You give us 75% or we'll torch the whole place and all the boats. The gasoline is ready!"[49] Whether the BAC took the threat seriously, the bank upped the offer from 50 percent to 60 percent.

On January 22, 1991, 542 workers belonging to SIP and to Sindicato Agua received indemnifications of 5.2 million colones (or roughly US$1 million). On average, the workers received less than US$2,000 a person. The money only went to permanent workers. All those years fighting for the rights of the *eventuales* in the plant and on the sea were for naught. The former plant workers and fishermen welcomed the money; they were all in dire straits. Yet, it hardly represented what they had struggled for all those years. Some used the severance pay to start very small businesses. Others used it to head to "el norte," especially the fishermen who had been blacklisted in the few remaining fishing companies in the country. Several Sindicato Agua activists joined forces with ex *guerrilleros*, their erstwhile political antagonists, to form a shrimp farming cooperative that still functions today.[50]

EMBITTERED MEMORIES

Most former plant workers are deeply embittered as they bemoan the loss of an industry that had allowed for a life in a town they remember as prosperous and decent compared to the dystopian present. The mostly female SIP militants evince little but contempt for the 1987–91 strike. More than anything else for the former plant workers, Benítez's slogan "todo o nada" synthesized Sindicato Agua ideology and action during the 1980s. On one level, the phrase refers to his maximalist stance, his rejection of any compromise with the company and later with the BAC. For Ana Alvarenga, who returns to the port from Montreal several

[49] Ruperto Torres, interview with the author, Puerto El Triunfo, 2013.
[50] The shrimp farming cooperative is still operating today. If there were lingering ideological discrepancies, they were long ago buried. It seems that the ex *guerrilleros* had been given the land in Sisiguayo as part of the Peace Accords, and they brought in Ruperto Torres and others due to their knowledge of shrimp and some prior friendship.

months a year, that stance led to a once-vibrant town left with "nothing," utterly devastated. "Todo o nada" also conjures up memories of Benítez's authoritarianism. Office staff who worked in the payroll department recall how the Sindicato Agua leader would storm in whenever there were any errors; he would loudly berate and threaten them.[51] Others remember that he went around armed with a pistol. Ana recalls that,

"[H]e was so overbearing with us that he insulted us ... calling us company stooges [*patronalistas*]. She adds, "Todo o nada – that was their slogan ... but that's no way to negotiate ... Benítez was not a friendly guy – only with his own people. I met with him a couple of times – but only on the docks. He refused to come to the plant."[52]

Ana, who, as we saw, had suffered unbearable domestic violence before and during her marriage, possessed perhaps an extra dimension of resentment against Benítez's chauvinistic treatment of her. Today anger still shapes her memories of him: "He was a drunk ... who knows where he came from?" That memory also derived from the official and unofficial SIP discourse about him. SIP militants also tried to delegitimize Benítez because he had only worked a brief time as an *eventual*. Ana commented, "He had nothing to lose. He didn't work for the company."[53]

Former fishermen, not surprisingly, remember key moments and practices from the 1980s differently and in so doing shed some light on the local *desencuentro* in the past and present. In particular, they interpret "todo o nada" in their own register. In this view, Benítez was willing to compromise; but he would not sacrifice the integrity of the union to do so. Sindicato Agua members fully agreed with their leader that the proposed subcontracting system would lead inevitably to the destruction of the union. Therefore, *todo* was a statement that the union had to survive and therefore subcontracting had to be stopped. And *nada* signified the destruction of the union.

The fishermen also remember the enunciator of that slogan as a remarkable individual who was sincere and dedicated to their cause. They laud Benítez's leadership skills and his achievements on behalf of the union. As Angel Escobar recalls, "He was a magnificent leader. He struggled with great determination; he did everything he could for the workers."[54]

---

[51] Ivette Bará, communication with the author, 2017.
[52] Ana Alvarenga, interview with the author, Montreal, 2016.
[53] Ana Alvarenga, interview with the author, Puerto El Triunfo, 2015.
[54] Ángel Escobar, interview with the author, Los Angeles, 2016.

FIGURE 7.5 Angel Escobar and family, 1980s
(courtesy Angel Escobar)

Benítez left a powerful impression on fellow Sindicato Agua leader, Migdonio Pérez:

The night before of an important meeting he would just read and read. The day of the meeting with the lawyers, he would not look at the book because he would have memorized it all. He had quite a mind ... not just anybody can memorize what you are going to speak.[55]

Indeed, he possessed a unique quality. As Ruperto Torres put it,

He had been a drunk. People would kick him when he was passed out on the street. And he quit drinking and began to put all that energy into reforming the union and winning a decent shake for the fishermen. But he never forgot where he came from or the pain and humiliation of those kicks.[56]

---

[55] Migdonio Pérez, interview with the author, Puerto El Triunfo, 2013.
[56] Ruperto Torres, interview with the author, Puerto El Triunfo, 2013.

The power and resonance of his populism derived in part from that deepest of resentments against the powerful. His personal transformation also gave luster and credibility to his crusade against corruption in the union and the company (with the exception of the illegal sales). They recall the final contract (1985) as a major achievement. His ability to negotiate and enlist the support of the powerful also won him respect.

Yet even to Benítez's former comrades, he had a downside. First, he allowed himself to become too closely identified with the Christian Democratic Party, thereby "politicizing" the union. Nevertheless, despite (or because) the government was on his side he was not an adept negotiator, particularly with regard to the 1987–91 strike. More significantly, his courage was not limitless. They recall that he left the country during the period around the November offensive of the FMLN, when guerrillas briefly occupied parts of the capital. None of his union comrades felt that their leader was in any particular danger. Ruperto Torres conjectures that he fled because he simply did not know how to move forward. Without the cooperative, the options were unpalatable to him. Whatever his motives, this action led to considerable dissent within Sindicato Agua and eventually led to his semi-enforced exile from the port and his emigration to Australia. He left embittered memories about the longest strike in the history of El Salvador (most likely in Latin American history), one that attempted to hold the line against the global advance of the casualization of labor and create noncapitalist labor relations on land and sea.

Notwithstanding that radical vision, as we have seen, the *desencuentro* ran deep. The red baiting of the mid-1980s had subsided as FENASTRAS and UNOC began to collaborate, but the memory of the Cold War–inflected venom lingered on, as did the memory of the machista scorn evinced by Sindicato Agua leaders for SIP members. Most fundamentally, SIP members had a hard time forgiving the fishermen for what they perceived to be their greed that had contributed to the destruction of everyone's livelihood. Before the strike, they had presciently argued that it would only bring "misery, hunger, pain, and desolation to Puerto El Triunfo."[57] That the strike fulfilled their prediction did not make it any easier to join forces with Benítez either at the time or today in their memories.

[57] Ricardo Jovel and SIP, "Carta Abierta," *Diario de Hoy,* July 29, 1987.

Conclusion

Tropical Deindustrialization and Its Discontents

Historians of the twentieth century ... are both "exiles" and "witnesses" because they are deeply involved in the events that constitute the object of their research. They do not explore a far and unknown past, and the difficulty of their task lies in taking distance with respect to a recent past, a past that they often have lived and observed that still haunts their environment.

Enzo Traverso, *Left-Wing Melancholia*

Gunshots ring out frequently as the two main *maras* (gangs) in Puerto El Triunfo battle over turf on which they can engage in petty extortions. One day in 2016 a group of *mareros* approached Ovidio Granadeño, 72-year-old former Sindicato de la Industria Pesquera (SIP) activist turned baker. They demanded that he start paying "la renta" or face serious consequences. He responded, "Look guys, you know I spent a lot of years dealing with death squads and the National Guard. So, now I'm just going to go about my business."[1] Perhaps the old man's response stirred a sense of respect or bafflement, but regardless they didn't demand "renta" again. He already pays a different kind of "renta" in the exploitative hours he labors to barely break-even; he works from 4 AM until 2 PM six days a week. Yet, Ovidio's story is one of the precious few bright spots in the bleak panorama of tropical deindustrialization that envelops the port.

---

[1] Ovidio Granadeño, interview with the author, Puerto El Triunfo, 2016. For a superb study of gangs and neoliberalism, see Deborah Levenson-Estrada, *Adiós Niño: The Gangs of Guatemala City and the Politics of Death* (Durham, NC: Duke University Press, 2013).

Although Ovidio's biography is unusual in Puerto El Triunfo, it synthesizes strands of solidarity that symbolize the strength of the SIP and, more generally, the Salvadoran labor movement at its apogee in the late 1970s. He was on the run when he arrived in the port toward the end of the February–March 1979 strike. The National Guard had marked him for elimination due to his activities as a member of the Bloque Popular Revolucionario (BPR), in particular his work fomenting cooperatives on occupied hacienda land. He combined his BPR work with his activism in his Christian Base Community (CBC). His work in the two organizations often overlapped.

As a young man, Ovidio could not provide for his new wife and child on the family *minifundio*, so he had traveled to the capital where he got a job in a bakery. Shortly after he started his job in 1967, his coworkers went on strike and he opted to become involved. He then met the secretary-general of the Bakery Workers' Union, Salvador Cayetano Carpio, also a Communist (and later guerrilla) leader, whose courage and intelligence influenced him profoundly.

These varied experiences in solidarity shaped Ovidio's thoughts and actions as a labor militant in the port. He remained a committed political militant and collaborated with the FMLN throughout the 1980s. Yet, his role as a rank-and-file SIP leader belonged to a separate sphere. He consciously avoided rising to the top of SIP ranks in part for fear of repression but mainly because he considered his union activity to be autonomous from and secondary to his revolutionary militancy.

Ovidio thus helped to guide the reconstruction of SIP following the lethal wave of repression in 1980–81. He infused the union with his moral and ethical sense, including a sense of responsibility toward the company machinery. Similarly, he urged his fellow union activists to take security precautions. He recalls with deep remorse how he had cautioned Manuel Rivera, following a negotiation session, not to go out that night. Plainclothes agents "disappeared" Rivera after picking up at a tavern in the port. Ovidio also denounced even the appearance of the slightest forms of corruption.

Ovidio guided SIP in a significant transformation into a "bread-and-butter" union, that is, one strictly focused on wages and benefits for its members. He also helped to shape SIP's largely negative response to the Sindicato Agua strikes and especially to their proposed cooperative. Ovidio's trajectory as a labor activist with leftist commitments and Christian roots raise difficult questions. How did a man so steeped in Christian radical and revolutionary notions of solidarity ultimately come to reject labor solidarity so close to home? How could a revolutionary and an eminently decent human being call for military intervention in the port?[2] He had his reasons: "*la movida*" deeply offended him, on the one hand, and Sindicato Agua's cheap and dangerous use of the epithet "subversive" to attack the SIP leadership angered him, on the other. Moreover, he received counsel from Federación Nacional Sindical de Trabajadores Salvadoreños (FENASTRAS) and from the FMLN that argued against any form of cooperativism as being counterinsurgent.

Ovidio's case is intriguing precisely because he combined a revolutionary ideology and practice with sensibilities rooted in a profound commitment to radical Christianity and to trade unionism. For a brief time, on his farming cooperative in 1977–78 and then during the high tide of labor successes in the port in 1979, Ovidio lived a unity among those three dimensions. Yet, by the mid-1980s, they were compartmentalized: his union militancy, his CBC work, and his clandestine activities on behalf of the FMLN became separate spheres of activity. The union focused on the plant; the CBC attempted to provide services to the impoverished war refugees in the port but shorn of its previous utopian aspirations; and the FMLN aimed to destroy or transform the state, but the guerrilla army operated in a sphere largely cut off from the union and from the CBCs. On a national level, while the FMLN was not at all cut off from the resurgent labor movement, it focused on recruiting militants and, to a lesser degree, disrupting the economy and challenging (e.g., delegitimizing) the government. For these reasons, the FMLN was incapable of promoting an emancipatory vision within the labor movement. Ovidio's biography encapsulates the complex nature of labor organizing in the port; against the backdrop of the Civil War, workers had multiple, coexisting affiliations and commitments, which contributed both to the achievement of labor solidarity at crucial moments and its eventual demise.

Moreover, Ovidio's transformation was also an early indicator of the spread of neoliberal rationality into the most remote ideological and geographical corners of the world. As Mathieu Hilgers writes, "The drive towards individual responsibility and the self as enterprise is a major principle of the neoliberal art of governing."[3] Indeed, we can see the disarticulation of his notions of solidarity as key to the emergence of

---

[2] Ovidio Granadeño, interview with the author, Puerto El Triunfo, 2014–15. Ovidio neither signed the document calling for the military intervention (it was signed collectively) nor does he recall it. That said, he was part of the SIP leadership.

[3] Mathieu Hilgers, "The Three Anthropological Approaches to Neoliberalism," *International Social Science Journal* 61, no. 202 (Oct. 2011): 358.

neoliberal rationality.[4] In particular, the reduction of the scope of meaning of the terms *interest* and *solidarity* from the geographical and social expansiveness of the late 1970s to the walls of Pezca S.A. in the 1980s reflected such a transformation. As we have seen, Cold War ideologies and practices (e.g., AIFLD) and the illicit financialization of capital were fundamental preconditions for the conflicts in the port that conditioned those dramatic changes.

Solidarity Under Siege offers a case study in what David Harvey has called "accumulation by dispossession."[5] The devastating bank fraud of 1985–86 involved two distinct forms of "financialization": a process analyzed by the Marxist geographer, whereby productive is superseded by financial capital. Fundamentally, it transferred funds from a highly productive enterprise into the financial sector, in so doing, transferring them from El Salvador to the United States. The fraud decapitalized the nationalized banking system and, therefore, facilitated the overall privatization of banks that previously had been a bulwark against neoliberalism and had achieved modest success in the limited redistribution of capital to the middle classes. The spread of neoliberal ideology and practice also hinged on the unmaking of labor solidarity.

This book has charted the practices and ideas that contributed to the making of solidarity in the port and the wider Salvadoran working class and its unmaking during the 1980s. The unraveling of working-class solidarity was a lengthy, multidimensional process, to a limited degree rooted in certain fractures that persisted despite the massive displays of solidarity during the late 1970s. In the port, as we saw, those had to do with labor segmentation and gender relations primarily between plant workers and fishermen. The other fissures were political. Recall, even during the mobilization of more than 1,000 port workers to the January 22, 1980 demonstration, SIP threatened workers with the loss of a day's pay if they did not participate and at least 25 percent or more of the labor force felt the coercion. Nationally, in addition to political antagonism, a significant sector of the industrial working class eschewed strikes or occupations for ideological opposition or for fear of precipitating a plant closure, a rapidly growing phenomenon.

---

[4] Kirsten Weld, *Paper Cadavers: The Archives of Dictatorship in Guatemala* (Durham, NC: Duke University Press, 2014), offers a highly developed generational account of the onset of neoliberalism and neoliberal rationality in Guatemala.

[5] David Harvey, *A Brief History of Neoliberalism* (New York: Oxford University Press, 2007), 161.

Notwithstanding those fissures that would remain embedded within it, the labor movement grew rapidly in the late 1970s to become proportionally among the largest and most militant in hemispheric history. That dramatic expansion depended on the ability of the radical Left to stimulate and to permit the flowering of subaltern consciousness without imposing rigid meanings upon it. Such consciousness is evident in the emergence of a proto-syndicalist consciousness in the port and in the capital traced in the first chapters of this book. Noé and Gloria, for example, pursued an agenda of absolute solidarity with the urban and rural labor movement, implacable opposition to management and bureaucracies, and a productivist ethos. Their anti-politicism did not prevent them from mobilizing intensively for the January 22 march that they interpreted, as did Alejandro Molina Lara, as an expression of workers' power. Similarly, the 46 factory *tomas* in the first 9 months of 1979 allowed for rank-and-file ideological expressions that emphasized solidarity at all costs. Those expressions would gather force early in 1980 when the revolutionary Left came to support a syndicalist-style demand for the *autogestion* of closed factories (or those on the verge of closure).

Nevertheless, the six-week period between November 6 and December 18, 1979 revealed problematic consequences that derived from the unspoken tensions between formal ideological statements and quotidian, grassroots consciousness and practice. During that understudied and undervalued period, the radical Left continued to express its unrelenting hostility to the government that they labeled the Junta Contrarevolucio-naria. Yet, as underscored in Chapter 3, there were neither death squad victims nor violent repression during those weeks. Rather the period witnessed not only successful union actions but, moreover, the explosion of a rural labor movement, proportionally among the largest and most militant in Latin American history. The very proclamations of the Junta Revolucionaria de Gobierno (JRG) in favor of rural labor, in part, spurred the movement that the radical Left was able to harness. Nonetheless, in the countryside and the cities, the disjunction between the radical anti-JRG discourse and the daily reality of governmental tolerance for dissent and the consequent giant strides toward labor emancipation had crippling effects on the Left. For they proved unable to connect the discourse and reality in such a way as to create a viable strategy to take advantage of this most unusual conjuncture in which their real antagonists were relatively weak and in disarray.[6]

---

[6] William Deane Stanley, *The Protection Racket State: Elite Politics, Military Extortion, and Civil War in El Salvador* (Philadelphia, PA: Temple University Press, 1996), 167–74, through a different analysis arrives at a similar conclusion.

Let us briefly reconsider the making of solidarity in the port whose workers would form a key contingent in the national movement. The packinghouse workers union achieved a high degree of what the sociologist Beverly Silver calls "associational power" – that is a high level of internal cohesion that translated into power at the point of production, in turn related to structural or workplace bargaining power due to their position in a "tightly integrated production process."[7] The union used both forms of power to better dramatically their members' standard of living and working conditions. They succeeded in large part because of their sustained resistance to early forms of what subsequently would become known as the flexibilization (or casualization) of labor, related to labor segmentation. Labor activists fought against the marginalization of a large, primarily female sector of the workforce thereby increasing union power. The case of the packinghouse workers suggests that a high degree of autonomy could be carved out under authoritarian rule, especially due to the legitimacy of a certain style of apolitical unionism committed to defending *interests*. Throughout the 1970s, SIP operated in an increasingly authoritarian political environment and yet, despite their established affiliation with a leftist federation, the union managed to attain influence at all levels of shop floor labor relations including the firing of high-level management and substantial control over work rhythms and conditions. SIP had also achieved a remarkable degree of legitimacy, a local form of hegemony, in the port. As we saw, local paramilitary rightists collaborated with the union leadership and that collaboration saved lives, as the ORDEN activists consistently informed the SIP leadership of impending raids by the National Guard or planned assassination attempts.

By the late 1970s, SIP had constructed a limited form of local hegemony. My use of the Gramscian term refers to the union's ability to command respect and consent from all sectors of port society and to neutralize the use of force by the state authorities. The enclave-like ambience of Puerto El Triunfo and the shrimp industry favored the union's hegemony. Unlike in other enclaves, however, the oligarchic owners and high-level managers resided in the capital.[8] Only the Partido

---

[7] Beverly Silver, *Forces of Labor: Workers' Movements and Globalization since 1870* (Cambridge: Cambridge University Press, 2003), 13. She borrowed the term from Erik Olin Wright.

[8] For the classic accounts of enclave labor in Latin America, see Charles Bergquist, *Labor in Latin America: Comparative Essays on Chile, Argentina, Venezuela, and Colombia* (Stanford, CA: Stanford University Press, 1986) and Phillipe Bourgois, *Ethnicity at Work: Divided Labor on a Central American Banana Plantation* (Baltimore, MD: Johns Hopkins University Press, 1989).

de Conciliación Nacional (PCN), the military party, in decline throughout the 1970s, could offer a challenge to SIP. Yet, the union's reach was extensive enough to encompass PCN members. The controlled incorporation of rightist elements into SIP, in turn, probably helped to stave off repression much longer than elsewhere in the country. Moreover, union activists built and promoted the value of a multidimensional solidarity that managed to filter through the boundaries of its formal apoliticism. SIP's limited control over port society resembled that of other unions throughout the hemisphere, particularly in those cities, towns, and enclaves dominated by one industry. The port union distinguished itself, however, by achieving so much when much of the country, suffering under a terrorist regime, was on the verge of civil war.

The mobilization of women was both cause and consequence of the construction of local hegemonic forms. We have noted how the union mobilized female *eventuales*, many of whom, like Gloria, found their voices and identities as union militants. Indeed, Gloria's story from her childhood in the cotton fields to her ascension to union leadership is significant precisely because it reveals the fluid construction of new forms of sociability within the old organizational structures. She overcame the stain and stigma of deep poverty and worse to achieve a level of dignity that symbolized that of the female working class.

SIP's local hegemony and the advance of female labor militancy nevertheless faced rigid limits. Labor segmentation rooted in the production process formed a series of barriers to solidarity. The two most fundamental divisions were between plant workers and fishermen and between permanent and temporary workers, the latter primarily used to peel and pack *chacalín*. Before the late 1970s, the female and male permanent workers generally considered themselves superior to the *eventuales* not only for their income but also for their social refinement – in particular their distance from the culture of the rural poor. The union mobilization of the female *eventuales* ultimately persuaded the permanent workers to recognize that their own empowerment accompanied and depended upon that of the temporary workers. The victory of August 1979 dealt a blow, however temporary, to management and its long-standing accumulation through the flexibilization of labor. Nevertheless, SIP's triumph could only last 15 months; it could not withstand the wave of death squad violence in December 1980 that killed or drove into exile most of the union leadership.

The Civil War, the Cold War, gender ideologies, and the global march of neoliberalism accentuated and overdetermined the rift between the port labor unions. Although labor's defeat ushered in the era of tropical deindustrialization, the history of the two unions permits us to resist the implicit teleology of neoliberalism's triumph in the region.

This book also offers a different perspective on US policy in El Salvador during the Civil War.[9] As is well known, the United States contributed upward of US$6 billion to defeat the FMLN insurgency. Every move the United States made in Central America aimed to defeat the guerrillas and the Sandinista government in Nicaragua. There was, however, a contradiction at the core of its Salvadoran policy, particularly under the Reagan administration. Counterinsurgency involved a total assault on the Salvadoran Left in all of its manifestations. The United States recognized that the most effective nonviolent counterinsurgency strategy hinged on support for Duarte and the Christian Democratic Party. That assessment was based on both the objective political strength of Duarte in 1984–85 and on US rejection of the extreme Right among whose innumerable crimes included the assassination of two AIFLD employees in 1980. The Christian Democratic program of cooperativism, robust government ownership, and support for labor nevertheless struck against the core values of the Reagan administration. Indeed, the administration compelled Duarte to modify his program significantly, by embracing the "modern" sector of capital and the recommendations of the IMF. As Ignacio Ellacuría observed, "Here is Duarte's paradox in a nutshell. Without U.S. aid, he cannot stay in power; but the more aid he receives, the tighter his straitjacket becomes, the less he can hope to carry out programs of his own that diverge from Reagan administration policy."[10] Although the contradiction between counterinsurgent and neoliberal goals played out in myriad ways that remain largely unstudied, we can see one iteration in the port. AIFLD's financial and political support for the 1985 Sindicato Agua strike that cost the government more than US$4.5 million in export income was at loggerheads with the Reagan

---

[9] See Greg Grandin, *Empire's Workshop: Latin America, the United States, and the Rise of the New Imperialism* (New York: Metropolitan Books, 2006), 103–4. Grandin underscores the contradiction between the broad counterinsurgent US strategy that encompassed Duarte's reformist program with the ideological imperatives of the Reagan administration. "Far from promoting industrialization and a more equitable distribution of the nation's wealth, the Reagan administration insisted that Duarte orient the economy toward free trade while at the same time cutting back on social spending, which only served to estrange the Christian Democrats further from their working-class supporters." Ibid., 104.

[10] *NACLA Report on the Americas* 20, no. 1 (Jan.–Mar. 1986).

administration's efforts to stabilize the economy. As we saw in Chapter 5, one unintended consequence of that strike was to prompt the massive fraud involving US$20 to $30 million that significantly weakened the banking system and further undermined the economy. AIFLD also supported the 1987–91 strike. Although they were not directly involved, it is doubtful Sindicato Agua would have launched the strike without counting on AIFLD's limited financial backing and political support.

The Cold War also directly heightened tensions between the two unions. AIFLD and Duarte provided a language of assault against the SIP leadership, some of whom did sympathize with and in some cases worked with the FMLN. Ovidio Granadeño, for example, found safe houses for guerrillas needing rest and relaxation. Other SIP activists also provided limited logistical support.[11] Yet throughout the Civil War there were no guerrilla attacks or fighting in the port. Sindicato Agua's charges of "subversion" against SIP activists could have been death sentences; they created additional fear and anxiety for the union militants. Conversely, FENASTRAS viewed every move by the CGT as an element of a counterinsurgent strategy that had to be defeated.

The Cold War accounted for only one aspect of the discord in the port. There was a sharp gender dimension to the conflict, whose origins were in the division of labor, pitting male fishermen and dockworkers against mostly female packinghouse workers. Cultural factors exacerbated the structural division: women resented the fishermen's machista lifestyle, which they blamed for the destabilization of families. There were also obvious work and leisure cultural differences. Whereas the SIP militants strove to achieve what sociologists would call a stable, middle-class existence (*una vida digna* is a common subaltern refrain), the shrimpers lived an almost caricature of macho heroism, drinking, womanizing, and flaunting their general disregard for societal norms – as one shrimper confided – "los pescadores somos degenerados."[12]

Like Gloria García, Ana Alvarenga suffered a brutalized childhood. Well into adulthood, she endured domestic violence, first perpetrated by her siblings and later by her husband, a shrimp boat captain. Ana experienced a sense of her own liberation through her union activity. Most significantly, after a lifetime of abuse, she found her dignity and established her equality with the male leaders through giving speeches and

---

[11] Ovidio Granadeño, interview with the author, Puerto El Triunfo, 2014. One explanation for the lack of armed action in the port was its use by the FMLN precisely for recuperation from injuries or exhaustion.

[12] Ruperto Torres, interview with the author, Puerto El Triunfo, 2013.

helping mobilize workers in other plants throughout the region. Moreover, she was a delegate to El Salvador's first feminist conference that devoted much energy to devising legal and psychological strategies for dealing with domestic abuse.[13]

Nevertheless, Ana's ascension to the union leadership occurred just as the port was sinking under the weight of the bank fraud and Sindicato Agua's strike against the company/bank's subcontracting plan that would eliminate the union. The depths of Ana's resentment against Sindicato Agua's machismo were but one factor in the *desencuentro* between Sindicato Tierra and Sindicato Agua. Most significantly, the form of *marinero* resistance – direct appropriation – created a realm of deep misunderstanding and impeded communication between the two groups. To speak openly about the practice was to invite serious problems: not only could crew members suffer criminal prosecution but also the military who profited from the enterprise could easily exact retribution. Thus, until the mid-1980s *la movida* was a realm of silence despite its significance for every aspect of labor relations and the port's survival.

These silences and *desencuentros* suggest an addendum to James Scott's concept of hidden transcripts. Typically, hidden transcripts reveal critiques of official and dominant forces. This study suggests that they also offer mutual critiques among subaltern forces. Such was the case of the transcripts of *la movida*. An analysis of those transcripts, however fragmentary, provides some insight into subaltern consciousness and the *desencuentros* (I and II) among different labor sectors. If indeed the dominant discourse is subject to a debate over meaning by elite and subordinate populations, meanings are also contested among subaltern groups especially those that are structurally divided.

Plant workers and fishermen had different understandings of key terms such as *cooperative* or slogans such as *todo o nada*. Those different understandings, rooted in distinct experiences and class positions, led to breakdowns in potential alliances. Many SIP leaders were socialists who believed workers could run the industry. Yet they opposed Sindicato Agua activists whose notion of a cooperative grew out of their hidden transcripts of primary accumulation and inspired by Christian Democratic trade unionism.

Both Sindicato Tierra and Sindicato Agua valiantly resisted neoliberal inspired managerial practices, but they did so at different times, with distinct

---

[13] "Primer Encuentro de Mujeres Para Analizar La Crisis Económico y Político," *El Mundo*, Sept. 21, 1988; Ana Alvarenga, interview with the author, Montreal, 2016.

methods and with precious little solidarity between the two unions. As we saw in Chapters 1 and 2, during the 1970s SIP successfully waged a struggle to transform the status of female casual labor. The active participation of the female *eventuales* radically changed the union both in its scope and militancy. They received no support from Sindicato Agua in their efforts [save during the 1979 strike]. During the 1980s, Sindicato Agua fought against neoliberal managerial practices. When open unemployment reached 33 percent, Sindicato Agua mobilized the fishermen *eventuales* and linked their interests to the permanent labor force. Sindicato Agua struggled above all else against the system of subcontracting that management – following the incipient but powerful global trend – sought to impose. Sindicato Tierra, however, embraced the new system, a harbinger of neoliberal management strategies, as the only way to keep the company afloat. The *desencuentro* impeded a potential alliance that might well have charted a different course through the storm of neoliberalism that swept up everything solidary in its wake.

A member of Sindicato Agua synthesized their cause: "It is better to struggle today than to live tomorrow like a modern slave in an unjust society that does not recognize the rights of working people."[14] A leftist plant worker might have spoken those same words. Uttered by a Christian Democratic fisherman, however, their meaning floated adrift on the bay.

Ana Alvarenga surveys the wreckage of tropical deindustrialization, the hollowed-out structures, the conveyor belts that convey nothing, the machinery strewn throughout the grounds of Pezca S.A.:

It disappoints me so much that a company that was once called the Central American monster [for its size] has left so many families without daily sustenance; people who struggled because we Salvadorans are hard-working people. We struggle to get ahead. I am so disheartened to see that all of the large-scale machinery that was here has all been destroyed ... It pains me that there are so many people here in need.[15]

Was another outcome really possible?[16] To respond we need to critically review the transformation of the Left leadership of SIP. Had they recognized the possibility of aligning with Sindicato Agua in their battle for a cooperative, SIP's extended webs of solidarity would have perhaps also resisted the onset of neoliberal rationality. At the same time, Sindicato

---

[14] Central Latinoamericano de Trabajadores, *CLAT Informativo*, Apr. 1988, 42.

[15] Ana Alvarenga, interview with the author, Puerto El Triunfo, 2015.

[16] In a response to my film, *Port Triumph,* Professor Daniel James posed this question: "[G]iven the extraordinary concatenation of overwhelming state violence, company hostility, a raging civil war what other outcome was possible?" Personal communication with the author, Feb. 2018.

Agua would have had to rein in its *caudillo,* Mauricio Benítez, so that horizontal relations between the two unions could be established. The creation of the cooperative, within their collective grasp, would have allowed for the formation of a space of solidarity, of egalitarian social relations. Such spaces of resistance, however limited and problematic, are the only extant levees built to withstand the global hurricane of neoliberalism. In 1998, Hurricane Mitch provoked devastation throughout Central America. The dams around the shrimp farms in Honduras burst and the torrents of polluted waters reached as far as the Bay of Jiquilisco. Against real and metaphorical hurricanes, the shrimp cooperative might not have survived.

The theorist Wendy Brown cautions against left-wing nostalgia in part because the object of mourning has been a deeply flawed welfare state. Moreover, she convincingly argues that such an affect impedes the development of a serious alternative to the status quo. Ana and other port workers and fishermen look back on their moments of liberation and of triumph with pride and nostalgia, mixed with the bitterness of an ultimate defeat whose causes have remained as murky as the polluted bay. This book has tried to shed some light through those turbulent waters of despair. A reader might recognize hope in the moments of liberation and solidarity shared by so many and strive to create new societal forms that mirror such values despite the pervasive neoliberal ideologies and policies that not only impede their development but also deny their very right to exist. Memories of solidarity contain their own radical potential: they evoke long-censored dreams and aspirations for a dignified life in a better world.

Epilogue

That's when I really felt hell come down on me.

Arnovis Guidos Portillo, detained at the US border in June 2018, upon
learning that his daughter had been taken by ICE to Florida or New York.
He had fled the Calle 18 gang in Puerto El Triunfo, following a soccer
scuffle with a sibling of a gang leader.

The Perez family sets sail at dawn. José, Marta, and their three kids aged 6 to
15 paddle in their *cayuco* (dugout canoe) from their island hut across the
Bay of Jiquilisco in search of *curiles* (a mollusk). The beauty of the dawn on
the bay dissipates as they enter into the deep shade of the mangrove swamp.
Marcos, the 15-year-old, ties up the *cayuco* as the rest of the family gather
their nets and buckets. The youngest children stay closest to the *cayuco* but
Marcos scrambles across low-lying tree branches until he locates a mud bank
deep in the jungle. The five of them labor in the heat and mud, digging out
curiles and placing them in hemp bags. They all puff on homemade cigars to
ward off the masses of insects. By mid-afternoon, they wash themselves off in
the bay, place their catch in the *cayuco*, and begin the trek across *Jiquilisco*
to Puerto El Triunfo, an hour away. At a cantina by the municipal pier, José
haggles with the owner before selling him the day's catch. The *curiles* that
the family worked so hard to collect do not have much value insofar as they
are a *boca* (snack) to accompany beer. The family earns between US$80 to
$120 a month for their arduous labors, 365 days a year. The children cannot
attend school, a casualty of their familial struggle for survival.[1]

---

[1] The author and a film crew spent the day with the family in May 2015. These names are
pseudonyms.

Like the Perez family, more than 3,000 area residents, mostly women and children, spend their days in these infrahuman conditions gathering *curiles* out of the mud in the mangrove forests. Another 5,000–8,500 people depend on artisanal fishing in the bay. Another 4,000 people are involved in shrimp farming. Close to half of the area's population, including in Puerto El Triunfo, survives thanks only to their labors in the Bay of Jiquilisco.[2] The closing of the processing plants during the 1990s swelled the ranks of these subsistence fishermen and harvesters. Yet, the same environmental forces of chemical contamination, overfishing and mangrove forest destruction that affected the shrimp industry are also threatening their precarious livelihoods.[3]

As early as 1976, a study showed that the population that lived near the bay had five times more residue from pesticides in their blood than the rest of the Central American population.[4] Those same contaminants from the neighboring cotton plantations along with overfishing directly contributed to the 50 percent decline from 1978 to 1992 in the capture of white shrimp (the contaminants affected the shrimp larvae in the bay).[5] During the 1990s, sugar substituted for cotton on the plantations (the largest still owned by the Wright family) bordering the Bay of Jiquilisco but that change did nothing to diminish the contamination through pesticide runoff.

In 1998, Hurricane Mitch tore through the area wreaking further havoc on the inhabitants of the zone and on the remaining industrial and artisanal shrimp enterprises.[6] Regardless of the exact nature of the damage, shrimp production (exclusively for the domestic market) fell from more than two million kilos in 1995 to less than 500,000 in 2000.[7] Subsequently shrimp production has recovered to its pre-hurricane levels but not nearly enough to sustain more than 250 non-unionized industrial fishermen.

---

[2] Rafael E. Cartagena, Elías Escobar, and Oscar Díaz, *La zona costera de Usulután: Retos para la gobernanza ambiental territorial* (San Salvador: PRISMA, 2012), 11. Shrimp farming that took off with the end of the war and takes place typically along the bay and on the edge of the mangrove forests.

[3] Ibid.

[4] Dirección General de Recursos Naturales Renovables, "Estudio de Contaminación Por Insecticidas en Bahía de Jiquilisco, 1975–1976," San Salvador, 1976, 84.

[5] The first *veda* (closed season) was only enacted in 2002.

[6] Mario Sáenz, president of Atarraya S.A., interview with the author, San Salvador, 2013.

[7] Dirección General de Pesca y Aquicultura, *Consideraciones técnicas sobre la pesca en zonas costeras de El Salvador* (San Salvador: MAG, Gobierno de El Salvador, 2012).

It would have been very difficult but not impossible for the cooperative that Benítez envisioned to have survived the combined effects of the hurricane's devastation, the environmental degradation, and the decades of overfishing. Yet, the cooperative spirit from the 1980s has endured around the Bay of Jiquilisco. The majority of artisanal fishermen and shrimp farmers are organized in cooperatives and former union activists are in the forefront of communal organizations that promote efforts to achieve safety in this gang-ravaged zone and the minimum requirements for a dignified life.

Not surprisingly, the exiles in North America have fared differently. Although they are better off economically, none of them are wealthy. They all feel nostalgia for the port and El Salvador. They know they had no choice but to leave and yet a sense of remorse about their absence from home remains embedded in their consciousness. They empathize strongly with the new immigrants from Central America who also had little or no choice about emigrating.

Alejandro Molina Lara fled into exile in August 1981. However, before he left, his remaining comrades in Federación Nacional Sindical de Trabajadores Salvadoreños (FENASTRAS), most of whom were in jail, informed him that they expected him back for their next congress at the end of the year so that he could be elected secretary-general. In Los Angeles he had a difficult time raising the money to return and thus arrived a few weeks late. He met with a Frente de Acción Popular Unificado (FAPU) militant who informed him that as a punishment for his late arrival he would have to work in a factory instead of assuming the leadership of the labor federation. At the time, FAPU was tied to the guerrillas and in virtual control of FENASTRAS. Angry and disillusioned, Alejandro made a clandestine trip to Puerto El Triunfo where his union *compañeros* raised enough money for his return trip to the United States.

Once in Los Angeles, he was contacted by FENASTRAS militants who apologized claiming the leader who had disciplined him had acted incorrectly. They then asked him to go on tour in support of his imprisoned comrades. He accepted their apology and spent 1982 traveling throughout the United States. Sponsored by the CISPES and progressive unions, he traveled from the coal mines of West Virginia to the copper mines of Arizona giving impassioned speeches to union members about Salvadoran labor struggles.[8]

---

[8] "Salvadoran Trade Unionist on Tour in U.S. Coalfields," *The Militant,* Nov. 26, 1982.

Alejandro returned to Los Angeles and immediately brought his four children and his estranged wife to live with him. A United Electrical Workers' Union (UE) contact from his tour got him a job as a welder in a small industrial wire factory. He became intensely involved with Local 1421 of the UE, at the time among the most progressive unions. Within a year, the Spanish-speaking rank and file elected him shop steward and eventually president of Local 1421 that encompassed seven factories. In 1998, he led a largely successful strike against the Industrial Wire Company for a wage increase (from US$9.30 an hour to US$13) and against 12-hour shifts with no overtime.[9] As in 1979 in the port, Molina Lara again guided a strike that lasted for months. Following the strike, management took reprisals against him by shifting him from his maintenance welding job to the production line. A confrontation with a regional union official estranged him from possible support just at this critical moment. The disciplinary shift to production line proved exhausting as it was suited for far younger people. At the time, Alejandro was pushing 60. Within two years, a large coil of industrial wire fell and struck him; he suffered serious back and shoulder injuries. After disability payments ended, he went into retirement and began living on Social Security benefits.

Looking back on his career in the international labor movement, Alejandro has nothing to regret. Nevertheless, his powerful and unwavering commitment took its personal toll. He did not have enough time to spare for his children. Today he feels estranged from most of his children and grandchildren who all live in the Los Angeles area.

Gloria also fled to Los Angeles in 1981. She had no support network in place though in 1988 her sister, also a Pezca worker, joined her. Gloria first found work in a Mexican restaurant. When she obtained residency in 1985, she got a job in a small non-union metalworking shop. In 1990, she suffered a severe back injury on the job. The company wouldn't help beyond disability payments. In 1991, they gave her US$1,000 in severance. After that, she could only get odd jobs that didn't further inflame her back injury, such as child care. She has had several operations but still suffers from the pain. Gloria regrets that she was so impoverished in Los Angeles for so long. "I couldn't give my kids anything special. They never got brand name clothes."[10] Nor did she ever enjoy vacations. During the filming of *Port Triumph*, we took her to the iconic observatory

---

[9] *The Militant*, Jan. 19, 1998; Molina Lara, interview with the author, Los Angeles, 2017.
[10] Gloria García, interview with the author, Los Angeles, Feb. 2017.

in Griffith Park. She smiled and commented, "First time I've ever been here." Her sons were able to stay in school and eventually obtain good employment. One son is a policeman and the other operates trains in the port of San Pedro. Her sons support her and periodically provide her a ticket to visit family and friends in Puerto El Triunfo. Despite the years of economic precariousness, her family life has been rewarding; she alternates living with the two sons and their spouses and children. Gloria thrives on her relationship with her five grandchildren, who bring her great joy.

Right after the FENASTRAS bombing of October 1989, Ana Alvarenga decided that she could no longer ignore the death threats she was constantly receiving. She managed to gain refugee status through the Canadian Embassy. The country's welfare system took care of her and her six children. They all received good educations and today they are trilingual professionals. Like Gloria, Ana is thrilled with her grandchildren. Ana's children support her well. She is able to return to Puerto El Triunfo annually where she maintains a house with air conditioning and participates in church and community organizations.

Her former union *compañeros* in Los Angeles are beginning to feel the anxiety of their communities in the aftermath of the Trump electoral victory. Alejandro interprets the victory as a reflection of anti-Latino racism. Angel Escobar thinks that the only solution to combat the desperation that haunts the Latino community would be a week-long general strike.[11] Gloria fears that the Trump administration could strip her and other Latinos of their citizenship. She had confided this anxiety to me in February 2017. As if confirming her worries about her status, the administration has recently escalated its border harassment of Central American refugees, criminalizing asylum seekers and detaining them in large numbers, separating them from their children, and deporting them. Among those separated from his six-year-old daughter and deported back to El Salvador is Arnovis Guidos Portillo, who fled out of fear of the Calle 18 gang in Puerto El Triunfo.[12] The US Citizenship and Immigration Service has also ramped up its investigation of naturalized citizens suspected of obtaining their status fraudulently with the goal of stripping

---

[11] Angel Escobar was blacklisted along with other Sindicato Agua activists and could not find work on the sea and thus forced to emigrate. Today he works as a cook at Universal Studios.

[12] Joshua Partlow, "U.S. Officials Separated Him from His Child," *Washington Post*, June 23, 2018 (accessed July 9, 2018), www.washingtonpost.com/world/the_americas/u-s-officials-separated-him-from-his-child-then-he-was-deported-to-el-salvador/2018/06/23/37b6940a-7663-11e8-bda1-18e53a448a14_story.html?utm_term=.9e7a1945dae7.

them of citizenship.[13] All these aspects of Trump's Zero Tolerance Immigration Policy substantiate Gloria's fears. For her it is time to put aside differences within the community and resist together, where possible.

In February 2018, Carlos Henriquez Consalvi and I presented the film, *Puerto El Triunfo* to some 50 port residents in an event hosted by the Casa de Cultura. I expected that the film would receive sharp criticism from both sides of the historic split between Tierra y Agua due to the documentary's balanced portrait of the conflict of the 1980s. As I awaited the first question, Carmen Minero stood up and walked toward the podium. I ceded my position and she commenced an impassioned tale of her travails as a worker and a fighter with SIP. In effect, she repeated much of her testimony in the film. Others also rose and offered their testimony. It struck me later that what the protagonists were doing was in a sense offering validation of themselves and the film, underscoring both the differences and continuities between their screen image and edited words and themselves as physical beings. Others who did not appear in the film also made similar comments about the value of their collective struggles. No one asked any questions about the film. Indeed, they did not need to ask any questions because they were authorities of their own experiences.

The terror that struck the SIP activists in 1980 and 1981 still haunts some people. Ovidio feels almost paralyzed by his ambivalence at seeing soldiers patrol the streets. And Gloria, from the relative safety of Los Angeles, reflects on the past. At a film showing at UC Irvine, in response to a question from the audience about terror and trauma, she commented, "The wounds don't bleed anymore but they still hurt."[14]

The memories of terror and of the loss of their livelihoods remain in the minds of the elder port residents and exiles alike. They all experience strong senses of ambivalence. Puerto El Triunfo seems to be emerging from the long night of gang violence, yet, like Ovidio, many view the military who patrol their streets with a mixture of gratitude and dread, gratitude for providing a sense of security against the gangs and dread for evoking memories of military repression during the civil war. They have overcome past divisions to make collective efforts to try to improve living conditions for all and to create opportunities for the area's youth. Yet, the

---

[13] Jamelle Bouie, "White Fight," *Slate*, July 8, 2018 (accessed July 9, 2018), https://amp .slate.com/news-and-politics/2018/07/donald-trump-is-leading-the-republican-charge-to-preserve-a-shrinking-white-majority.html.

[14] Gloria García, comments to film audience, UC Irvine, Mar. 2018.

dreams of equality and prosperity incarnated in their union struggles now seem almost unimaginable.

The exiles in the United States feel pride and a tinge of resentment against the "all-absorbing system," in Alejandro's words, as they witness the thoroughgoing Americanization of their children and grandchildren. They are relatively comfortable, if alienated from the larger cultural mainstream. After decades in the United States, they desire to remain part of the Salvadoran fabric. They do so by returning home when they can, aiding local projects with whatever resources they can spare, and by defending their diasporic community against what they perceive to be unrelenting aggression, however different from 1980. Some suggest that the hostility and aggression come from the same place then and now. In response, they still know how to cast a net of solidarity.

Bibliography

ARCHIVAL SOURCES

Puerto El Triunfo – All Digitized

Sindicato de la Industria Pesquera (SIP) General Archives
Sindicato General de Trabajadores de la Industria Pesquera (SGTIPAC- Sindicato
   Agua) Archives
SIP Departamental Archives
Subseccional Atarraya Archives
Subseccional Pezca Archives

San Salvador

Archivo de la Asamblea Legislativa (AAL)
Universidad Centroamericana (UCA)
   Centro de Información, Documentación y Apoyo a la Investigación (CIDAI)
   Centro Intercultural de Documentación (CIDOC)

The Netherlands

Erasmus University Rotterdam
   Kooster Collection, International Institute of Social Studies

United States

Digital National Security Archive (DNSA)
   El Salvador: The Making of U.S. Policy, 1977–1984 collection

El Salvador: War, Peace, and Human Rights, 1980–1994 collection
North American Congress on Latin America (NACLA) Archive

GOVERNMENT DOCUMENTS

Corte Suprema de Justicia
Diario Oficial
Juzgado Segundo de lo Penal
Ministerio de Agricultura y Ganadería (MAG)
US Congress, Senate
US Department of Labor
US Department of State

INTERVIEWS AND CORRESPONDENCE

Alvarenga, Ana
Amaya, Adela
Bará, Ivette
Caifás
Campos, Fidel
Castellón, Elsie
Chavarría, Migdalia
de Zelaya, Maura
Escobar, Ángel
Escolástico
Franco, Roberto
Franco, Rolando
Galileo, Amilcar
García, Gloria
Granadeño, Altagracia
Granadeño, Ovidio
Grande Preza, José Luis
Huezo Mixco, Miguel
Jovel, Ricardo
Mena Lagos, Alfredo
Minero, Carmen
Molina Lara, Alejandro
Palma, Evelio Ortiz
Paniagua, Ana
Parada, Carmen
Pérez, Migdalia
Pérez, Migdonio
Quinteros, Noé
Reyes, Virginia
Sáenz, Mario

Scanlon, Francis
Schipull, Norman
Segovia, Eloísa
Torres, Ruperto

NEWSPAPERS AND MAGAZINES

Agence France-Presse
Associated Press
Central America Report
Christian Science Monitor
Diario Latino
Dissent (United States)
El Diario de Hoy
El Faro
El Independiente
El Mundo
El Salvador Times
Executive Intelligence Review
La Crónica
La Prensa Gráfica
Latin American Weekly Report
Los Angeles Review of Books
Los Angeles Times
The Militant
New York Times
New York Times Magazine
Panama City ACAN
Proceso (El Salvador)
Pueblo
Pueblo Internacional
Radio Reloj (Costa Rica)
Slate
United Press International
Washington Monthly
Washington Post
Víspera

Albiac, María Dolores. "Los ricos más ricos de El Salvador." In *El Salvador: La transición y sus problemas*, edited by Rodolfo Cardenal and Luis Armando González, 153–83. San Salvador: UCA Editores, 2002.
Alexander, Robert. *A History of Organized Labor in Panama and Central America*. Westport, CT: Praeger Publishers, 2008.
Almeida, Paul. *Waves of Protest: Popular Struggle in El Salvador, 1925–2005*. Minneapolis: University of Minnesota Press, 2008.
American Arbitration Association Commercial Arbitration Tribunal. "Award in the Matter of the Arbitration between Beckman Instruments, Inc. and

Overseas Private Investment Corporation," *American Society of International Law* 27, no. 5 (Sept. 1988): 1260–80.

Anaya, Eugenio. "Crónica del mes," *Estudios Centroamericanos* 34, no. 374 (Nov./Dec. 1979): 1088–93.

Arias Segundo, José Isidrio. *Puerto El Triunfo: 487 años de antología histórica.* Puerto El Triunfo: Centro de Tecnología, 2009.

Bataillon, Gilles. *Génesis de las guerras intestinas en América Central (1960–1983).* Mexico City: Fondo de Cultura Económica, 2008.

Bayard de Volo, Lorraine. *Women and the Cuban Insurrection: How Gender Shaped Castro's Victory.* New York: Cambridge University Press, 2018.

Bayertz, Kurt. "Four Uses of Solidarity." In *Solidarity,* edited by Kurt Bayertz, 3–28. Dordrecht, The Netherlands: Kluwer Academic Publishers, 1999.

Bergquist, Charles. *Labor in Latin America: Comparative Essays on Chile, Argentina, Venezuela, and Colombia.* Stanford, CA: Stanford University Press, 1986.

Bollinger, William. "El Salvador." In *Latin American Labor Organizations,* edited by Gerald Michael Greenfield and Sheldon L. Maram, 307–88. New York: Greenwood Press, 1987.

Bosteels, Bruno. *Marx and Freud in Latin America, Politics, Psychoanalysis, and Religion in Times of Terror.* London: Verso Press, 2012.

Bourdieu, Pierre. *Sociology in Question.* London: Sage, 1993.

Bourgois, Phillipe. *Ethnicity at Work: Divided Labor on a Central American Banana Plantation.* Baltimore, MD: Johns Hopkins University Press, 1989.

Brockett, Charles D. *Political Movements and Violence in Central America.* New York: Cambridge University Press, 2005.

Cabarrús, Carlos Rafael. *Génesis de una revolución: análisis del surgimiento y desarrollo de la organización campesina en El Salvador.* Mexico City: Centro de Investigaciones y Estudios Superiores de Antropología Social, 1983.

Cabrera, Mario E. *Piruetas.* San Salvador: Palibrio, 2012.

Cáceres Prendes, Jorge. "Estado, sociedad y política de un contexto de insurgencia popular: El Salvador 1980–1987." *Anuario de Estudios Centroamericanos* 14, nos. 1–2 (1988): 25–49, 51–68.

Campos, Rodolfo R., ed. *El Salvador entre el terror y la esperanza: los sucesos de 1979 y su impacto en el drama salvadoreño de los años siguientes.* San Salvador: UCA Editores, 1982.

Campos, Tomás (Ellacuría). "La iglesia y las organizaciones populares en El Salvador." *Estudios Centroamericanos* 33, no. 359 (Sept. 1978): 692–702.

Cartagena, Camelia. *El silencio de los culpables: El Salvador, luchas sindicales, dos décadas de oro (1970–1989).* San Salvador: Servicios Gráficos El Salvador, 2015.

Cartagena, Rafael E., Elías Escobar, and Oscar Díaz. *La zona costera de Usulután: Retos para la gobernanza ambiental territorial.* San Salvador: PRISMA, 2012.

Casper, Norman. "El IADSL y la corrupción del movimiento sindical de El Salvador." *Estudios Centroamericanos* 41, no. 449 (Mar. 1986): 205–29.

Caulfield, Sueann, Sarah Chambers, and Lara Putnam, eds. *Honor, Status, and Law in Modern Latin America.* Durham, NC: Duke University Press, 2005.

Chávez, Joaquín. *Poets and Prophets of the Resistance: Intellectuals and the Origins of El Salvador's Civil War.* New York: Oxford University Press, 2017.

Ching, Erik. *Stories of Civil War in El Salvador: A Battle over Memory.* Chapel Hill: University of North Carolina Press, 2016.

Colindres, Eduardo. *Fundamentos económicos de la burguesía salvadoreña.* San Salvador: UCA Editores, 1977.

Cruz, Ernesto. "Crónica del mes, marzo–abril." *Estudios Centroamericanos* 41, no. 450 (Mar.–Apr. 1986): 342–53.

Dardot, Pierre and Christian Laval, *The New Way of the World: On Neoliberal Society.* New York: Verso, 2014.

Díaz, Arlene J. *Female Citizens, Patriarchs, and the Law in Venezuela, 1786–1904.* Lincoln: University of Nebraska Press, 2004.

Duarte, José Napoleón. *Duarte: My Story.* New York: Putnam, 1986.

Eisenbrandt, Matt. *Assassination of a Saint: The Plot to Murder Óscar Romero and the Quest to Bring His Killers to Justice.* Berkeley: University of California Press, 2017.

Ellacuría, Ignacio. *Veinte años de historia de El Salvador (1969–1989), tomo II, escritos políticos.* San Salvador: UCA Editores, 1991.

"Las organizaciones populares ante la nueva situación." In *El Salvador entre el terror y la esperanza: Los sucesos de 1979 y su impacto en el drama salvadoreño de los años siguientes,* edited by Rodolfo R. Campos, 613–15. San Salvador: UCA Editores, 1982.

Estudios Centroamericanos 454–55 (Aug.–Sept. 1986).

Farnsworth-Alvear, Ann. *Dulcinea in the Factory: Myths, Morals, Men, and Women in Colombia's Industrial Experiment, 1905–1960.* Durham, NC: Duke University Press, 2000.

Fitzsimmons, Tracy and Mark Anner. "Civil Society in a Postwar Period: Labor in the Salvadoran Democratic Transition." *Latin American Research Review* 34, no. 3 (1999): 103–28.

Freeman, Carla. *High Tech and High Heels in the Global Economy: Women, Work and Pink Collar Identities in the Caribbean.* Durham, NC: Duke University Press, 2000.

French, John D. *Lula's Politics of Cunning: From Trade Unionism to the Presidency. Part 2.* Chapel Hill: University of North Carolina Press, forthcoming.

French, John D. and Daniel James, eds. *Gendered World of Latin American Women Workers: From Household and Factory to the Union Hall and Ballot Box.* Durham, NC: Duke University Press, 1997.

García Linera, Álvaro. "Indianismo y marxismo: El desencuentro de dos razones revolucionarias." *Revista Donataria,* no. 2 (Mar.–Apr. 2005): 477–500. http://bibliotecavirtual.clacso.org.ar/ar/libros/coedicion/linera/7.3.pdf.

Gill, Lesley. *A Century of Violence in a Red City: Popular Struggle, Counter-insurgency, and Human Rights in Colombia.* Durham, NC: Duke University Press, 2016.

Gould, Jeffrey L. "Ignacio Ellacuría and the Salvadorean Revolution," *Journal of Latin American Studies* 47, no. 2 (May 2015): 285–315.

To Die in This Way: Nicaraguan Indians and the Myth of Mestizaje, 1880–1965. Durham, NC: Duke University Press, 1998.

To Lead as Equals: Rural Protest and Political Consciousness in Chinandega, Nicaragua, 1912–1979. Chapel Hill: University of North Carolina Press, 1990.

Gould Jeffrey L. and Aldo A. Lauria-Santiago. *To Rise in Darkness: Revolution, Repression, and Memory in El Salvador, 1920–1932.* Durham, NC: Duke University Press, 2008.

Grandin, Greg. *The Last Colonial Massacre: Latin America in the Cold War.* Chicago: University of Chicago Press, 2011.

"Living in Revolutionary Time: Coming to Terms with the Violence of Latin America's Long Cold War." In *A Century of Revolution: Insurgent and Counterinsurgent Violence during Latin America's Long Cold War,* edited by Greg Grandin and Gilbert M. Joseph, 1–43. Durham, NC: Duke University Press, 2010.

Empire's Workshop: Latin America, the United States, and the Rise of the New Imperialism. New York: Metropolitan Books, 2006.

Gross, George B. "Shrimp Industry of Central America, Caribbean Sea, and Northern South America," *Marine Fisheries Review* 35, nos. 3–4 (1973): 36–55.

Guerra, Tomás. *El Salvador, octubre sangriento: Itinerario y análisis del golpe militar del 15 de octubre de 1979.* San José: Centro Víctor Sanabria, 1979.

Guerra y Guerra, Rodrigo. *Un golpe al amanecer: la verdadera historia de la proclama del 15 de octubre de 1979.* San Salvador: Indole Editores, 2009.

Guido Béjar, Rafael. "El movimiento sindical después de la Segunda Guerra Mundial," *Estudios Centroamericanos* 45, no. 504 (Aug. 1990): 871–92.

Harvey, David. *A Brief History of Neoliberalism.* New York: Oxford University Press, 2005.

Herrera Schlesinger, Ana Eloisa. "Los trabajadores de la industria pesquera." Law thesis, Universidad de El Salvador, May 1980.

Hilgers, Mathieu. "The Three Anthropological Approaches to Neoliberalism." *International Social Science Journal* 61, no. 202 (Oct. 2011): 351–64.

James, Daniel. *Doña Maria's Story: Life, History, Memory and Political Identity.* Durham, NC: Duke University Press, 2000.

Resistance and Integration: Peronism and the Argentine Working Class, 1946–1976. Cambridge: Cambridge University Press, 1988.

Joseph, Gilbert M. "Latin America's Long Cold War: A Century of Revolutionary Process and U.S. Power." In *A Century of Revolution: Insurgent and Counterinsurgent Violence during Latin America's Long Cold War,* edited by Greg Grandin and Gilbert M. Joseph, 397–414. Durham, NC: Duke University Press, 2010.

Kantor, Mark, Michael D. Nolan, and Karl P. Sauvant. *Reports of Overseas Private Investment Corporation Determinations.* Oxford: Oxford University Press, 2011.

LaFeber, Walter. *Inevitable Revolutions: The United States in Central America.* 2nd ed. New York: Norton, 1993.

LeoGrande, William M. *Our Own Backyard: The United States in Central America, 1977–1992.* Chapel Hill: University of North Carolina Press, 1998.

Levenson-Estrada, Deborah. *Adiós Niño: The Gangs of Guatemala City and the Politics of Death*. Durham, NC: Duke University Press, 2013.

———. *Trade Unionists against Terror: Guatemala City, 1954–1985*. Chapel Hill: University of North Carolina Press, 1994.

Lindo-Fuentes, Héctor and Erik Ching. *Modernizing Minds: Education Reform and the Cold War, 1960–1980*. Albuquerque: University of New Mexico Press, 2012.

Lungo, Mario. *El Salvador in the Eighties: Counterinsurgency and Revolution*. Translated by Amelia Shogun. Philadelphia: Temple University Press, 1996.

———. *La lucha de las masas en El Salvador*. San Salvador: UCA Editores, 1987.

Majano, Adolfo Arnoldo. *Una oportunidad perdida: 15 de octubre 1979*. San Salvador: Indole Editores, 2009.

Martí, César. "LP-28: Unidad revolucionaria y perspectivas de poder." In *El Salvador: alianzas políticas y proceso revolucionario*. Cuadernos de Coyuntura, no. 5, 21–25. Mexico City: Sociedade de Economia Política Latinoamericana, 1979.

McAllister, Carlota and Diane M. Nelson, eds. *War by Other Means: Aftermath in Post-Genocide Guatemala*. Durham, NC: Duke University Press, 2013.

———. "Aftermath: Harvests of Violence and Histories of the Future." In *War by Other Means: Aftermath in Post-Genocide Guatemala*, edited by Carlota McAllister and Diane M. Nelson, 1–46. Durham, NC: Duke University Press, 2013.

Menjívar Larín, Rafael. *Formación y lucha del proletariado industrial salvadoreño*. San Salvador: UCA Editores, 1982.

———. *El Salvador: El eslabón más pequeño*. San José: Editorial Universitaria Centroamericana, 1980.

———. "BPR: Para una política revolucionaria." In *El Salvador: alianzas políticas y proceso revolucionario*. Cuadernos de Coyuntura, no. 5, 15–20. Mexico City: Sociedade de Economia Política Latinoamericana, 1979.

Menjívar Ochoa, Rafael. *Tiempos de locura: El Salvador, 1979–1981*. San Salvador: Facultad Latinoamericana de Ciencias Sociales, 2006.

Montgomery, David. *The Fall of the House of Labor: The Workplace, the State, and American Labor Activism, 1865–1925*. Cambridge: Cambridge University Press, 1987.

Morales Velado, Oscar A. *La resistencia no violenta ante los regímenes salvadoreños que han utilizado el terror institucionalizado en el período 1972–1987*. San Salvador: UCA Editores, 1988.

———. "El movimiento laboral atenazado," *Estudios Centroamericanos* 42, nos. 463–64 (May–June 1987): 344–48.

NACLA Report on the Americas 20, no. 1 (Jan.–Mar. 1986).

National Labor Committee in Support of Democracy and Human Rights in El Salvador. *El Salvador 1990: ARENA Repression Unites the Salvadoran Labor Movement*. El Salvador and New York: Labor Campaign (Sept. 1990).

———. *Labor Rights Denied in El Salvador: An On-Site Investigation by a Delegation of Labor-Legislative-Religious Leaders*. El Salvador and New York: Labor Campaign (Dec. 1988).

Nevins, M. Eleanor. "Intertextuality and Misunderstanding." *Language &*
Communication 30, no. 1 (Jan. 2010): 1–6.

Norton, Chris. "Build and Destroy," *NACLA Report on the Americas* 19, no. 6
(1985): 26–36.

Paige, Jeffrey. *Coffee and Power: Revolution and the Rise of Democracy in*
Central America. Cambridge, MA: Harvard University Press, 1998.

Phillips, Peter and Charles Cole, "Fisheries Resources of Jiquilisco Bay, El Salvador." Proceedings of the Gulf and Caribbean Fisheries Institute, 30th Annual
Session (Nov. 1977).

Pirker, Kristina. *La redefinición de lo posible: Militancia política y movilización*
social en El Salvador, 1970–2012. Mexico City: Instituto Mora, 2017.

"Radicalización política y movilización social en El Salvador: los frentes
de masas," *Observatorio Latinoamericano* 9 (Nov. 2012): 62–77.

Ramos, Julio. *Divergent Modernities: Culture and Politics in Nineteenth Century*
Latin America. Durham, NC: Duke University Press, 2001.

Romero, Óscar A. *Archbishop Oscar Romero: A Shepherd's Diary.* Translated by
Irene B. Hodgson. Cincinnati, OH: St. Anthony Messenger Press, 1993.

Samayoa, Salvador and Guillermo Galván, "El movimiento obrero en El Salvador
¿resurgimiento o agitación?" *Estudios Centroamericanos* 34, nos. 369–70
(July–Aug. 1979): 591–600.

"El cierre patronal de las empresas: Prueba de fuego para el sindicalismo
revolucionario en El Salvador." *Estudios Centroamericanos* 34, no. 371
(Sept. 1979): 793–800.

Sánchez Ramos, Irene. "El Salvador, 1986: El carácter global de la contrainsurgencia." *In El Salvador: Proceso político y guerra.* Cuaderno de Divulgación,
no. 4, 44–73. San Salvador: Centro de Investigación y Acción, 1987.

Scipes, Kim. *AFL-CIO's Secret War against Developing Country Workers:*
Solidarity or Sabotage? Lanham, MD: Lexington Books, 2010.

Silver, Beverly J. *Forces of Labor: Workers' Movements and Globalization since*
1870. Cambridge: Cambridge University Press, 2003.

"El sistema financiero de El Salvador: Análisis y perspectivas," *Cuadernos*
de Investigación. San Salvador: Centro de Investigaciones Tecnológicas y
Científicas, May 1989.

Stanley, William Deane. *The Protection Racket State: Elite Politics, Military*
Extortion, and Civil War in El Salvador. Philadelphia, PA: Temple University
Press, 1996.

Stern, Steve J. *Secret History of Gender: Women, Men and Power in Late Colonial*
Mexico. Chapel Hill: University of North Carolina Press, 1995.

Stewart, Stephen O. and Danilo Jiménez. "Final Report: Midterm Evaluation:
AIFLD-AID cooperative agreement in El Salvador." June 1993. El Salvador.
Submitted to USAID, Washington DC.

Thackray, Arnold and Minor Myers Jr. *Arnold O. Beckman: One Hundred Years*
of Excellence. Philadelphia, PA: Chemical Heritage Foundation, 2000.

US Department of State. "Telegram from the Embassy in El Salvador to the
Department of State, 'Updating Our Strategy for El Salvador.'" May 26,
1980. In *Foreign Relations of the United States, 1977–1980, vol. XV: Central*
America, 1977–1980. Washington, DC: Government Publishing Office.

"Telegram from the Embassy in El Salvador to the Department of State, Subject: High Level Dialogue with GOES." May 29, 1979. In *Foreign Relations of the United States, 1977–1980, vol. XV: Central America, 1977–1980.* Washington, DC: Government Publishing Office.

Viterna, Jocelyn. *Women in War: The Micro-Processes of Mobilization in El Salvador.* New York: Oxford University Press, 2013.

Volosinov, V. N. *Marxism and the Philosophy of Language.* Translated by Ladislav Matejka and I. R. Titunik. Cambridge, MA: Harvard University Press, 1973.

Weinstein, Barbara. *For Social Peace in Brazil: Industrialists and the Remaking of the Working Class in São Paulo, 1920–1964.* Chapel Hill: University of North Carolina Press, 1996.

Weld, Kirsten. *Paper Cadavers: The Archives of Dictatorship in Guatemala.* Durham, NC: Duke University Press, 2014.

Whitfield, Teresa. *Paying the Price: Ignacio Ellacuría and the Murdered Jesuits of El Salvador.* Philadelphia, PA: Temple University Press, 1995.

Winter, Jay. *Dreams of Peace and Freedom: Utopian Moments of the Twentieth Century.* New Haven, CT: Yale University Press, 2006.

Wood, Elisabeth Jean. "Conflict-Related Sexual Violence and the Policy Implications of Recent Research." *International Review of the Red Cross* 96, no. 894 (Sept. 2014): 457–78.

Index